SPONTANEOUS
HEALING

Andrew Weil, M.D., a graduate of Harvard Medical School, has worked for the National Institute of Mental Health and was for fifteen years a Research Associate in Ethnopharmacology at the Harvard Botanical Museum. He has travelled extensively throughout the world collecting information about the medicinal properties of plants, altered states of consciousness and healing. He is currently Associate Director of the Division of Social Perspectives in Medicine and Director of the Program in Integrative Medicine at the University of Arizona in Tucson, where he practises natural and preventive medicine.

Andrew Weil is the author of several books on health-related subjects. *Spontaneous Healing* is his sixth book.

Books by Andrew Weil, M.D.

THE NATURAL MIND:
A New Way of Looking at Drugs
and the Higher Consciousness

THE MARRIAGE OF THE SUN AND MOON:
A Quest for Unity in Consciousness

CHOCOLATE TO MORPHINE:
Understanding Mind-Active Drugs
(with Winifred Rosen)

HEALTH AND HEALING

NATURAL HEALTH, NATURAL MEDICINE:
A Comprehensive Manual for Wellness and Self-Care

SPONTANEOUS HEALING

SPONTANEOUS HEALING

*How to Discover and Enhance
Your Body's Natural Ability to
Maintain and Heal Itself*

ANDREW WEIL, M.D.

WARNER BOOKS

A *Warner* Book

First published in the United States of America
by Alfred A. Knopf, Inc. 1995
First published in Great Britain by
Little, Brown and Company 1995
This edition published by Warner 1997

A CIP catalogue record for this book
is available from the British Library.

ISBN 0 7515 1680 5

Printed and bound in Great Britain by Clays Ltd, St Ives plc

Warner Books
A Division of
Little, Brown and Company (UK)
Brettenham House
Lancaster Place
London WC2E 7EN

For Diana

CONTENTS

Contents

SPONTANEOUS HEALING

INTRODUCTION

A MAN WHOSE lungs are filled with cancer is sent home to die, having been told that medicine can do nothing for him. Six months later he reappears in his doctor's office, tumor free. A young woman—diabetic, a heavy smoker—lies unconscious in a coronary care unit following a bad heart attack. Her doctor anguishes over the fact that her cardiac function is rapidly declining and he is powerless to save her. But the next morning she is awake and talking, clearly on the way to recovery. A neurosurgeon tells grieving parents that their son, who is in a coma following a motorcycle accident and severe head injury, will never regain consciousness. The son is now fine.

Most doctors I know have one or two stories of this sort, stories of spontaneous healing. You will uncover many more of them if you seek them out, yet few medical researchers do. To most doctors, the stories are just stories, not taken seriously, not studied, not looked to as sources of information about the body's potential to repair itself.

Meanwhile, modern medicine has become so expensive that it is straining the economies of many developed nations and putting itself beyond the reach of much of the world's population. In many countries politicians argue about how to pay for health care, unaware that a philosophical debate about the very nature of health care has been ongoing throughout history. Doctors believe that health requires outside intervention of one sort or another, while proponents of natural hygiene maintain that health results from living in harmony with natural law. In ancient Greece, doctors worked under the patronage of

Asklepios, the god of medicine, but healers served Asklepios's daughter, the radiant Hygeia, goddess of health. Medical writer and philosopher René Dubos has written:

> For the worshippers of Hygeia, health is the natural order of things, a positive attribute to which men are entitled if they govern their lives wisely. According to them, the most important function of medicine is to discover and teach the natural laws which will ensure a man a healthy mind in a healthy body. More skeptical, or wiser in the ways of the world, the followers of Asklepios believe that the chief role of the physician is to treat disease, to restore health by correcting any imperfections caused by accidents of birth or life.

Political debates about how to cover the costs of medical care mostly take place among followers of Asklepios. There has been no argument about the nature of medicine or people's expectations of it, only about who is going to pay for its services, which have become inordinately expensive because of doctors' reliance on technology. I am a dedicated follower of Hygeia and want to interject that viewpoint into any discussions of the future of medicine.

Let me give an example of how these different philosophies lead to very different courses of action. In the West, a major focus of scientific medicine has been the identification of external agents of disease and the development of weapons against them. An outstanding success in the middle of this century was the discovery of antibiotics and, with that, great victories against infectious diseases caused by bacteria. This success was a major factor in winning hearts and minds over to the Asklepian side, convincing most people that medical intervention with the products of technology was worth it, no matter the cost. In the East, especially in China, medicine has had a quite different focus. It has explored ways of increasing internal resistance to disease so that, no matter what harmful influences you are exposed to, you can remain healthy—a Hygeian strategy. In their explorations Chinese doctors have discovered many natural substances that have such tonic effects on the body. Although the Western approach has served us well for a number of years, its long-term usefulness may not be nearly so great as the Eastern one.

Weapons are dangerous. They may backfire, causing injury to the user, and they may also stimulate greater aggression on the part of the enemy. In fact, infectious-disease specialists throughout the world are now wringing their hands over the possibility of untreatable plagues of resistant organisms. Just today I received a copy of *Clinical Research News for Arizona Physicians,* a publication of the university medical center where I teach, that featured an article on "Resistance to Antimicrobial Agents: The New Plague?" It reads in part:

> While antimicrobial agents have been considered the "wonder drugs" of the 20th century, clinicians and researchers are now acutely aware that microbial resistance to drugs has become a major clinical problem. . . . A variety of solutions have been proposed. The pharmaceutical industry is attempting to develop new agents that are less susceptible to current resistance mechanisms. Unfortunately, the organisms appear to rapidly develop new resistance mechanisms. . . . In the inpatient setting, strict adherence to infection control procedures is essential. Health care workers need to understand that antimicrobial resistance is an accelerating problem *in all practice settings* that can directly compromise patient outcomes.

The phrase "can directly compromise patient outcomes" is euphemistic. It means patients will die of infections that doctors formerly could treat with antibiotics. In fact, antibiotics are rapidly losing their power, and some infectious-disease specialists are beginning to think about what we will do when we can no longer rely on them. We might have to revert to methods used in hospitals in the 1920s and 1930s before there were antibiotics: strict quarantine and disinfection, surgical drainage, and so forth. What a reversal that will be for technological medicine!

Meanwhile, resistance does not develop to the tonics of Chinese medicine, because they are not acting *against* germs (and do not therefore influence their evolution) but rather are acting *with* the body's defenses. They increase activity and efficiency of cells of the immune system, helping patients resist all kinds of infections, not just those caused by bacteria. Antibiotics are only effective against bacteria; they are of no use in diseases caused by viruses. Western medicine's powerlessness against viral infections is clearly visible in its ineffectiveness against AIDS. Chinese herbal therapy for people infected with HIV looks much more promising. It is nontoxic, in great contrast to the Western antiviral drugs in current use, and may enable many of those with HIV infection to have relatively long, symptom-free lives, even though the virus remains in their bodies.

The Eastern concept of strengthening internal defenses is Hygeian, because it assumes that the body has a natural ability to resist and deal with agents of disease. If that assumption were more prominent in Western medicine, we would not now have an economic crisis in health care, because methods that take advantage of the body's natural healing abilities are far cheaper than the intensive interventions of technological medicine, as well as safer and more effective over time.

Asklepians are most interested in treatment, while Hygeians are interested in healing. Treatment originates outside; healing comes from within. The word "healing" means "making whole"—that is, restoring integrity and balance. I have long been interested in stories about healing, and I assume you are too. Perhaps you know someone who experienced a spontaneous remission of cancer, in which widespread malignant disease disappeared, to the amazement of doctors in charge of the case. Maybe the disappearance was temporary or maybe it was permanent. What happened? Or perhaps you know someone who was healed by prayer or by religious fervor.

I have titled this book *Spontaneous Healing* because I want to call attention to the innate, intrinsic nature of the healing process. *Even when treatments are applied with successful outcomes, those outcomes represent activation of intrinsic healing mechanisms, which, under other circumstances, might operate without any outside stimulus.* The main theme of this book is very simple: The body can heal itself. It can do so because it has a healing system. If you are in good health, you will want to know about this system, because it is what keeps you in good health and because you can enhance that condition. If you or people you love are sick, you will want to know about this system, because it is the best hope for recovery.

Part One builds a case for the existence of a healing system and presents evidence for its operation, including its interactions with the mind. At every level of biological organization, from DNA up, mechanisms of self-diagnosis, self-repair, and regeneration exist in us, always ready to become active when the need arises. Medicine that takes advantage of these innate mechanisms of healing is more effective than medicine that simply suppresses symptoms. This section includes stories of people I have known who have recovered from illness, often in spite of the predictions of doctors who saw no possibility of recovery or insisted that improvement could occur only with a great deal of Asklepian effort. As I have made it known that I am interested in cases of this sort, I have found more and more of them, and I believe that anyone who looks will find others. Spontaneous healing is a common occurrence, not a rare event. We may marvel at stories of spontaneous remissions of cancer but pay little attention to more commonplace activities of the healing system, such as the repair of wounds. In fact, it is the ordinary, day-to-day workings of the healing system that are most extraordinary.

Part Two of the book tells you how to optimize your healing system. You will find here specific information on modifying lifestyle to increase your healing potentials, including facts about food, environmental toxins, exercise, stress reduction, vitamins, supplements, and tonic herbs that can help you maintain your well-being. I will also suggest an eight-week program for gradually changing lifestyle in a manner that will enhance your natural healing power.

Part Three gives advice on managing illness. It analyzes the strengths and weaknesses of conventional and alternative treatments and identifies a number of strategies used by successful patients. I give suggestions here for using natural methods to ameliorate common kinds of illnesses and also include a chapter on "Cancer as a Special Case," because that disease poses a unique challenge to the healing system, and the selection of treatments for it requires careful analysis of each individual's condition. An afterword, "Prescriptions for Society," considers how existing medical institutions would have to change to accommodate Hygeian philosophy.

Until now few doctors and scientists have looked for examples of healing; therefore, it is not surprising that the phenomenon of spontaneous healing seems obscure and the concept of an internal healing system odd. I contend that the more we embrace that concept, the more we will experience healing in our lives, and the less reason we will have to use medical interventions that are unnecessary, sometimes damaging, and consume so much money. Healing-oriented medicine would serve us much better than the present system, since it would be safer and surer as well as cheaper. I have written this book in an effort to help bring it into existence.

Part One

THE HEALING SYSTEM

1

PROLOGUE IN
THE RAIN FOREST

LET ME TAKE YOU with me to a faraway place I visited more than twenty years ago: the sandy bank of a wide river on a sultry afternoon in 1972. The river was a tributary of the Río Caquetá in the northwest Amazon, near the common border of Colombia and Ecuador, and I was lost. I was searching for a shaman, a Kofán Indian named Pedro, who lived in a remote hut somewhere in the huge, dense forest, but the trail that was supposed to take me there left me at an uncrossable river with no sign of how to proceed. It was getting late in the day.

Two days before, after a long, hard drive, I left my Land-Rover at the end of a dirt road and took a motorboat to a tiny frontier settlement, where I spent a restless night. The next day, I found some Indians who took me by canoe to the beginning of a trail they said would eventually bring me to the clearing where Pedro lived. "Half a day's walk," they told me, but I knew that half a day's walk for an Indian might be more for me. I had a backpack with essentials, but not much food, since I expected to be staying with the shaman. After several hours in dark forest, the trail forked. No one had said anything about a fork. I listened for the whisper of intuition and decided to go to the right. After another hour I came upon a clearing with several huts and five Kofán men painting each other's faces.

I was terribly hot and thirsty and asked in Spanish for water. The men ignored me. I asked again. They said they had no water. "No water?!" I exclaimed. "How can that be?" They shrugged and continued to apply their makeup. I asked for the shaman. "Not here," said one of the Indians. "Where can I find him?" There was an offhanded indication of a trail beyond the huts. "Is it far?" I asked. Another shrug.

This was a new experience for me. In the hinterlands of Colombia I had always found Indians to be exceedingly hospitable. It was the inhabitants of the rough frontier towns, the mestizo fortune hunters, who were unfriendly and intimidating. Once I passed through them to Indian territory, I always felt safe, assured that the native people would take in a stranger, help him find his destination, and certainly give water to a thirsty traveler.

The five Kofán men were young, handsome, and, obviously, vain. They wore simple cotton tunics, had long, glossy, black hair, and were intently devoted to their cosmetic art. After one would apply new markings to forehead or cheek, the recipient would spend long minutes evaluating the additions in a broken piece of mirrored glass, grunting approval or requesting further embellishment. This was clearly going to take all afternoon. My presence held not the slightest interest for them, and after half an hour of being ignored, I put on my pack and continued down the trail, until, several hours later, it disappeared in a dense thicket at the edge of the big river, leaving me stranded.

It was strikingly beautiful there, although I was inclined to view the river and forest more as obstacles than as sources of sensory pleasure. Big, billowy cumulus clouds floated above the canopy of trees. The river was swift and clear. There was not a sign of human presence, no sounds except those of insects and birds. Were it not for the sandflies, small biting pests that are out in great numbers from dawn to dusk, I would not have minded camping there. I had a hammock and mosquito net in my pack and could have spent the night if necessary, but I felt anxious at the prospect of being lost, and discouraged by the fruitlessness of my quest.

This shaman, so difficult to reach, was said to be a powerful healer. In a year I spent wandering in South America, most of the shamans I met were disappointing. Some were drunks. Some were clearly out for fame and fortune. One, when he learned I was a doctor from Harvard, was interested only in persuading me to obtain for him a certificate from that institution testifying to his powers so that he could one-up his rivals. I had plenty of adventures during these travels, but in the end, none of them had taught me how to be a better doctor.

Pedro was my last hope. He was unknown to the outside world. I would be the first gringo to visit him, and I had high hopes that he would teach me the secrets of healing I had so long been searching for.

But now I was lost, and the brilliant Amazon sun was taking on the rich golden tones of the end of afternoon. Night would come quickly here, meaning surprising chilliness along the river and no chance of reaching a habitation. I'm not a smoker, but I lit up three cigarettes at once, Pielrojas ("Redskins"), the local cheap brand, with a picture of a North American Indian in full war bonnet on the pack. I puffed on them and blew smoke all around me, hoping for the usual temporary relief from biting sandflies that tobacco smoke brings.

When in doubt, eat. I broke into my meager stores and found a packet of cocoa mix and some dried fruit. I set up a little butane stove, boiled some river water, and soon was sipping the hot liquid, which never tasted better – a bit of comfort and familiarity in this, for me, strange environment.

I was in this remote part of South America because I was searching for something I believed to be exotic and extraordinary, something worlds away from my ordinary experience. I was looking for insight into the source of healing power, and the interconnectedness of magic, religion, and medicine. I wanted to understand how the mind interacts with the body. Above all, I hoped to learn practical secrets of helping people to get well. I had spent eight years in a prestigious institution of higher learning, four studying botany and four studying medicine, but I had found no clear answers to my questions. My botanical studies awakened a desire to see the rain forest, meet native practitioners, and help rescue fast-disappearing knowledge of medicinal plants. My medical training made me want to flee from the world of invasive, technological treatment toward a romantic ideal of natural healing.

Three years before, in 1969, when I finished my basic clinical training, I made a conscious decision not to practice the kind of medicine I had just learned. I did so for two reasons, one emotional and one logical. The first was simply a gut feeling that if I were sick, I would not want to be treated the way I had been taught to treat others, unless there were no alternative. That made me uncomfortable about treating others. The logical reason was that most of the treatments I had learned in four years at Harvard Medical School and one of internship did not get to the root of disease processes and promote healing but rather suppressed those processes or merely counteracted the visible symptoms of disease. I had learned almost nothing about health and its maintenance, about how to prevent illness—a great omission, because I have always believed that the primary function of doctors should be to teach people how *not* to get sick in the first place. The word "doctor" comes from the Latin word for "teacher." Teaching prevention should be primary; treatment of existing disease, secondary.

I am uneasy about the suppressive nature of conventional medicine. If you look at the names of the most popular categories of drugs in use today, you will find that most of them begin with the prefix "anti." We use antispasmodics and antihypertensives, antianxiety agents and antidepressants, antihistamines, antiarrhythmics, antitussives, antipyretics, and anti-inflammatories, as well as beta blockers and H_2-receptor antagonists. This is truly antimedicine— medicine that is, in essence, counteractive and suppressive.

What is wrong with that? you may ask. If a fever is in the danger zone, or an allergic reaction is out of control, of course those symptoms should be counteracted. I have no objection to use of these treatments *on a short-term basis for the management of very severe conditions*. But I came to realize, early in my hospital days, that if you rely on such measures as the main strategy for treating illness, you create two kinds of problems. First, you expose patients to risk, because, by their nature, pharmaceutical weapons are strong and toxic. Their desired effects are too often offset by side effects, by toxicity. Adverse reactions to the counteractive drugs of conventional medicine are a great black mark against the system, and I saw more than enough of them in my clinical training to know that there has to be a better way. Botanical medicine appealed to me because it offered the possibility of finding safe, natural alternatives to the drugs I had been taught to use.

The second problem, less visible but more worrisome, is the chance that over time suppressive treatments may actually strengthen disease processes instead of resolving them. This possibility did not occur to me until I read the writings of a great medical heretic, Samuel Hahnemann (1755–1843), the German prodigy and renegade physician who developed homeopathy, one of the major schools of alternative medicine. Homeopathy relies on very small doses of highly diluted remedies to catalyze healing responses. I am not a homeopath. I disagree with some key points of homeopathic theory (its opposition to immunization, for example) and find the system as a whole puzzling as well as incompatible with current scientific models of physics and chemistry. Nonetheless, I have experienced and observed homeopathic cures and admire the system for its use of treatments that cannot harm. What is more, I find some of Hahnemann's ideas useful.

One of his most important teachings concerns the danger of suppressing visible symptoms of illness. Hahnemann used the example of an itching, red rash on the skin. Better to have disease on the surface of the body, he taught, because from the surface it can exit outward. Suppressive measures may drive a disease process inward toward more vital organs. The itching rash may disappear, but worse trouble may appear down the road, trouble that may resist the strongest suppressive treatments.

Hahnemann had this insight long before the discovery of corticosteroids, the very powerful anti-inflammatory hormones that conventional doctors now dispense without much thought for the harm they can do. Topical steroids are very effective suppressants of skin rashes and are now even sold over the counter in the United States. Again and again I see patients who become dependent on them. As long as they use the steroid creams and ointments, their rashes are held in check, but as soon as the treatment is stopped, the symptoms reappear more severely than before. The disease process is not resolved but merely held at bay, gathering power for renewed expression as soon as the outside, counteractive force is removed.

When steroids are given systemically, their suppressive power and toxicity is even greater. Patients who take drugs like prednisone for months or years to control rheumatoid arthritis, asthma, and other autoimmune and allergic disorders commonly suffer terrible toxicity (weight gain, depression, ulcers, cataracts, weakened bones, acne), but cannot stop taking the drugs because their symptoms will return in full force. What happens to the energies of such suppressed diseases? Where do they go?

My experience with patients confirms Hahnemann's warning. Recently I saw a woman in her mid-thirties who, two years before, had developed symptoms of a serious autoimmune disease: scleroderma. The disease began with episodes of painful blanching of the hands on exposure to cold. This is Raynaud's phenomenon, a sign of neurovascular instability that can exist by itself or herald deeper disturbances of nervous and circulatory function. In this case it was followed by joint pain and swelling of the fingers. Then the skin of her fingers and hands began to thicken and harden, the classic, visible manifestation of scleroderma (the word means "hard skin"). The hands of patients with advanced scleroderma are often cold, purplish, shiny, hard, and immobile, but this external change, while disfiguring, is not the worst effect of this disease. When scleroderma involves internal organs of the digestive and cardiorespiratory systems, it can kill.

Doctors quickly diagnosed the problem and started the patient on high doses of prednisone and other immunosuppressive drugs. She responded dramatically. Within a few months, her skin returned to normal, all joint pain disappeared, and her physician pronounced her to be "in complete remission." Unhappily, a year later she developed shortness of breath. X-rays revealed pulmonary fibrosis, a progressive disease in which normal lung tissue is replaced by abnormal fibrous tissue. She was told that this condition was not related to the previous scleroderma; but, in fact, pulmonary fibrosis is a well-known, albeit uncommon, manifestation of the same process, only in a much more vital area of the body and much more resistant to treatment. Her hands were warm, pink, and soft. There was no visible sign of disease on the surface of her body. Inside, however, she was being crippled by a disease in her lungs that now resisted all the counteractive power of conventional medicine.

By the time I completed my medical internship, I had seen enough variations on this theme to convince me that I did not want to practice conventional medicine or take any further training in it. I did not know what else to practice, however, and that uncertainty led me to undertake my present quest. But after two difficult years of searching, I had learned little about healing. Shortly before coming to Kofán territory I had concluded that I must not have made a sufficient effort to explore new terrain. The healers and shamans I had located were already discovered, too well known, too easy to find. What I was looking for must be still farther away, I thought, still harder to reach, more obscurely hidden in the Amazon forest.

And so there I was, cocoa finished, day coming to an end, lost.

I did eventually find Pedro the shaman, and I remember our meeting very well, even though it happened long ago, because it was a major turning point in my life. Of course, at the time I had no idea of its real significance, regarding it as just another in a long series of frustrations. In fact, it was the first step of a new path, one that would take me back to a place where I would discover what I had known all along but had been unable to recognize.

Having packed up my equipment and shouldered my pack, I noticed a sandbar a short distance upriver. I thought that from its vantage point, I might get a better view of the area and be able to make an educated guess as to the direction of Pedro's hut. I waded to the sandbar, and as I scanned the shore I spied what looked like a bit of trail farther upstream. It was. I got to it by walking just at the water's edge and, once on it, felt my anxieties melt away, even as the sun got low in the west. After forty-five minutes I came to a clearing where a small river entered the big one. At the junction, elevated on stilts, was a lone, thatched hut of ample size. I ran up to it just as the sky was blazing with the colors of a tropical sunset, and climbed a rude staircase up to a deck overlooking the confluence of the rivers.

There was no shaman in sight. The only inhabitant was a young Indian girl, who spoke Spanish hesitantly and looked at me as I might regard an extraterrestrial. She told me that Pedro was gone. He had left ten days ago and should have been back the day before. I asked if I could stay. She did not object, so I took off my pack and strung my hammock between two poles at the edge of the deck.

For the next four days and nights, I stayed mostly in my hammock, Pielroja cigarettes blazing in my fingers, watching the long, hot days pass into clear, starry nights. Occasionally I would brave the sandflies to go for an afternoon swim in the river. I tried, unsuccessfully, to engage the young woman of the house in conversation. And I sought refuge from the world of heat, humidity, blinding sun, and dense forest in a collection of Jack London's tales of the Far North that I had brought with me for just such a circumstance. It was an inspired choice, the perfect literary escape into a world with igloos, ice fields, and numbing cold. But sadly, it came to an end, so I reread it and reread it again.

There was one other diversion. Pedro had killed a jaguar shortly before he left. The jaguar had a young cub that was now in a cage in the house. It was appealingly cute and kittenish and wanted interaction. On one occasion I had it out of the cage and was playing with it on the floor until its play became too rough for me. I wanted it to stop, but my attempts to push the cub away and calm it down stimulated the wild-animal circuit in its brain. Suddenly it was no longer a cute kitten but a vicious hellcat. The Indian girl came at it with a broom and together we managed to get it back in its cage. I came away with nasty scratches and two good bites on my arms.

Then, one afternoon, Pedro appeared and greeted me matter-of-factly. He was a vigorous, solemn man in his early forties. I liked him at once, but he told me soon into our conversation that there would not be any point in my staying, because he had stopped practicing his profession. Instead of working as a healer, he had become a political activist and was trying to organize his fellow Kofán to fight a great threat to their way of life, the presence in their forest of "La Texas." This was the local name for Texaco, which had come to the northwest Amazon to exploit its rich reserves of oil. I had once stayed briefly in a frontier town that served as Texaco's base and was appalled by what I saw and heard: it was a center of noise, mud, fumes, thieves, whores, and roughnecks that was spreading devastation from its margins. But the town was hundreds of miles from this peaceful region, and I could not imagine how it impacted on Pedro's life.

He told me that the noise of Texaco's helicopters had driven game from the forest and that, at the same time, fish were disappearing from the rivers. Hunting and fishing had declined drastically in the past two years, which he blamed entirely on the oil explorations. All of his efforts were now going to collecting signatures on a petition demanding reparations from Texaco. He was sorry I had come such a long way for nothing. I was, too. At least, I now understood why Kofán men would not be hospitable to a gringo walking through their forest.

The next morning I left. Eventually I got back to my Land-Rover and left Kofán territory for good.

I was to spend another year wandering in Colombia, Ecuador, and Peru, but I never again made such an arduous journey in search of an exotic, magical healer. Instead I studied medicinal plants in Ecuador and Peru, learned about the cultivation and use of coca leaf, worked with a Colombian filmmaker to document the use of drug plants by shamans, and looked for unusual fruits, spices, and dyes. Although I did not admit it to myself consciously, on some level I realized that what I was searching for was not to be found in the wilds of Amazonia or any other exotic location. I remained as committed as ever to finding answers to my questions: What is the source of healing? What is the relationship between treatments and cures? How can doctors and patients access healing more of the time? What my search for Pedro taught me was that I was looking for answers in the wrong way, that I did not have to turn from my own land and culture, my formal education, and my own self to find the source of healing. But I did have to spend those years wandering in order to figure that out.

Almost a quarter of a century has passed since I left Pedro's hut at the junction of the two rivers. In that time the destruction of the rain forest caused by the removal of oil has reached levels that Pedro and his people could never have imagined. Road building, oil spills, the dumping of toxic chemicals into rivers, and a cynical disregard for native cultures by both national governments and foreign businesses have damaged vast areas of Colombia and Ecuador irreparably. Simply put, the Kofán people have been put out of business. They are finished, terminated, and any knowledge held by their wise elders and traditional healers is soon to be lost forever. Other tribes now face the same threat. Whether they can avoid the fate of the Kofán is uncertain.

The years have been much kinder to me. I found what I was looking for and more, found it much closer to home in ways both unexpected and satisfying.

THE FACES OF HEALING:
KRISTIN

KRISTIN KILLOPS SHOULD not be alive today. Certainly she should not have children. Not only did her doctors send her home to die; they were quite clear that the treatments she received had destroyed her reproductive capacity.

Kristin's story begins with the appearance of unexplainable bruises on her body in 1974. She was nineteen and living with friends on the island of Maui in Hawaii. A doctor suggested she take iron supplements, but after two weeks without improvement, she underwent blood tests that yielded alarming results. All her blood counts were very low: red cells, white cells, and platelets. Platelets are the elements in blood responsible for clotting, and their low level was the cause of the bruising that attracted Kristin's attention. She was scheduled for a bone-marrow biopsy to determine why she lacked blood cells, and this result was even more ominous. Her marrow had almost no cells in it, only two percent of the normal number. The diagnosis was aplastic anemia—a medical calamity, because it represents loss of one of the body's most vital tissues, the source of all the formed elements of the blood. Kristin was evacuated to a Southern California hospital for full-scale technological intervention in an attempt to save her life.

The word "aplastic" means "without form"—a good description of a process that wipes out the normal components of bone marrow, leading to "empty marrow syndrome," in which there are empty spaces and fat where blood-forming cells should be. Bone marrow produces the red cells that carry oxygen, the various white cells that are central to the body's defenses, and the platelets. Normally, there is continuous production of all these elements, each one arising from its own ancestral cell line, maturing in stages, and finally migrating from the marrow cavity of large bones into the bloodstream. The ancestral cells themselves have a common ancestor called the stem cell, a "primitive," embryonic cell, native to the marrow, with the potential to differentiate into all other forms. Presumably, aplastic anemia results from failure of this stem cell, as a result of injury or suppression of some kind.

In Kristin's case, failure of bone marrow had no identifiable cause, but there was suspicion of a toxic exposure. Six other people on Maui developed marrow and blood abnormalities at the same time; all of them were dead within months. Such a cluster of cases suggests an environmental cause. Agricultural chemicals are used immoderately and carelessly in Hawaii, especially on the ubiquitous sugar cane and pineapple fields. Might these unfortunate people have had some genetic susceptibility to a pesticide or herbicide that entered their systems? We will never know.

Kristin arrived in Santa Barbara, California, desperately ill. Imagine the plight of someone with almost no functioning marrow. Severe depletion of red cells can damp down metabolism and stress the heart, which has to work harder to compensate for the low oxygen content of the blood. Deficiency of white cells knocks out resistance to infection. The hospital had to keep Kristin in a protective "reverse isolation" environment to minimize her contact with germs, as well as maintain her on antibiotics and give her daily washes with disinfectants. Absence of platelets creates the risk of abnormal bleeding, internally and externally.

Treatment of aplastic anemia requires drastic measures. Doctors often give high doses of steroids and other immunosuppressive drugs, which work in some cases but not others. Such treatment seems irrational, given the fact that the immune system is already crippled by the disappearance of its armies of white cells; but it is possible that some form of autoimmunity mediates the damage to the marrow, and steroids would suppress that. Maybe exposure to certain chemicals or viruses sets off an autoimmune reaction in which the immune system attacks marrow stem cells; the reaction then becomes self-perpetuating, independent of the triggering event.

Kristin's doctors began steroid treatment but thought she was too critically ill to survive. Instead they sent her to UCLA Medical Center in Los Angeles for a bone-marrow transplant. This operation may be the best hope for people with aplastic anemia, especially young people, who often respond well; but it is a major procedure, with uncertain results, limited by the availability of a suitable donor: preferably an identical twin or a sibling who is antigenically compatible. Luckily, Kristin had both a brother and a sister who matched and were willing to donate marrow, but she wanted to avoid the ordeal of a transplant. "I did many things to try to avoid it," she says, "including visualizations, meditation on healing, and taking a lot of vitamins and supplements. Then I found a healer to work on me, but it was just too late. The doctors gave me a firm deadline, and the healer did not have enough time to help me." Kristin received two bone-marrow transplants, but here she was not so lucky; her body rejected both of them. That was the medical profession's best shot. There was nothing else to offer her but general support and comfort. Her doctors had no hope.

Not so, Kristin. She was determined to find other sorts of treatments, and her inclination was to experiment with psychic healing and visualization. The hospital psychologist had referred her to a researcher at UCLA who studied psychic healing. Through him she found a healer who used hypnotherapy as well as the laying on of hands. While still hospitalized Kristin had two sessions a week with him for two weeks. At the end of that time, tests showed a modest increase in bone marrow, which her doctors told her was unheard of. But although her blood counts rose dramatically, they did not get high enough for her to escape isolation rooms, and she required transfusions. Finally, the doctors said they could do nothing more. After discussions with the patient and her mother, they discharged her from the hospital. Her mother understood that her daughter was being released so she could die at home.

Kristin persevered in her search for healers. She saw another who came five days a week to do the laying on of hands. After two weeks, results were again miraculous: blood counts rose and bordered on low normal. She hung on. Then she contracted serum hepatitis from the transfusions and became very ill, with a fever that remained over 100 degrees for a month.

She heard of a woman who could prescribe healing diets by psychic intuition. The diet prescribed for her was not easy to follow: no sugars or starches of any kind, two eggs and an extra yolk each day with steamed vegetables, vegetable broth and salad without oil, a little steamed fish or chicken, and one glass a day of pomegranate or grape juice, diluted fifty percent with water. Kristin followed this regimen for nine months. "It was the hardest thing I've ever done," she said. She lost weight. "But it pulled me through. Within a few days, there was dramatic improvement in the symptoms of the hepatitis."

In all, Kristin spent half a year in the hospital. One year from the onset of her illness, she knew she was going to live, although the road back to health remained slow and difficult. "They told me I would never have children, due to the drug they had given me to suppress rejection of the marrow transplants," she remembers. "Because of the risk of uncontrollable bleeding, they couldn't let me have periods, so they also gave me high doses of female hormones. In addition I got prednisone to try to control reactions to the transfusions and male hormones to try to stimulate my bone marrow. I didn't have a period for a year, and one psychic healer who put her hand over my pelvis said she sensed 'total blackness' there. But then I went on a fast for a week, and my period started! It's been completely regular ever since."

Twenty years later, Kristin is a healthy, vital woman, and the mother of four natural, healthy children. Her recovery was so unusual from the medical point of view that one of her doctors presented her case at an international conference on aplastic anemia. Kristin writes: "I am not just alive but quite healthy and strong. I've always thrived on physical activity and found as I got better that I could become as strong as I wanted to be. Daily bicycling, regular running, and ocean swimming helped get me over the final hurdle to excellent health.

"Today I am happy and busy raising my four children. I am a licensed naturopathic doctor but have not practiced since becoming a mother. I teach yoga and am writing and illustrating a children's book. Our family is very active—we ski, and windsurf, and I run regularly. Unless I mention my medical history, others do not suspect it; in fact those I do tell are quite surprised to learn that I was ever seriously ill."

What reserves of healing power did Kristin draw on to reactivate her bone marrow, neutralize whatever was the original cause of the disease, and undo the toxic effects of invasive treatment? I am fascinated by her unwavering confidence through her ordeal. "I always believed there was a way to live," she told me. "I just had to find it in time. That belief and the search fueled my undying optimism and made me an active participant in the healing process."

And what would she tell others facing grave medical crises?

"There may be different ways to healing for different people," she says, "but there is always a way. Keep searching!"

2

RIGHT IN MY
OWN BACKYARD

WHEN I FINISHED my South American travels in 1973, I began a long process of settling down in the vicinity of Tucson, Arizona, where I live to this day. I felt a strong affinity with the natural environment of the desert and made good connections with people and places in the area. One of those connections was with Sandy Newmark, a graduate student in anthropology at the University of Arizona, who became one of my neighbors in Esperero Canyon in the foothills of the Catalina Mountains. Sandy subsequently left anthropology to be a farmer in the White Mountains of central Arizona; then he returned to Tucson to enroll in medical school. Today he is my family's pediatrician.

Sandy and his wife, Linda, now a clinical psychologist, have a daughter, Sophia, who is developmentally retarded. When Sophia was a baby, many of the Newmarks' friends offered suggestions for treatment. One was to take the baby to an unusual osteopathic physician named Robert Fulford, who had a good record of working with children suffering from all sorts of problems. Sandy and Linda were so impressed with him that they took Sophia for a number of his gentle sessions of "cranial therapy," and Sandy, then in his first year of medical school at the University of Arizona, worked with Dr. Fulford for a time. He kept telling me I should meet him, but I was not interested, partially due to my ignorance about osteopaths. With the usual prejudices of medical doctors, I considered them second-rate M.D.'s who dabbled in the kind of manipulation of the body more frequently done by chiropractors. I was also probably still attached to the romantic notion of finding a healer/teacher in some far-off, very different culture—this despite my repeated experience of coming back emptyhanded from trips to remote places. It took many people telling me many times that I had to meet Dr. Fulford before I finally paid him a visit.

Bob Fulford was then in his late seventies. He had come to Tucson from Cincinnati in retirement from an overwhelming practice. One night, after spending a year recovering from exhaustion, he received a desperate call from a friend whose baby was severely ill with pneumonia. The baby was in the hospital, not responding to antibiotics. Dr. Fulford went to the hospital, gave hands-on treatment, and the next morning the baby was out of danger. Within hours people began calling him with requests for treatment, and he found himself drawn inexorably out of retirement and back into the practice of his own special form of osteopathic medicine.

I was struck by the simplicity of Dr. Fulford's office: a waiting room with a nurse-receptionist and two treatment rooms. Except for a diploma from the Kansas City College of Osteopathy on the wall, there were no distinguishing features and none of the equipment normally associated with a medical office. Dr. Fulford appeared kind and grandfatherly. He was tall, strong, and relaxed, with large, wonderful hands. He spoke quietly and sparingly. I told him I had heard much about his effectiveness and wanted to experience his treatments for myself.

"Well, what's wrong with you?" he asked.

"Not much," I told him. "My neck's been bothering me a little; sometimes it gets pretty stiff and sore."

"Well, let's see what we can do about it," he said.

He asked me to stand, put his hands on my shoulders, and observed my breathing. Then he moved my head in different directions. "Just get up here on the table," he directed. I lay on my back and watched him wheel over a stand with a curious instrument on a long power cord. The instrument was his "percussion hammer," a modified dentist's-drill motor with a thick, round metal disk that vibrated up and down. Dr. Fulford sat on a stool next to the table, adjusted the vibration rate, and put the disk in contact with my right shoulder. I could feel the vibrations through the whole right side of my body, pleasant and relaxing but hardly major therapy. After several minutes, Dr. Fulford's hand gave a little jerk and he muttered, "There she goes." With that he removed the percussion hammer and placed it in a new spot on my right hip. He continued this routine for twenty minutes, while I drifted in and out of daydreams; then he turned off the machine, moved his stool to the end of the table, and put his hands on the sides of my head, his fingers around my ears.

For the next few minutes, he cradled my head, applying the gentlest of pressure, now here, now there. It was one of the least dramatic forms of body work I had ever felt, so much so that I doubted it could accomplish anything. At the same time it felt reassuring to be held by such experienced, confident hands.

When this phase of the treatment was over, Dr. Fulford checked the mobility of my limbs, then asked me to sit up. He finished with a few, more familiar manipulations to crack my spine.

"There, that should do it," he said.

"What did you find?" I asked.

"Not much," he replied. "A few little restrictions in the shoulder that were probably causing your neck to get sore. Your cranial impulses are very good."

I had no idea what cranial impulses were, but I was glad to hear mine were good. As for "restrictions in the shoulder" and how they might cause a stiff neck, I was equally in the dark. But no further explanation was offered, and Dr. Fulford indicated that our time was up. He told me I was welcome to come back anytime and watch him work.

I was pleasantly surprised to learn that the charge for this session was only thirty-five dollars, clearly a bargain, if only for the relaxation it provided. Still, I failed to see how this minimal intervention could account for all the stories I had heard about Dr. Fulford's clinical successes. I resolved to come back and watch him treat others.

The next day I was surprised to find that I was fatigued and sore. I called Dr. Fulford to ask if this could be a result of his work. "Oh, yes," he said, "that's perfectly normal; you might feel it for a couple of days." And so I did. After that I felt fine, and my neck did, indeed, bother me less, but I did not notice any other change.

About a month later, I began spending a few hours a week in the doctor's little office on Grant Road, watching the old man work with patients. His office was always full, often with parents and children, representing a cross-section of the diverse groups that populate southern Arizona, including Hispanics and Asians, city folk and country folk. All came with high expectations and gratitude just for the chance to see this man. At the least, Dr. Fulford was a wonderful

role model of the old-fashioned, caring family doctor who made people feel better just by the warmth of his presence and his own personal example of good health.

Observing him, I was surprised by the brevity of his histories and
physical examinations. He asked very few questions when a new
patient walked in the door—"What's the problem? . . . How long
has it been bothering you? . . . Did you ever take any bad falls in
childhood? . . . Do you know anything about the circumstances of
your birth?" and maybe a few more. Then he stood people up,
checked the patients' limbs and breathing, rotated their heads, and
asked them to lie on the table. He administered to most people the
same kinds of treatments I received: a slow going-over with the percussion hammer, held to various parts of the body until some sort of
release occurred (when his hand holding the instrument would jerk
suddenly), then slow, imperceptible hands-on manipulation of the
head, and finally a few adjustments of the back. He rarely volunteered explanations of what he thought was wrong or what he aimed
to do; but if people asked, he would do so in a few words. Most people did not ask; they just seemed to entrust themselves or their children to the doctor and let him work in silence. Everyone relaxed in
Dr. Fulford's hands, even restless, fussy children, who would calm
down almost as soon as he touched them.

Often, at the end of the session, he gave people strange daily exercises to perform, exercises that I had never seen before. One he recommended frequently went like this: Stand with your feet apart at
shoulder width and extend the arms to the side fully with the left
palm facing up and the right palm facing down. Breathe deeply and
regularly, holding this position until the strain in the upper arms and
shoulders becomes unbearable. Then, as slowly as you can, raise the
arms above the head, keeping them fully extended, until the hands
touch. Then lower the arms and relax. What was that supposed to
do? I asked him. "It opens the chest and allows the breath to
expand," was the answer. Another Fulford exercise was to sit on the
edge of a chair with feet flat on the floor and shoulder width apart,
then bend forward and, with the arms inside the legs, grasp the bot-
toms of the feet with the hands. Hold this position for a few minutes,
and it gently stretches the lower vertebrae, allowing for greater
motion of the spine. Sometimes when patients came back, Dr. Fulford, on examining them, would say, "You haven't been doing your

exercise," or "Good, you've been doing your exercise," and the patients would confirm that this was so.

He often told patients not to come back. "When do you want to see me again?" they might ask as they got off the table. "I don't need to see you again," Dr. Fulford would say. "You're fixed." "But don't I need any follow-up?" they might persist. Dr. Fulford smiled and shook his head. "I took the shock out of your system," he would say. "Now just let old Mother Nature do her job." If there was any disappointment among Dr. Fulford's patients, it had to do with their not having to see him again, since the experience of his treatment was so satisfying.

Gradually, I began to realize that I was seeing something quite extraordinary. This old man of strong hands and few words was, in fact, fixing people who came to him with a wide range of disorders, often in one session of therapy that, on the surface, seemed minimal. I heard tale after tale of longstanding problems resolved after one or two visits to Dr. Fulford, problems that had not responded to conventional medicine. And these were not just aches, pains, and other musculoskeletal ailments but also hormonal and digestive disturbances, sleep disorders, asthma, ear infections, and more. How could such undramatic treatment give such dramatic results?

I began to ask Dr. Fulford about the why and wherefore of his methods. What was the theory behind them? Just what was he doing? The answers I received sounded like nothing I had learned at Harvard Medical School.

Bob Fulford was a pure, old-time osteopath in the tradition of the man who founded the system, Andrew Taylor Still (1828–1917) of Kirksville, Missouri. A. T. Still, "the Old Doctor" to his contemporaries, was a renegade physician who disowned the toxic drugs of his colleagues in favor of a drugless system of therapy based on manipulation of bones. His idea was to adjust the body mechanically in order to allow the circulatory and nervous systems to function smoothly, bringing natural healing power to any ailing part. The new profession that he founded in 1874 was very successful in its early years, but by the middle of the twentieth century it was eclipsed by the spectacular rise of modern scientific medicine, also known as allopathic medicine. In response, osteopaths abandoned Still's teachings and began to behave increasingly like M.D.'s. Today the M.D. and D.O. degrees are equivalent; most osteopaths rely on drugs and surgery, and few use manipulation as a primary modality of treatment.

Nevertheless, there has always existed within the osteopathic profession a minor tradition of healers who use no drugs and continue to refine A. T. Still's insights into the nature of the human body and its potential to heal itself. One of those was William Sutherland, who in 1939 announced to his colleagues his discovery of an aspect of human physiology he called the primary respiratory mechanism, and a technique for modifying it that became known as cranial therapy, or craniosacral therapy. Sutherland worked on his theory for many years to ensure its correctness before going public. Nonetheless it met with great resistance, and only a small percentage of osteopaths accepted it. One of those was the young Robert Fulford, then just beginning his general practice in Cincinnati.

Sutherland's insight was that the central nervous system and its associated structures were in constant rhythmic motion, and that this motion was an essential feature—perhaps the most essential feature—of human life and health. He identified five components of the mechanism:

- Motion at the cranial sutures, the joints linking the twenty-six bones of the skull
- Expansion and contraction of the hemispheres of the brain
- Motion of the membranes covering the brain and spinal cord
- A fluid wave within the cerebrospinal fluid that bathes the brain and spinal cord
- Involuntary, subtle motion of the sacrum (tailbone).

Sutherland thought the rhythmic expansion and contraction of this system resembled breathing, but since it was occurring in the most vital, most essential organs, he called it "primary respiration" to indicate its importance in the hierarchy of body functions and distinguish it from "secondary respiration," the familiar motions of the chest, lungs, and diaphragm associated with the exchange of air. He postulated that an intact, freely moving primary respiratory mechanism was necessary to full health; any restrictions in it could lead to disease, since the central nervous system regulated all other organs.

One of the main heresies in Sutherland's formulation was the notion that the cranial bones move. Generations of anatomists had taught that the joints of the skull are fixed and immobile. Not only

M.D.'s but also most D.O.'s refused to consider the idea of cranial motion. Dr. Fulford was not one of them, and he started training himself to feel those motions by putting his hands on people's heads.

It is only in recent years that researchers at Michigan State University's College of Osteopathic Medicine have confirmed Sutherland's theory with X-ray films of living skulls that show cranial motion. Those motions can be measured by sensitive instruments. Bob Fulford would argue that the most sensitive instruments are the hands of a practiced physician. He trained himself to feel a human hair under seventeen sheets of paper, and he says that anyone can develop similar touch sensitivity with enough practice.

Under Dr. Fulford's guidance I began feeling heads myself to see if I could detect cranial impulses. At first I felt mainly my own pulse, but as I practiced I began to feel the subtle breathlike motion that Dr. Fulford considers the most vital expression of life. At least I felt it in people who had well-running primary respiratory mechanisms. Once he asked me to feel the head of a woman who, he said, had no detectable cranial impulses. She had been in several bad accidents, one twenty years before, and now suffered extreme fatigue, insomnia, migraine headaches, weak vision, poor digestion, and increased susceptibility to infection. Her head felt like a bag of cement, a dead weight, the rhythm of life not present. After several sessions of treatment, her cranial motions began to return, and as they did, her health began to improve.

"What causes impairment of this system?" I asked Dr. Fulford.

"Trauma," was the answer. "Three kinds of trauma. The first is birth trauma. If the first breath of life is not perfectly full, the cranial rhythms are restricted from the start. That first breath is so important. In my lifetime I've seen problems of this sort increase steadily, which, I think, is a black mark against our obstetrical practices. The second common reason is physical trauma, especially in early life. Any fall or blow that knocks the wind out of you, that causes the breath cycle to be interrupted, even for a moment, can cause permanent, lifelong restriction in the primary respiratory mechanism. It's possible to feel and identify and undo those restrictions with your hands. That's what I call taking the shock out of the body. And a third reason, maybe less common, is major psychological trauma—again, especially in early life. I estimate that ninety-five percent of people have restrictions of one degree or another in this function."

Around the time Dr. Fulford was teaching these new concepts to me, I was helping a friend through a medical crisis. Kim Cliffton was a thirty-four-year-old marine biologist who spent most of the year on the Pacific beaches of southern Mexico, trying to save an endangered species of sea turtle that was being hunted to extinction. He directed a World Wildlife Fund project that kept him in the field leading a rough, adventurous life except for the summer months, when the turtles headed out to sea. Then he would come up to Tucson, looking bedraggled, to tell his stories and gather his strength. For several years he had suffered from intestinal problems: episodes of severe diarrhea in Mexico, inability to digest many foods, and abdominal pain. He would routinely take courses of antibiotics and antiparasitic drugs, but year by year the episodes became more frequent and more intense. Now he came to me having lost twenty pounds, saying that he had not had a formed bowel movement in months, that his stool frequently contained blood and mucus, that he had constant abdominal pain and increasing debility. He did not think he would be able to continue his turtle work.

Kim wanted prescriptions to knock out what he thought were more parasites in his gut, but the picture he presented was not one of infection. Instead, he seemed to me to have chronic inflammatory bowel disease, possibly ulcerative colitis, and I urged him to see a highly recommended gastroenterologist at the University of Arizona Health Sciences Center. Kim was the son of a pulmonary surgeon in New York, and he had great faith in conventional medicine. That faith was tested, however, when, after a long and expensive series of tests, culminating in a biopsy of the colon, the gastroenterologist could not identify the nature of the problem, except to say that Kim's colon was severely and chronically inflamed. Ulcerative colitis was definitely a possibility. "I think we should go in and take out more tissue," the gastroenterologist told me. "Then maybe we'll find out what the hell he's got." This did not sound encouraging, and since Kim was paying for it out of his own pocket, I suggested looking for another approach. Then it occurred to me to send Kim to Dr. Fulford.

Kim had a long history of playing contact sports, including boxing—he had been a heavyweight in the army—and had suffered many traumatic injuries. I noticed that he always breathed through his mouth. In addition to the intestinal problems he complained of episodes of bad back and neck pain. It seemed to me that Dr. Fulford might be able to make sense of this whole picture, but I foresaw two problems. The first was that Dr. Fulford was now only seeing patients under thirty, a limit he imposed because his practice was again getting out of hand as his reputation grew. "I'm almost eighty," he said to me one day, "and·I can't work myself to exhaustion anymore. My energies go further with younger folks; their healing responses are stronger." He had invented the percussion hammer to make things easier on himself, too. What it accomplished could be done by hand, he said, but with much more effort.

A second problem was that Kim, having grown up with conventional medicine and lacking any experience with alternative practitioners, might be reluctant to trust himself to one. I did my best to explain to both Dr. Fulford and Kim why they should see each other, and I succeeded, except that Kim couldn't see how an osteopath was going to help his colon. "Just tell him all your symptoms," I urged him, "all the intestinal symptoms as well as the pains in your back and neck."

I was unable to be in the office that day and waited expectantly to see Kim when he came home. "He's a quack," were Kim's first words. "I mean, he's a nice old man, but he doesn't do anything."

"What did he tell you?" I asked.

"He said I was in critical condition, that my cranial motions were completely shut down because of old injuries, and that the cranial nerve controlling the digestive system was not functioning as a result. Also that the same injuries make me breathe through my mouth, and that doesn't nourish my brain as breathing should."

"Did he say he was able to help you?"

"He said he took care of most of it and that I should come back in three weeks. But he seemed so feeble, and he's got all these nervous tics; I felt sorry for him. At least it didn't cost much."

"What do you mean by 'nervous tics'?" I asked.

"You know, when he has that vibrator on you, every few minutes his hand flies up in the air and his whole body jerks."

"Really?"

"Yes, it's kind of sad."

I called Dr. Fulford for his view of the session. "Mr. Cliffton came in not a moment too soon," he told me. "His whole primary respiratory mechanism was shut down. I think he would really have gone downhill fast."

"Were you able to help him?"

"Oh, yes, I got major releases from many parts of his body, undid a lot of the trauma, and got the impulses flowing again. Once the vagus nerve kicks in, he'll be all right. He should just take it easy now and let old Mother Nature do her job."

Six hours after the treatment, Kim's diarrhea stopped for the first time in eight months, never to return. Over the next three months he regained all of his lost weight and energy. The back and neck pain disappeared, and he stopped breathing through his mouth.

"He saved my life," Kim told me later. "I'm convinced that man saved my life." He has since become a passionate convert to alternative medicine in general, and osteopathy in particular. This cure was so impressive that I tried to arrange a conference to discuss the case with Dr. Fulford, Kim, myself, and the university gastroenterologist. That doctor said he was interested but failed to show. When I asked him why, he told me, "Look, I'm not going to argue with success, but I can't believe that osteopathic treatment had anything to do with the outcome."

Shortly afterward I had another opportunity to witness Dr. Fulford's skill with the human body, this time firsthand. I was working in my garden with a friend. In a freak accident that I could never reconstruct, he stood up as I bent down, and his shoulder hit me hard in the right side of my face, just forward of my ear. There was a sharp pain, and I could neither open nor close my mouth fully. It felt as if my jaw were partially dislocated, and I couldn't get it to go back, no matter what I did. I called Dr. Fulford and told him what had happened. "Get on down here," he said. I drove myself to his office and walked in, still in pain and still unable to make my jaw work. He made time in his lineup of patients and told me to get on the table.

As soon as he put his hands on my head, he named the bone in my skull that was out of place. Then he began the gentlest of manipulations. After a few minutes, he said, "There, it's back." I felt nothing happen and no change in the discomfort. He said I could get up. "It still hurts," I said, disappointed.

"Oh, the muscles will be sore for a little while," he replied. "Well, I've got to get busy."

I left, unconvinced that I had been helped, contemplating a visit to the emergency room of the university hospital. But ten minutes later, as I was sitting at a stop light, I suddenly realized that the pain was not there, and that I could open and close my mouth normally. Incredible! Thank you, Dr. Fulford! Then I thought: What would you have done if you didn't know about him? Probably, I would have visited an emergency room, undergone X-rays, and been sent home with painkillers, muscle relaxants, and the expectation of a large bill. Possibly I would have remained unhealed for weeks or months.

Now I was truly inspired to learn everything I could from Dr. Fulford. I also became increasingly frustrated in trying to explain my excitement to colleagues. Most doctors were no more interested in my stories than the gastroenterologist had been. It was especially annoying to try to talk with pediatricians about the Fulford approach to ear infections in children.

Recurrent infection of the middle ear—otitis media—is the bread and butter of pediatricians; so common is it that an ever-growing number of people in our society accept it as a normal part of growing up. The conventional treatments are antibiotics and decongestants and sometimes surgical placement of tubes through the eardrums to equalize pressure. Commonly the drug treatments end episodes of infection sooner or later, only for new episodes to recur at frequent intervals.

Bob Fulford was outstandingly successful at permanently ending this cycle in young children, often with just one session of treatment in which he concentrated on freeing up the sacrum. "I just beat the heck out of their tailbones" was the way he put it, because he found that the sacral end of the craniosacral system was often the one that was locked up in children, probably from trauma suffered during birth. Here is how he explained the situation:

"When the sacrum is restricted, the whole primary respiratory mechanism is impaired. Along with this goes a pattern of restricted breathing, and it is the force of the breath—the rhythmic pressure changes in the chest—that pumps the lymphatic circulation. With inadequate lymphatic circulation there is poor fluid drainage from the head and neck. Stagnant fluid builds up in the middle ear, providing an ideal breeding ground for bacteria. You can wipe out the bacteria all you want with antibiotics, but if you don't correct the underlying problem of fluid stagnation, they're just going to come back." Certainly that is the usual experience of kids, parents, and pediatricians; the bacteria just come back.

I saw case after case go through Dr. Fulford's office in which this simple treatment cured otitis media permanently. Often I could see a change in breathing as soon as the child got off the table: greater, more symmetrical expansion of the chest, deeper breaths. Yet I could not get one pediatrician from the Tucson medical community to come to Dr. Fulford's office and watch. Instead of being interested in my accounts of his treatment, the medical men seemed threatened. Finally, one practitioner, an Englishwoman, agreed to watch. She even sent a patient, with such good result that she consented to help me make a documentary film of Dr. Fulford with the biomedical communications department of the University of Arizona.

The more I watched Bob Fulford work, the more I was impressed by his own health and vigor. At eighty he was an inspiration for successful aging. Once I asked him for his personal secret of good health. "I'll show you," he said, and with that took a deep, slow breath that went on so long that I stared in disbelief. His chest expanded enormously. Then he exhaled as spaciously. "The' more air you can breathe in and out, the more nourishment you can give to the central nervous system," he said afterward. "Good breathing is the key."

The medicine I saw Bob Fulford practice was the kind of medicine I had longed for during my years of clinical training and my years of wandering. It was nonviolent medicine that did not suppress disease but rather encouraged the body's own healing potential to express itself. Dr. Fulford was the first practitioner I met who adhered religiously to the two most famous admonitions of Hippocrates: "First, Do No Harm" (*Primum non nocere*) and "Honor the Healing Power of Nature" (the *vis medicatrix naturae*).

I learned so much by simply watching him work, being worked on by him, and having informal discussions with him. His answers to my questions were always brief and in ordinary language, unsophisticated by the standards of academic medicine but bright with wisdom and full of useful practical information. Here are some ideas I took away from my time with him that I have found most useful in my own work as a physician:

- *The body wants to be healthy.* Health is the condition of perfect balance, when all systems run smoothly and energy circulates freely. This is the natural condition, the one in which least effort is expended; therefore, when the body is out of balance, it wants to get back to it. Treatment can and should take advantage of this tendency to return to the condition of health.

• *Healing is a natural power.* When Dr. Fulford told patients to relax and "let old Mother Nature do her job," he was expressing in a folksy way his great faith in the *vis medicatrix naturae* of Hippocrates, a concept missing from conventional medicine. Never in my years at Harvard Medical School did anyone mention it to me and my classmates, nor do medical school professors talk about it to students today. That seems to me to be the greatest single philosophical defect of modern medicine, a defect that has immense practical significance, since it underlies our inability to find cost-effective solutions to common health problems.

My friend Linda Newmark said that Dr. Fulford told her the best thing she could do for her husband, Sandy, while he was in medical school, was to take him out in nature for regular walks. He explained to her, "He'll need that to balance all the other stuff they're putting into his head."

• *The body is a whole, and all of its parts are connected.* Dr. Fulford had a brilliant, intuitive understanding of the body as a unified functioning system. When a patient came in complaining of pain in the knee, he did not automatically conclude that the problem was in the knee and proceed to work there. He knew that the knee is the compensating joint for both the ankle and the hip. If there is a restriction in an ankle, as a result of an old injury, the ankle will not be able to respond as it should to gravity and motion and will transmit a distorted force up the leg. The knee will compensate for the distortion in order to keep the pelvis in its normal position, and the strain of the compensating effort might be experienced as knee pain. If the knee is locked for any reason, the distortion from the ankle can reach the hip, causing lower back pain. How many knee and back operations were performed, Dr. Fulford wondered, for problems that actually originated in locked-up ankles? I saw him cure cases of chronic knee and back pain by unlocking ankles with his percussion hammer.

Bob Fulford thought the restrictions he talked about occurred in the fascia, the tough connective tissue that covers muscles and separates spaces inside the body. Anatomists teach that fascia exists as separate sheets, but Fulford worked on the premise that all of the fascia throughout the body is one big, convoluted piece. If a restriction occurs anywhere in it, it distorts the fabric of the whole; hence local changes can have global effects.

Similarly, when Kim Cliffton came with his complaints of back and neck pain, mouth breathing, and chronic bowel disease, Dr. Fulford looked at this whole picture of disturbed physiology and identified a common root in an old traumatic injury of the head. The gastroenterologist, who looked only at Kim's colon, could make no sense of the problem and had no treatments to offer except drugs to suppress the inflammatory process in the colon.

• *There is no separation of mind and body.* Just as Dr. Fulford believed that psychological trauma could interfere with the respiratory motions of the central nervous system, so also did he presume that physical interventions, by their effect on the nervous system, could improve psychological function. He regularly raised IQs of learning-disabled children by his cranial therapy; in fact, he was so successful at this that a state hospital for developmentally retarded children in Louisiana had him come for a few weeks every year to work on its patients.

• *The beliefs of practitioners strongly influence the healing powers of patients.* Dr. Fulford believed that the patients he treated could get better. He had a simple, genuine, and very beautiful faith in their potential for healing, which he communicated in many ways, both verbal and nonverbal. That was one reason so many people gravitated to him. He was also careful to select those cases he thought he could help. If you had a broken bone, he would tell you, "There's nothing I can do for a broken bone. Let nature heal it, then come to me, and I'll take the shock of the injury out of your system." Neither would he treat problems requiring surgery or other forms of emergency care.

As he got older, and the demands on him increased steadily, he kept lowering the age limit of patients he accepted. Soon it was twenty-five, then twenty. Ideally, he would have liked to restrict his practice to infants, "because their healing potential is so great, and the restrictions have not had time to become fixed in body structures." He also thought all newborns should have prophylactic treatment, because "so many illnesses in later life are long-term consequences of traumatic birth, and for the first twenty-four hours of life, the bones are just like jelly; it takes no effort to put them back the way they should be."

Dr. Fulford did not succeed with everyone, but he had a higher percentage of successful outcomes than any other practitioner I have met.

Eventually, the workload became overwhelming, and Bob Fulford, to the great dismay of his patients and followers, announced that he was going into permanent retirement and moving back to southern Ohio. He did so; but, as I write this, he is still, at the age of ninety, actively teaching cranial therapy. He travels around the country lecturing, instructing students in technique, and inspiring new generations of physicians to become true doctors.

Discovering Dr. Fulford in my own backyard after chasing all over the world was a powerful lesson: I did not have to look Out There for what I wanted. Neither do most people have to look Out There for healing. Of course, it is worth searching for the best treatment, since treatment comes from outside. But healing comes from within, its source in our very nature as living organisms.

THE FACES OF HEALING:
HARVEY AND PHYLLIS

IN THE SUMMER of 1992, when he was fifty years old and six months into a happy second marriage, Harvey Sandler developed a disturbing set of symptoms. His vision became blurred, he would wake up in the middle of the night drenched in sweat, he began to urinate frequently, and he became impotent. The last change was the most disturbing, because he and Phyllis, his new wife, had enjoyed a passionate sexual relationship for some time. "It got more and more difficult for me to perform," Harvey remembers, "so I just stopped coming to bed." He chalked it all up to stress and did not visit a doctor.

Phyllis says, "I didn't want to pressure him, but after a while it got me down." Harvey's job as a money manager gave him some stress; but in Phyllis's words, "Really, our lives were pretty good." After several months, Harvey sought help from a psychiatrist specializing in sexual dysfunction. She suggested blood tests, one of which, for a pituitary hormone, was abnormal. Then an eye doctor ordered an MRI scan of the brain, and this test revealed a tumor directly behind Harvey's eyes. In this location it was pressing on the hypothalamus, a vital center that controls the pituitary gland, and through it, many involuntary functions of the body. It was also affecting the optic nerves.

From its location and appearance, Harvey's doctors thought the tumor was benign—either a glioma or a craniopharyngioma. The former is a solid tumor arising from cells that support neurons. The latter arises from embryonic cells left over from fetal development and tends to be cystic, containing fluid-filled sacs in addition to tissue; it usually appears in people younger than Harvey, but may grow slowly for a long time before it reaches a size that affects brain function.

The brain is one part of the body where the distinction between benign and malignant tumors is not as immediately important as it usually is. The problem here was a space-occupying lesion, exerting pressure on vital centers in a confined area. It would have to be removed or shrunk.

Harvey and Phyllis made the rounds of neurosurgeons in New York. Most were "very alarmist" about the tumor and prospects for removing it without causing permanent brain damage. "Finally we found one neurosurgeon who told us what we wanted to hear," Phyllis says. "He told us the operation would be 'a piece of cake,' and he could have Harvey in and out of the hospital in two days. We decided to go with him."

The operation took place in November 1992. When exposed, the tumor turned out to be the size of a small egg, situated between the optic nerve and the hypothalamus. The surgeon, unable to remove the tumor because of its location, drained fluid from it to reduce the pressure it was causing and took a sample of the tissue, which identified it as a craniopharyngioma. He then sent Harvey for thirty radiation treatments to shrink the tumor, ending just around Christmas.

To everyone's dismay, the patient got worse as treatment progressed. His vision deteriorated to the point of near blindness, leaving him unable to read anything or see what was on a television screen. To prevent brain swelling, doctors had prescribed Decadron, a strong steroid; it caused Harvey to gain forty pounds and changed his personality. "He was angry, aggressive, and nasty and slept most of the time," Phyllis says. Harvey says only, "I don't remember any of it." He began to lose his memory and his mind. He would get lost in his apartment, describe events that never happened. "I didn't know who this person was," Phyllis recalls. According to the doctors, none of this should have happened, and they had no explanation for the deterioration. "Nobody would take responsibility for it, either," Phyllis says. "The surgeon said, 'I'm only the carpenter here; my job is done'; the endocrinologist told us to see the neurologist, and the neurologist told us to see the endocrinologist. I got really scared."

About this time, a counselor named Deborah, who is skilled at working with seriously ill people, took Phyllis away for a weekend break, arranging for Harvey's son to come in and care for him. Deborah's brother was a distinguished neurosurgeon in Philadelphia, and he was called in for another opinion. After reviewing the case, this doctor told his sister: "Harvey Sandler will never make an independent decision again in his life. He will never recover. You should try to prepare Phyllis to accept his condition; it will be lucky if he stays the same and doesn't deteriorate further."

Phyllis became hysterical when Deborah reported this conversation, and as Deborah recalls: "Phyllis screamed, 'There's no way he's not coming back!' I said, 'Okay, I'm with you,' but in my heart I didn't believe it."

Phyllis returned home feeling she could not afford to waste time. "I called all the smartest and best-connected people I knew," she says, "always asking for help. I told them I had to find the one doctor in the world who had done more of these procedures than any other. Well, I got sent on one wild-goose chase after another. I talked to doctor after doctor. Finally, I found one who seemed right, but he specialized in aneurysms, not tumors. Then the eye doctor called me and said, 'Time is of the essence. What vision he has left is going.' I dragged my poor husband from doctor to doctor, even though he was exhausted and never wanted to go out. Usually, I had to dress him and half-carry him, and usually he fell asleep in the doctors' offices; once he wandered out of an office and got lost. Finally, I found a neurosurgeon who was willing to operate, one who had done a lot of these procedures and wasn't put off by such a high-risk case."

The second operation to remove the tumor took place in mid-February 1993. Harvey did not wake up for a long time after the surgery. Then he almost died from fluid filling his lungs. On the fourth day after the operation he lapsed into a coma, and the doctors again were at a loss.

It was Phyllis who saved the day. She wondered whether Harvey's coma might be the result of withdrawing him from Decadron too quickly. The drug is used short-term to prevent brain swelling after surgery, but this team of doctors did not know that Harvey had been maintained on very high doses of Decadron since the previous operation. When Phyllis pointed that out to them, they tried giving Harvey some Decadron intravenously. The next morning he was sitting up and talking. He stayed in intensive care for two weeks, in a regular hospital room for another two weeks, then began a long and steady recovery.

"It took him a whole year to catch up," Phyllis says, "and he remained amnesic for the three months prior to the second operation. Slowly he got stronger physically and recovered some of his memory. He had to develop a whole new way of thinking and approaching life. He had to learn what had happened to him, then to be frightened about it, then to be reborn."

Deborah remembers Harvey's frustration during this period. "Everyone expected him to be transformed by the experience," she recalls, "but it seemed that everyone *but* him got transformed. Harvey had had it all. He was rich, successful, good-looking, enjoying life immensely. His friends were deeply affected by what happened. Almost overnight, he turned into one of life's unfortunates: brain-damaged, overweight, angry and abusive, disoriented, with a good chance of dying or being a vegetable. People said, 'If this can happen to him, it could happen to me.' It really got people thinking about their vulnerability and motivated them to clean up their acts. Now, after the second operation, the more Harvey heard about the effect he had had on others, the more he resented the fact that nothing magical had happened to him."

Phyllis spent time every day trying to help Harvey learn to walk again. He would fight with her a lot and remembers her asking him constantly, "So what's different now? How is your life changed as a result of all this?" All he could think to say was, "I just want to get back on the tennis court."

About a year after the second operation, the magic happened. In Harvey's words: "I started thinking. I had always let Phyllis do the thinking for me, and I had always shied away from power and responsibility. Now it seemed the tumor and the surgery had reawakened parts of me that had been asleep and at the same time lessened other parts of me. My ability to perform sexually came back six weeks after the operation, but my sexuality in general was diminished. It think it had been too dominant before. On the other hand, thinking and emotion increased. In general, I felt more balanced. To make a very long story short, I've assumed responsibility for my life. I'm a more responsible human being now, and I'm using my power appropriately. This illness is one of the biggest gifts I've ever had.

"On a practical level, my vision is better than it was before, and my memory is excellent. I'm working and playing and living much more the life I want to live. I've changed my work so that I can stay at home and don't have to go in to an office. I play tennis every morning."

I also talked to Phyllis about her perspective on the saga. She said, "Throughout the darkest days I remember thinking, 'There are going to be gifts coming from this, and I'm going after every one of them.' We were very isolated during that period; I didn't let many people into our lives. If I had believed the doctors all knew more than me, I would have accepted their pessimistic outlook and not kept pursuing the possibility of a cure. It's hard to believe they don't know it all. The surgeon who finally took us on told me he couldn't guarantee that Harvey would live or have any vision or even recover consciousness. He is as surprised and thrilled at the extent of the recovery as anyone else. A year after the operation, we invited him and his wife to come for dinner and celebrate with us.

"Really, Harvey has been reborn. He was given a chance to redesign himself, and he's come out a more generous person, someone who is more sensitive to people and wants to be the best person he can be. I've been reborn in the process too. Our adventure has inspired both of us to keep trying to heal the parts of ourselves that are not yet healed. We are still processing it and appreciating it."

Phyllis wanted me to know that this was not the first dramatic healing she had witnessed. "Seven years ago I developed excruciating sciatic pain. I had it for two and a half years and went to more than twenty doctors but could get no relief with any of the treatments they prescribed. Then my first grandchild was born, and I really wanted to be with the baby. I knew I had to make myself better if I was going to be able to enjoy being a grandmother. I listened to tapes, visualized, got acupuncture, ate healthy food, and took vitamins. In just four weeks I was pain free, a hundred percent. I think the most important thing I did was to visualize more blood going to my back. That and telling myself, 'I really want to be healed.' "

3

TESTIMONIALS

AS A PHYSICIAN with botanical training and a long-standing interest in medicinal plants, I work as an advisor to several groups promoting research on herbal medicine, one of which is the American Botanical Council in Austin, Texas. Recently, the director of the council, Mark Blumenthal, asked me to comment on a letter he received from a woman in Chicago, extolling the health benefits of ginkgo. She was taking pills containing an extract of the leaves of a tree, *Ginkgo biloba*, native to China and now widely planted in cities throughout the world, because it is resistant to air pollution. The tree has attractive, fan-shaped leaves, used for centuries in traditional Chinese medicine, and the female trees provide edible nuts. Only in recent years has a concentrated, standardized extract of ginkgo leaves become available in the West. This product has become very popular in Germany as a treatment for circulatory disorders and now is available in all health food stores in this country. The medical profession here remains mostly ignorant of it.

Let me quote at length from the letter:

An 84-year-old friend of mine (I am 60) called to ask me if I knew anything about Ginkgo biloba. I said no, but I would do some research on it. My research led me to two books. . . . Then I did a little research elsewhere, coming up with a few things.

My own reaction to Ginkgo was so astounding that I became a walking advertisement for it. I started noticing activity on the third day I started taking it (one pill a day in the beginning). In a few days there was more activity. During the second week I began taking three a day, one with each meal. I believe it was the third week that I lost my depression and began feeling like the world was a wonderful place in which to live.

I began having more energy. In a six-week period I noticed more and more changes. . . . One of the most outstanding was when the Ginkgo reached my equilibrium. I had been walking with a cane because my gait was so unsteady. Suddenly, while walking in a store, I noticed that I wasn't using my cane, and I had a longer stride, a steady stride. Not minutes later I ran into someone I knew and excitedly told her what had just happened to me. I was *swinging my cane instead of using it to steady myself.* I was so excited that I made a spontaneous rapid turn-around (something I hadn't done in years!). (I know people must have thought I was crazy!) I was all smiles—as was the person I met!

I lost the pain in my legs and feet. I was regaining normal breathing action. Now, a year later, I have lost my night blindness (and have gotten my ophthalmologist interested in Ginkgo). My vision is better, and my hearing has improved immensely. (My TV is now on low sound rather than loud.)

I called and wrote to people I knew. People needed to know what was happening to me. Those who saw me after I was on Ginkgo were amazed.

A beautician had a lot of pain in her wrists from working with her hands so much. After listening to me she began taking Ginkgo and claims she not only has eliminated her pain but also sleeps much better. A woman in her late 40s could rarely get out of her house, and when she did, she needed to have a wheelable can of oxygen with her and be using it all the while she was out. Now she uses the oxygen very little—and is able to go many places. This shocks a lot of people who know her and her background.

I have TMJ (temporo-mandibular joint) problems—or I should say *I did have them.* Suddenly I no longer suffer from the pain! It had to be Ginkgo! It just *had to be!* I figure as long as I am on Ginkgo I'm not going to be bothered by it. Even the clicking sound is gone!

I have a 94-year-old mother in a nursing home and this year she changed doctors. . . . The new doctor was agreeable to Mom taking Ginkgo if I would pay for it. I certainly was willing to do that.

The last Wednesday of January 1994 this doctor okayed the Ginkgo. He allowed her only one pill a day. I wasn't concerned about that since I had seen the 84-year-old woman who originally talked to me about Ginkgo do amazingly well with only one pill a day!

Mom started with Ginkgo the very next day. From Thursday to Sunday she changed amazingly! She was no longer depressed. She was happy. She was filled with life. Her voice volume had changed from a weak, soft voice (you could hear illness in its tone) to a strong, solid voice. I could feel electricity in that room between us! I was so happy to see her changes and she was thrilled to feel so much better! She also had a very miraculous improvement in her hearing! This placed her life in an entirely new category! Previously she walked in her own little world—not being able to hear others speak unless they yelled loudly (and few bothered to do that), and not being able to think clearly (short-term memory loss, confusion, anxiety, etc.). . . .

Suddenly she was hearing! For the first time she wanted to know how to fix her hearing aid! And one day she started talking to the people at her dining room table—something she had never done before! . . . It was obvious that her short-term memory loss was improving. . . . Her hemorrhoids also have improved. I expect a lot more things to improve. . . .

IT IS SO WONDERFUL TO BE ABLE TO FEEL LIFE AS IT SHOULD BE FELT—BE WILLING TO BREATHE AND ENJOY LIFE AS IT SHOULD BE ENJOYED! A PERSON JUST DOESN'T WANT TO STOP!

A man I know took one Ginkgo a day for approximately six months. He suffered from ringing in the ears. At six months he lost the ringing. He quit the Ginkgo. The ringing returned.

I believe it is necessary to continue taking Ginkgo if you intend to retain any of the benefits it offers. For those who suffer greatly it certainly is worth the cost! Far too many people feel that life isn't worth living. I wish I could reach them all and tell them the wonders of Ginkgo!

This letter is a classic example of a testimonial to a health product. As such it would likely be dismissed by most medical scientists, who tend to drop all testimonials into wastebaskets labeled Anecdotal Evidence. In medical usage, "anecdotal evidence" means "of no scientific value or importance." I take a different view of this material, and I am interested in why so many doctors have a hard time with it.

I suppose the simplest answer is that doctors and scientists do not like to be made to look like fools, and they sense danger in endorsing products or techniques whose claimed effects may turn out to be false or unprovable by controlled experiments. But it is equally foolish to ignore testimonial evidence, because it may suggest directions for experimental inquiry as well as provide clues to the nature of healing.

Many scientists reject testimonials out of hand on the assumption that the information is false, that people are either deluded or have simply made up the stories for one reason or another. The essence of good science is open-minded inquiry, so would it not make sense to try, at least, to verify the stories? My experience, overwhelmingly, is that whenever I have met and interviewed persons who have written testimonial letters to me, I have found no reason to disbelieve them, although I may not agree with their interpretations of their experiences. For example, I believe the writer of the letter quoted here experienced the positive changes she reports in her own health and the health of relatives and friends. I am not sure I agree with her statement that "it had to be Ginkgo! It just *had to be!*"

Science is the orderly gathering of knowledge by methodical inquiry and experiment, but where do you get ideas to inquire about or experiment with except through your experience of the world around you? Experimenting blindly, without starting from reasonable hypotheses suggested by experience, often wastes time, money, and effort. I became interested in Dr. Fulford and through him in cranial osteopathic theory and practice as a result of paying attention to testimonials about his work. Testimonials have led me to discoveries of other useful practices as well.

Some years ago I got a letter from a man in California describing remarkable experiences with a preparation of an herb called bloodroot, which he said miraculously dissolved moles and other growths on the skin, including, in at least one case he had witnessed, a malignant melanoma. He urged me to order the product from an old man in Utah who prepared it, and to experiment with it. I did order it (it was quite inexpensive), and shortly afterward a container of oily, blood-red paste arrived in the mail with no instructions. I went to my bookshelf to read about the plant.

Bloodroot is a small woodland herb, *Sanguinaria canadensis,* native to the North Central United States and Canada. Its taproot exudes a bloody juice, which probably inspired Native Americans to experiment with the plant as a medicine. Bloodroot was one of the most popular herbal remedies among Plains Indians and the European settlers who came later, used internally for sore throats and respiratory ailments and externally for growths on the surface of the body. The plant fell into disfavor in modern times with the demonstration that it was toxic: taken internally, it interferes with cell division and may promote mutations and cancer. The Food and Drug Administration has it on a list of most dangerous herbs. But I was able to find a number of references to its peculiar ability to dissolve abnormal growths on the skin without harming normal tissue, even to dissolving some breast cancers that had eroded through the skin, in the days before current cancer treatments were available. As a topical application, it seemed safe.

Since I had no immediate use for the paste, I put it in my refrigerator and forgot about it. I only remembered it six months later, when I had to make a decision about veterinary treatment for my dog, Coca, a female Rhodesian ridgeback, six years old and in good health except for a growth that had developed on her right side, near the shoulder. It had started as a black skin tag but had steadily enlarged until it was now the size of a marble and looked like a little black cauliflower. My vet told me it should come off. "These things can turn into melanomas," he said. Taking it off would mean putting the dog under general anesthesia, which I did not want to do, since general anesthesia is a risky procedure, more so in dogs than humans. I did nothing, and the tumor kept growing.

Then I remembered the container in my refrigerator. Here was a perfect opportunity to test the power of bloodroot. I smeared a thin coating of the paste over the growth, and repeated the application every morning for three days. On the fourth day, when I called Coca over for the treatment, I was alarmed to see blood running down her side. The tumor had turned grayish and seemed to be separating from the skin, leaving a gaping wound underneath. I stopped applying bloodroot, cleaned the area with hydrogen peroxide, and resolved to keep an eye on the area. Two days later, the whole tumor, then whitish gray, fell off, leaving a raw, circular area that quickly healed over. The end result was a perfectly circular, slightly depressed area of skin, with no trace of tumor. The bloodroot had removed it more neatly than one could have done with a scalpel. Later, hair grew over the spot, concealing it completely. I could not have asked for a better outcome, especially as the dog had showed no signs of discomfort.

So much for my animal trial; I was ready to go on to humans. Shortly afterward a friend came to visit who showed me a mole he was worried about on his chest. His name is John Fago, a photographer, who had lost a leg to bone cancer some years before. He had been an avid downhill skier before the operation and now was an avid and very skillful one-legged skier. Statistically, John's chances of being cured of his cancer were excellent, and he was careful to follow a lifestyle that increased them even more. Still, he was understandably nervous about strange growths. This one was a pigmented mole that had been enlarging. When I told John about the bloodroot cure of my dog, he did not hesitate. "Let's do it," he said.

Unlike my dog, John had no coat of fur, so it was easier to watch the process. On the second day of applying the paste, the skin around the base of the mole became inflamed, an obvious immune reaction, and John said it was quite sore. On the third day, the mole turned pale and began to swell. On the fourth day, it fell off, leaving a perfectly circular wound that healed quickly. Later I asked John to describe his experience to a group of medical students. He did so, with the result that I began getting requests for nonsurgical removal of moles. Over the years, I have given out bloodroot paste and instructions on how to use it to a number of medical students, and the outcomes have been consistent and satisfactory. The most recent was a young woman with a large mole at the collar line at the base of the neck. A dermatologist wanted to take it off, but his description of the size of the incision he would have to make put her off, and she knew that healing would be difficult because of the location. She asked me if I knew any alternative to surgery. Bloodroot solved her problem. "It got pretty scary-looking on the third day," she told me afterward, "but I remembered your description of what would happen, and I tried not to worry. Now the mole is gone completely, and I think it's a much better job than the dermatologist could have done. I'm amazed."

So here is an example of a discovery made by paying attention to a testimonial. I would hope it would inspire scientific inquiry into the mechanism by which bloodroot is able to stimulate rejection of abnormal tissue and into possible applications of it for treatment of growths other than moles.

Talking about herbal cures with doctors is particularly difficult because they have no training in medical botany and because the subject is highly polarized, with some authorities claiming that the use of plants in medicine is not only unscientific, being based on purely anecdotal evidence, but also dangerous. This is an uninformed position. Not only do many pharmaceutical drugs in current favor come from plants; there is quite an active effort today to study traditional plant remedies by the methods of modern science. In general, herbal medicines are safer than pharmaceutical drugs simply because their active constituents are diluted by inert material and modified by secondary components. On the other hand, manufacturers of herbal products often make unsubstantiated claims for them in order to sell their wares in a competitive and largely unregulated market.

Take *Ginkgo biloba.* Dozens of scientific articles about its chemistry and pharmacology, based on both animal and human experiments, have appeared in good, peer-reviewed journals, although the journals are not ones read by American physicians. (I cannot think of one physician I know who reads *Planta Medica,* a German journal and one of the best.) If you will review the hefty technical literature on ginkgo, you will find experimental evidence that it increases blood flow throughout the body, especially in the head. It has been shown to be an effective and nontoxic treatment for disorders of hearing and equilibrium due to impaired circulation to the ear and for deficits of memory and mental function due to impaired blood supply to the brain. Its lack of toxicity is in great contrast to pharmaceutical drugs used to treat these conditions.

The known actions of ginkgo extract are consistent with some of the favorable results reported in the testimonial letter from the woman in Chicago, but the effects she says she has experienced go beyond those known actions. Besides, the dose she was using is low. The effective dose range is two tablets of the standardized material taken three times a day. Even with that, patients are advised to be patient; the beneficial effects of ginkgo usually do not appear before six to eight weeks of continuous usage. So even if we accept the stories as true, there is a question about the assignment of cause and effect. Did ginkgo cause the beneficial changes?

This question raises a thorny issue that leads even more doctors to throw testimonials into wastebaskets. It is well known that belief in medicines can cause favorable outcomes even if the medicines are ineffective. This is the placebo response, which most doctors dislike because it muddies their experiments and seems inherently unscientific from the point of view of the biomedical model. I regard the placebo response as a pure example of healing elicited by the mind; far from being a nuisance, it is, potentially, the greatest therapeutic ally doctors can find in their efforts to mitigate disease. I believe further that the art of medicine is in the selection of treatments and their presentation to patients in ways that increase their effectiveness through the activation of placebo responses. The best way to do this as a physician is to use treatments that you yourself genuinely believe in, because your belief in what you do catalyzes the beliefs of your patients.

Unfortunately, this view of placebo medicine is very much out of fashion today. Most doctors want nothing to do with placebos, favoring instead "real" treatments that work through identifiable biochemical mechanisms. They also like treatments that produce very specific effects ("magic bullets"). If a drug begins to work in too many different conditions, most doctors lose interest in it, because they think lack of specificity means lack of an underlying mechanism. In other words the drug could be—perish the thought!—merely a placebo.

I might mention that this way of thinking is unique to Western medicine. In traditional Chinese medicine, drugs, which are mostly herbal, are classified into three categories, called superior, middle, and inferior. Inferior drugs are those with specific effects in specific conditions, the magic bullets that are Western medicine's highest therapeutic ideal. Middle drugs have broader powers because they strengthen body functions. Superior drugs are the tonics and panaceas, those that work for everything. Ginseng is an example; its Latin name, *Panax,* comes from the same root as *panacea,* meaning "all heal." In the Chinese conception, superior drugs work by stimulating the defensive functions of the body, making it more resistant to assaults of all kinds. These drugs are not toxic, not weapons against specific diseases; but by increasing resistance, of course they work for everything.

This short digression into medical philosophy and the differences between Western and Eastern medicine is meant simply to point out the many reasons why most scientifically minded doctors in this country would ignore testimonials such as the one above. In short: they tend to disbelieve the stories without attempting to verify them, possibly out of fear that someone is trying to put something over on them; they are unwilling to endorse (or even consider) types of treatments falling outside their area of experience, such as herbal remedies; and they are reluctant to put cause-and-effect interpretations on anecdotes of this sort because they fear the reported benefits, even if true, may turn out to be "nothing more" than placebo responses.

Over the years that I have been writing and speaking in public I have received hundreds and hundreds of testimonials. For every testimonial letter that has come to me I have heard dozens more stories that were not written down. In these accounts patients have sung the praises of an astonishing variety of therapies: herbs (familiar and unfamiliar), particular foods and dietary regimens, vitamins and supplements, drugs (prescription, over-the-counter, and illegal), acupuncture, yoga, biofeedback, homeopathy, chiropractic, surgery, prayer, massage, psychotherapy, love, marriage, divorce, exercise, sunlight, fasting, and on and on. I collect this material, save it, and take it seriously. In its totality and range and abundance it makes one powerful point: *People can get better.* More than that, they can get better from all sorts of conditions of disease, even very severe ones of long duration.

Like my colleagues, I also question the simple cause-and-effect interpretations placed on these reports and hesitate to endorse products and practitioners; but unlike most of them, I do not throw out the reports. Testimonials are important pieces of evidence. They are not necessarily testimony to the power or value of particular healers and products. Rather, *they are testimony to the human capacity for healing.* The evidence is incontrovertible that the body is capable of healing itself. By ignoring that, many doctors cut themselves off from a tremendous source of optimism about health and healing.

THE FACES OF HEALING: AL

OF THE PEOPLE I have interviewed for their personal accounts of healing, Alan Kapuler is one of the most unusual and delightful. A molecular biologist turned New Age gardener, he combines a formidable intellect and wide-ranging knowledge of life processes with a deep sensitivity to and reverence for the natural world. Al is the co-founder and director of Peace Seeds in Corvallis, Oregon, a family business specializing in the preservation, propagation, and distribution of heirloom and other unusual varieties of flowers and vegetables. He is also research director of Seeds of Change, a national organic seed company. Al works hard, loves his plants, collects and packs thousands of packets of seeds by hand, and is committed to nonviolence as a general principle.

Al Kapuler was graduated summa cum laude in biology from Yale University in 1962 at the age of nineteen. He considered going to medical school and remembers that in an admissions interview for New York University, he was asked why he wanted to be a doctor. "I want to cure cancer," he replied. Instead he studied cancer at Rockefeller University for six years, eventually earning a Ph.D. in life sciences. Much of his research experience was devoted to developing new chemotherapy agents and understanding their mechanisms of action on DNA.

Soon after completing his studies, Al dropped out of what he now calls the "whole materialistic system." He moved to the country, became a most-of-the-time vegetarian, and started farming. Since then, he has lived simply and worked the soil. In 1987 he settled with his wife and young children in Corvallis, where he set up Peace Seeds as a for-profit endeavor. "I was really working compulsively at that point," he recalls, "doing twenty-five thousand packets of seeds, growing and cleaning hundreds of seed crops, trying to solve the problem of 'right livelihood,' and all this with only part-time help; I was under a lot of stress."

You would think that given his biomedical background, he would have been alarmed by the appearance of swollen lymph nodes in his groin in June 1989, but the nodes were painless, and Al thought they would go away. They didn't. He tried putting hot and cold compresses on them with no success and just continued with his exhausting work. "I had no idea what they were," he told me. The enlarged nodes were on both sides, the size of quarters. Eventually he sought the advice of a physician friend he had known since graduate school. The friend recommended a CT scan of the whole body; it revealed between twenty-five and thirty abnormal nodes from the neck to the groin, two of which were biopsied and sent off for diagnosis. The result was mixed cell lymphoma, cancer of the lymphatic system. "They told me I had a seven-year life expectancy, that it would probably be two to three years before it got bad, and that I had to start chemotherapy."

Al's mother-in-law, an advocate of natural foods, sent him a book on healing cancer with a macrobiotic diet. He read it along with other books on dietary approaches to cancer. The books on macrobiotics made the most sense to him. "They used less pseudoscience than the others. They just said that certain patterns of eating cause cancer, and here's what you can do to reverse it. I thought I ate a pretty healthy diet, but, in fact, we consumed a lot of sugar in the form of honey and fruit juice, and I smoked tobacco. I also drank coffee—two cappuccinos a day with honey. From the macrobiotic point of view, all this is terrible. I realized I had to cut out everything unhealthy from my life." In November 1989 he went on a strict macrobiotic diet: brown rice, miso soup, beans, cooked vegetables, and sea vegetables, or in his words, "your basic Oriental monastic diet." The diet allowed no fruits or salads, no oils, no bread, no dietary supplements, and, of course, no meat or milk products, no sugar, and no alcohol.

"Did you ever consider doing chemotherapy?" I asked.

"Are you kidding? I'm a molecular biologist. I know what that crap does to people. And I knew that poisoning myself made no sense. Besides, I remembered telling that medical school interviewer years before that I wanted to cure cancer. I thought to myself, 'Ha! Now I've got a chance to do it.'

"Actually, I've come to love brown rice and vegetables, and on this program, I could have as much of those as I wanted. I had to chew my food very well. The diet agreed with me. I've been macrobiotic ever since, becoming more or less strict as changes in my health dictate."

For the first eleven months of this regimen, Al saw no change in his lymph nodes: no new ones developed, but there was no improvement. During this time he went to an oncologist in Eugene, Oregon, who did blood work every two months to look at the numbers of abnormal lymphocytes in Al's circulation. The numbers would fluctuate, and the oncologist pressured Al to start chemo. "He told me he'd just give me a 'light dose.' But I'd look around his office, and everyone was eating candy all the time. There were candy boxes on the counter where patients met the receptionists and receiving nurses. The secretaries and nurses and patients were all into it, and then you'd see the patients going into the chemo room. I told him, 'Never mind; the diet will take care of me.' "

In September 1990, just around the time of his forty-eighth birthday, Al noticed that the nodes in his groin seemed to be shrinking. By the end of October they were gone, and his groin was completely back to normal. His blood work returned to normal too, and the oncologist was amazed. Al recalls, "And another well-known oncologist told me I was the only patient he knew with a confirmed diagnosis of cancer who got into complete remission as a result of diet therapy alone."

There was no sign of abnormality in Al's lymphatic system until the beginning of 1993, when he was again under unusually heavy stress as a result of his work. His income had dropped, he was trying to work with another organization, and he felt he was at a crossroads in his career, with the future direction uncertain. In response to this stress, he abandoned his strict diet and began to eat sweets. Shortly afterward he developed a gum infection on the right side of his mouth. This was followed by an infection in his left ear. As the ear infection drained, the lymph nodes in the left side of his neck swelled. They were tender, suggesting reaction to infection rather than any malignant process; but when the infection resolved, the lymph nodes remained enlarged. Al now had six abnormal nodes in his neck. He also developed a rash on three fingers of his right hand; it would come in cycles, beginning with itching and developing into weeping pustules that would eventually become crusted and disappear. Having his hands in the soil made it worse. Al decided he had to take further action.

"My diet had become looser in the previous couple of years when I was feeling completely well. I decided I would go back on the strict regime. Also, I saw a documentary film that a friend of mine had made about the Hoxsey cancer therapy, and another friend, an acupuncturist, told me he had seen a patient cured by this method. I decided to go to Mexico, to a clinic in Tijuana that offers it."

The Hoxsey treatment is a tonic, composed of seven herbs and potassium iodide, and a diet. The diet, which prohibits pork, tomatoes, and vinegar, among other things, was much less restrictive than Al's macrobiotic regimen, which he continued. The idea of an herbal tonic appealed to Al's sympathies with plants, especially since many of the plants in the Hoxsey formula have anticancer properties.

"I went to Tijuana in the spring of 1993, and I must say I got better treatment at that clinic than anything I've seen from the medical profession in this country. The staff were very humane, very caring. You've got to remember that my father was a doctor, and I've had a lot of conventional treatment in my life. I had polio as a kid—in the 1949 epidemic—and was out of school for six months. Then I had chronic tonsillitis and was on endless cycles of antibiotics for years. So I'm very familiar with that kind of medicine, and I liked the kindness and patience of the doctors in Tijuana much better. They were so impressed with my diet that they told me I'd respond very quickly to the herbal therapy."

Al returned home with a supply of the Hoxsey formula and took a small amount of it after each meal. Within two months the nodes in his neck were down, and he has had no problems since. "Actually, I think I'm in better health now than I was five years ago," he says. "I've got incredible energy now." Having visited with him recently, I can confirm this. Al gives every appearance of being in excellent health.

"What have you learned from all this?" I asked him.

"Oh, so much, so much," he replied. "First of all, the cancer was a great gift, truly one of the best things that's ever happened to me. As a result of it, I understand so much more about how the body works. I've become really sensitive to the effects of food on my system, for instance. If I eat the wrong food, I know it within a half hour by how I feel. Also, I discovered something very interesting about the process of healing from cancer. It's not a simple one-step thing. I think there was a relationship between that rash on my fingers and the nodes in my neck. Something was being discharged through the skin, as if the internal aspects of the disease were moving to the surface and then out of the body. No conventional doctor would see that relationship, but I'm sure of it. Now I have nothing on my skin; it's completely clear.

"Most of all, I've learned that you are your own physician and have to heal yourself. The trick is to get your ego out of the way, get your concepts out of the way, and just let the body heal itself. It knows how to do it."

4

MEDICAL PESSIMISM

IT IS DIFFICULT for me to write about the failings of my profession, but these failings have negative consequences for all of us. Simply put: too many doctors are deeply pessimistic about the possibility of people getting better, and they communicate their pessimism to patients and families. Many of the patients who come to see me have been told by doctors, in one way or another, that they will not get better, that they will have to learn to live with their problems or expect to die from them, that medicine has nothing more to offer them.

I see patients from all over the country as well as from other countries, the vast majority of them refugees from conventional medicine. About ten percent of them are well—they have no immediate problems and want preventive lifestyle counseling. I wish more people would come to me before they get sick, because I have a great deal of information about how to reduce risks of heart disease, cancer, stroke, and other diseases that kill and disable us prematurely. I also know of ways to protect and enhance the body's healing system, which are set forth in the second part of this book. My advice concerns diet, patterns of activity and rest, and ways of handling stress, along with intelligent use of vitamins, supplements, herbs, and practices that take advantage of mind/body interactions.

Of the remaining ninety percent of my patients, about half have routine complaints: allergies, headaches, insomnia, anxiety, sinus trouble, arthritis, back pain, and so forth. To these people I offer genuine alternatives to conventional medicine. From my extensive travels and studies of many different therapeutic systems, I have assembled a large collection of methods and remedies that I find to be safer, more effective, and certainly more cost-effective than the drugs and surgeries offered by mainstream medical practitioners. For the management of common, everyday ailments, conventional methods are best described as therapeutic overkill—heavy artillery that should be used only as a last resort, after simpler and safer methods have failed. The problem is that doctors are not trained in the use of simple methods that take advantage of the body's own healing potential.

The last group of patients are those with serious illnesses, where the probability of healing is less. I see many people with cancer, many with chronic degenerative diseases. Often, these people tell me they regard me as their last hope, since they have exhausted all other possibilities for medical help. In such cases I act as an advisor, helping patients weigh their options and make intelligent choices about how to use conventional medicine selectively and how to combine it with alternatives. For example, many of the cancer patients decide to undergo surgery and chemotherapy or radiation therapy, but they want to know what else they can do to prevent recurrences. Typically, their oncologists tell them they do not need to do anything else once they have been treated. The patients know better. They want to learn about anticancer foods and supplements, ways of using the mind to boost immune defenses, and so forth. My job is to make that information available.

Whether they are relatively healthy or relatively sick, the patients who come to my office are highly motivated to take responsibility for their own health. Motivated patients are a pleasure to work with. They are seeking information, which they will act on once they obtain it. Such patients tend to be intelligent and well educated, attributes consistent with the findings of surveys here and abroad of people who go to alternative practitioners. Finally, many of them have suffered physically, emotionally, or financially as a result of encounters with conventional medicine. Here are the complaints I hear most commonly:

"Doctors don't take time to listen to you or answer your questions."

"All they do is give you drugs; I don't want to take more drugs."

"They said there was nothing more they could do for me."

"They told me it would only get worse."

"They told me I would just have to live with it."

"They said I'd be dead in six months."

The last four statements are particularly disturbing, because they reflect deep pessimism about the human potential for healing. At its most extreme, this attitude constitutes a kind of medical "hexing" that I find unconscionable. Anthropologists and psychologists have studied medical hexing in shamanistic cultures, where, on occasion, a shaman or witch doctor will curse someone (usually at the behest of the person's enemy), and the victim of the curse then withdraws from society, friends, and family, stops eating, and weakens. The medical literature contains reports of chronic illness and death resulting from this process, with some speculation about physiological mechanisms that might account for it, such as derangement of the involuntary nervous system. So-called voodoo death is the ultimate example of a negative placebo response. Although it is easy to identify this hexing phenomenon in exotic cultures, we rarely perceive that something very similar goes on every day in our own culture, in hospitals, clinics, and doctors' offices.

Two years ago a man in his mid-thirties came to me for a second opinion about his illness. After several months of worsening episodes of diarrhea and abdominal pain, his family doctor referred him to a gastroenterologist, who diagnosed the problem as ulcerative colitis and started the patient on a standard suppressive drug but gave him no information about modifying his lifestyle. The man disliked the side effects of the drug and did not think it controlled the symptoms very well. He also suspected that his problem had something to do with stress. He complained about the drug treatment and persisted in questioning the gastroenterologist about other possible strategies, without success. "Do you know what that doctor said to me on my last visit? He said, 'Listen, I've got nothing else to offer you, and, anyway, the chances are you'll eventually develop colon cancer.' "

People with ulcerative colitis are statistically more likely than others to get colon cancer, it is true, probably because chronic inflammation and destruction of the lining of the colon leads to increased cell division and with increased cell division comes increased risk of malignant transformation; but the probability of colon cancer in any individual with ulcerative colitis is low, especially if the disease is controlled and, as in this case, mild. Besides, even cases of not-so-mild ulcerative colitis can respond dramatically to changes in lifestyle and outlook. I remember a woman in her mid-forties who had suffered for years with a severe form of the disease, managed imperfectly with high doses of prednisone and other suppressive drugs, who was told that surgical removal of the entire colon was her only option. She went on a macrobiotic diet, and the disease promptly disappeared. Fifteen years later, when she consulted me about an unrelated problem, it had still not returned.

How did the gastroenterologist's words of doom affect my patient? "I didn't sleep for three nights," he reported. "All I could think was, 'I'm going to get cancer of the colon,' and, frankly, the idea still haunts me." I gave him a program to follow, including referral to a hypnotherapist to help undo the medical hex and teach him how to use his mind to improve his condition. Had it been feasible, I would have put him in touch with the woman whose colitis had disappeared. That was the second opinion he really needed.

Here is another instructive story: Five years ago a fifty-three-year-old man from Canada came to see me. Actually, it was his wife who came to see me. He stayed in his car in the driveway, because, his wife said, he was terrified of doctors and couldn't bring himself to see another one. I took the history from her, then went out and persuaded him to come in. He had had several years of urinary disturbances, which he had ignored. When he did finally go to a urologist, the problem turned out to be prostate cancer that had already escaped the gland and gone to the bones of the pelvis, making for a poor prognosis. He went to a university hospital, where the only treatment offered him was female hormones to antagonize the growth of the tumor.

The main impression I had of this man was of someone in the grip of fear. He had seized on visualization therapy as his best and only hope and told me that he spent two hours a day in fierce concentration, trying to visualize his immune cells gobbling up the cancer cells. But he had made no effort to change his lifestyle in a manner that might have improved his general health and immunity; he continued to smoke cigarettes at the rate of two packs a day, for example. When

I asked about the smoking, he said: "Three months ago, I was at University Hospital, in the office of the chief urologist. He explained the hormone therapy to me and said that it was not worth doing any other treatment. I asked him, 'Should I stop smoking?' and he said, 'At this point, why bother?' "

Were I to ask that urologist about his reply—assuming he even remembered making it—he would probably say that he was doing the patient a favor by sparing him further trouble. What the patient heard, however, was "You are going to die soon." A high priest of technological medicine, enthroned in his temple, had uttered the equivalent of a shamanistic curse, for doctors in our culture are invested with the very same power others project onto shamans and priests. Those words were the source of the patient's terror, a terror that paralyzed him and prevented him from making constructive efforts for his own survival and well-being. Yes, metastatic prostate cancer has a poor prognosis, but this patient was still in relatively good general health, and it is not hard to find examples of people with metastatic prostate cancer who remain relatively healthy for years. Why prejudice the outcome?

There is a difference worth noting between the hex in this case and in the previous one. Here the urologist revealed his pessimism in an unthinking way, without any intent to upset the patient. The gastroenterologist who predicted colon cancer for the man with early ulcerative colitis may have been annoyed by a patient who questioned his treatment and repeatedly demanded information he was not able to provide. My experience is that thoughtless medical hexing is much more common than intentional hexing, though it is no less harmful.

Some of the stories I hear are so outrageous that all I can do is laugh; when I can get patients to laugh as well, I feel that the curses are dispelled. A woman from Helsinki in her late forties came to see me one February. She had early multiple sclerosis that had caused muscle weakness in one leg. I was more alarmed by her emotional state. She was depressed and wooden throughout the telling of the story, which she related as if it had all happened to someone else. It did not take much to make her feel better; traveling from Helsinki to Tucson in February was salutary in itself. Since she was able to stay for a while, I put her in touch with several therapists who worked with her on matters of body, mind, and lifestyle. After a month, she had brightened considerably and had adopted a more hopeful outlook.

"You wouldn't believe what those doctors did to me in Finland," she confided. I asked for details. "It took them a long time to make the diagnosis, many tests. Then finally, the head neurologist took me into his office and told me I had multiple sclerosis. He let that sink in; then he went out of the room and returned with a wheelchair. This he told me to sit in. I said, 'Why should I sit in your wheelchair?' He said I was to buy a wheelchair and sit in it for an hour a day to 'practice' for when I would be totally disabled. Can you imagine?" She related this tale with a healthy laugh that I strongly encouraged. Wheelchair practice, indeed!

I could go on and on recounting stories of medical hexing, intentional or unintentional, funny or—more often—sad, but I believe I have made my point. I have more uplifting subjects to write about. I cannot help feeling embarrassed by my profession when I hear the myriad ways in which doctors convey their pessimism to patients. I would like to change this pattern and am working to require instruction in medical school about the power of words and the need for physicians to use extreme care in choosing the words they speak to patients. A larger subject is the problem of making doctors more conscious of the power projected onto them by patients and the possibilities for reflecting that power back in ways that influence health for better rather than for worse, that stimulate rather than retard spontaneous healing. As I said earlier, we have thrust medical doctors into the roles served by shamans and priests in more traditional cultures, but doctors are poorly trained to play out those roles constructively. The good shamans I have met in my travels have been master psychotherapists who know both intuitively and by their training how to take projected belief and turn it back to patients in the service of healing.

On rare occasions a medical hex may motivate an exceptional patient to prove the doctor wrong by getting well. I remember one old woman who had survived uterine cancer years before telling me with a toothless grin, "That doctor told me I had less than a year to live, and now he's dead and here I am!" Unfortunately, that is the exception. The usual effect of a medical hex is despair, and I cannot believe that despair has beneficial effects on the human healing system. It is not a good idea to stay in treatment with a doctor who thinks you cannot get better.

It seems most strange that practitioners of the so-called healing art should have such little faith in healing. What are the roots of medical pessimism? One that I identify is the lopsided nature of medical education, which focuses almost exclusively on disease and its treatment rather than on health and its maintenance. The preclinical portion of the medical curriculum is top-heavy with detailed information about disease processes. Here the word "healing" is used rarely, if ever; the term "healing system" not at all. As I will explain in the next chapter, we already know some of the mechanisms of healing, but without the concept of a healing system, we cannot take this knowledge and put it together into any useful constructions.

The biomedical model from which conventional medical theory and practice derive makes it very difficult to present a view of the healing system to doctors-in-training. Its materialism leads to emphasis on form rather than function. The healing system is a functional system, not an assemblage of structures that can be neatly diagrammed like the digestive or circulatory systems. Here again, Eastern medicine has the advantage over its Western counterpart. Traditional Chinese medicine emphasized function over structure and, as a result, was able to understand that the human organism had a defensive sphere of function that could be stimulated, long before Western doctors realized that the "functionless" organs of the body—tonsils, adenoids, thymus, and appendix—were components of the immune system.

Worse, the biomedical model discounts or entirely writes off the importance of the mind, looking instead for purely physical causes of changes in health and illness. My experiences and observations of healing suggest that the mental realm is often the true locus of cause. Despite growing public interest in mind/body interactions, professional interest remains at a low level.

It is not only teaching that suffers as a result of these limitations but also research. Research produces the information that enters the medical curriculum; without research there is just anecdotal evidence. The disease focus of medical inquiry is obvious. Look at our National Institutes of Health. Really they are National Institutes of Disease: the National Cancer Institute, the National Institute of Allergy and Infectious Disease, the National Institute of Arthritis and Skin Diseases, the National Institute of Diabetes and Digestive and Kidney Diseases, the National Institute of Neurological Disorders and Stroke, and so on. Where is the National Institute of Health and Healing?

Very little research exists on healing, and what has been done is too narrow in scope. Investigators have paid some attention to one impressive phenomenon, spontaneous remission, but remission is not synonymous with healing. The word "remission" implies a temporary abatement of a disease process that may well recur. Moreover, remission is strongly associated with cancer, and cancer, in my view, is a special case. If we look only or mostly at spontaneous remission of cancer, we come away with a distorted picture of the healing system that in no way reveals its full range of activities and potentials.

The first comprehensive search of the medical literature for case reports of spontaneous remission was published in 1993 as a thick, annotated bibliography, containing hundreds of references. Fully seventy-four percent of them concern cancer, and the authors note that "a review of the remission literature reveals that almost all, if not all, the papers on remission have been about cancer." A first—and only—World Conference on Spontaneous Remission took place in 1974 at Johns Hopkins University School of Medicine. It was exclusively about cancer.

Healing is a researchable phenomenon. For years I have been asking my colleagues to look at and study folk cures of warts as examples of healing responses. Wart cures are common, dramatic events in which the healing system, activated by belief, rids the body of virus-infected tissue precisely and efficiently, making conventional treatments for warts look clumsy and barbaric. Still, the whole subject is regarded more as an amusement by medical scientists than as a serious field for investigation.

When medical students finish their preclinical studies and go on to work in the wards of teaching hospitals, the lopsidedness of their education is reinforced by their experience of illness. Third- and fourth-year students, along with interns, residents, and fellows, are immersed in the world of hospital medicine. The patients they see there are not representative of the total spectrum of illness. Rather, they constitute a skewed sample—the very sick. In that group, healing responses occur less frequently than in the general population. If you treat predominantly people with life-threatening crises and end-stage chronic disease, naturally you are going to be pessimistic about outcomes.

These facts of life of medical training—its unbalanced focus on disease rather than health, the limitations of its conceptual model, the deficiencies of research, and its skewed experience of illness toward the very worst possibilities—are sufficient to account for medical pessimism. Yet underlying all this are deeper motivations, never discussed and rarely considered, that have to do with why people become doctors in the first place.

When I ask students why they chose medical school, the usual kinds of answers I get have to do with helping others, enjoying prestige and power, and having job and financial security. I believe there is another reason that is less conscious. The practice of medicine provides an illusion of control over life and death. One way to deal with fears of life and death is to seek comfort in that illusion. But every time a patient fails to get better or, especially, dies, doctors must confront the fact that their control is illusory. The prediction of a negative outcome may offer psychological comfort to the physician: if the patient gets better, the doctor can be pleasantly surprised and take credit for it, whereas if the patient gets worse or dies, the doctor predicted it and therefore still seems to be in control. Medical pessimism may thus be a psychological defense against uncertainty, which does not excuse it or lessen its impact on patients. The fact is that we live in an uncertain universe, and do not have controlling power over life and death. What we do have is the ability to understand how the human organism can heal itself, a subject that is inherently comforting and gives reason for both doctors and patients to be optimistic.

THE FACES OF HEALING: JOHN

THE ONLY REMNANT John Luja has of his disease is a two-inch patch of itchy skin on his right lower leg, and he thinks that might not even be related to his prior problem. Now seventy-five, John runs a landscaping business outside St. Louis. He says he doesn't go to doctors and he has always used home remedies, probably because he grew up in Lithuania in a culture that was much more self-reliant than ours in matters of health.

In 1980 John developed an unusual problem: the skin on the front of both his lower legs became red and itchy. After four weeks it turned "kind of yellow and dead looking," and he did go to a doctor, who told him the problem looked like scleroderma, a potentially serious autoimmune disease. The doctor performed a skin biopsy to be sure, and the biopsy result was indeed scleroderma. To be absolutely sure, he sent John to a specialist, who did another biopsy and confirmed the diagnosis. "They told me there was no real cure," John recalls. "They said I could use cortisone cream to control the itching, and they said I should take cortisone pills, too, because it would give me some insurance against involvement of my internal organs."

John found that the cortisone cream worked immediately to make the skin on his legs feel better. "Then after two weeks, it stopped working; in fact, it made things worse. I think I might have been allergic to it. I found a cortisone lotion that seemed to be better." He also started taking prednisone pills. Now the skin started to harden, and new affected areas appeared on his back, arms, and chest. "The doctor told me the scleroderma would probably start inside me and that I'd probably die from it."

On learning this, John's daughter and son-in-law, then living in Arizona, decided to move back to the St. Louis area to be near him. Mike, his son-in-law, says that much of John's skin at that time "looked and felt just like plastic, like the surface of a mannequin. They had told him that he had a fatal illness, and we just accepted that."

In fact, John never accepted the doctors' prognosis. He had little faith in the prednisone and stopped taking it after six weeks. Instead, he decided he would research the subject himself. "I thought what I had was something like arthritis," he says, "because I noticed that I would get worse before it rained. About three or four days before rain, the itching would get real bad. I also thought it had something to do with nerves, because I was having a lot of trouble with the business and was very nervous when it started. And I figured it had something to do with too much calcium."

So John started reading about home remedies for arthritis and excess calcium in the system. He decided to try vinegar and lemons, washing the affected skin with vinegar and eating fresh lemons. I asked him how he ate the lemons. "I just ate them straight," he said. "The other thing I tried was aloe vera juice. I bought it at the health food store and started drinking it every day. Soon the itching was gone. I never used the cortisone lotion again.

"Still, I thought something was wrong inside me. I felt I needed to shock my system, and I got the idea from a book of using a high dose of vitamin E. I took 5,000 units of vitamin E a day for two weeks." That is definitely a high dose of vitamin E, since the recommended daily allowance is 30 international units, and a megadose, advocated by proponents of antioxidant therapy, is 800 to 1,000 units a day.

John says: "I think that really started something."

His disease had been present for six months. Two months after he started his home remedies, it stopped spreading. Then the hardened skin began to soften. "The doctor was surprised to see the change. He told me, 'I don't know what you're doing, but whatever it is, keep doing it!' After six months, the condition started to disappear on my arms and chest. After two years it was gone and has never come back."

I asked John what he had done about the nervous component of his illness. "I just settled down," he replied. "Whenever your nerves are involved in a disease, you've got to make a change in your life; you've got to change your thinking."

Mike thinks his father-in-law's attitude had a lot to do with the outcome. "I think it was the way he was raised, in a culture that valued home remedies more than professional treatment. He never bought into the doctors' pessimism. And he really had faith in his aloe juice. He always had a gallon of the stuff with him and drank it by the glass."

"My health today is pretty good," says John Luja. "I still use vinegar if I get any itching. I still eat lemons from time to time. And I try not to go to doctors."

5

THE HEALING SYSTEM

IF THE HEALING SYSTEM is invisible or difficult to see from the vantage point of clinical medicine, its existence is clear from other points of view. Simply as an evolutionary necessity, organisms must have mechanisms of self-repair to counteract the forces that create injury and illness. For most of our existence as a species, we have not had doctors, whether conventional, alternative, or otherwise. The survival of the species alone implies the existence of a healing system.

My purpose in writing this book is to convince more people to rely on the body's innate potential for maintaining health and overcoming illness, but I cannot easily give you a picture of this system. Lacking organized research, we know few of the details of its components and mechanisms. Also, the human organism is dauntingly complex, and its ability to repair itself is one of its most complex functions. Mind/body interactions frequently appear relevant to peoples' experiences of healing, but we lack a model that integrates mind into biological reality.

There is an aphorism that I find useful in such situations: "As above, so below; as below, so above." This means that patterns of truth observed at any level of reality will be true at every level of reality. Therefore, if we can discern the operation of the healing system at any level of biological organization, we should be able to infer the nature of its operations at other levels. I will describe what we know about mechanisms of self-repair at a few key points of the human organism, beginning with DNA, the macromolecule that defines life. The tone of this chapter will be a bit more technical than that of the previous ones. Do not be discouraged if you cannot absorb all the details presented here, because what matters are the general principles.

DNA takes the same form in all organisms, from human beings to viruses—an enormous molecule with a double-helix structure made up of two chains of sugar molecules, twisted about each other, with "rungs" linking the two chains. The rungs form between complementary pairs of nitrogen-containing subunits (nucleotides), whose specific sequences differentiate the DNA of one organism from that of another. Only four different nucleotides occur in DNA; they are the "letters" of a genetic code spelling out "words" of information that direct the construction and operation of all forms of life. The so-called Central Dogma of modern molecular biology states that DNA *replicates* itself in order to pass its genetic information on from one cell to another and from one generation to the next; DNA also *transcribes* its information into another macromolecule, RNA, that can travel out of the cell nucleus; RNA, in turn, *translates* this information into the manufacture of specific proteins that determine the structure and function of organisms. These three processes—the replication, transcription, and translation of genetic information—are the most basic processes of life. They are also amazingly intricate and risky, because there are so many points at which things can go wrong.

For example, in order for DNA to replicate or transcribe itself, the long double helix must unwind and separate, so that each strand can act as a template on which a new, complementary strand can form. During this process, DNA is susceptible to injury from certain forms of energy (ionizing radiation and ultraviolet light) and matter (chemical mutagens). Also, mistakes can occur in the assembly of the new strands, such as the placement of wrong nucleotides. Damage to DNA can have disastrous consequences for organisms. Therefore, sophisticated mechanisms have evolved for the repair of this molecule in order to assure nearly error-free transmission of genetic information from one generation to the next, even in the simplest forms of life.

All of the mechanics of replication, transcription, and translation are directed by a special class of proteins called enzymes. A great deal of the genetic code specifies the manufacture of enzyme molecules, which, in turn, oversee the chemical reactions that develop the genetic code into biological reality. In a sense, enzymes are the "hands" that carry out DNA's instructions. It was not until 1965 that scientists, using a technique called X-ray crystallography, were able to picture the three-dimensional structure of an enzyme (one in the white of a hen's egg), but since then our knowledge of enzymes has expanded rapidly. The more we know about them, the more magical they seem.

Enzymes catalyze the chemical reactions of life—that is, they speed up the rates at which these reactions reach equilibrium but are not themselves changed in the process. Enzymes are necessary because if left to themselves, the reactions would not take place fast enough to support life. Chemists can speed up indolent reactions by subjecting them to high temperatures and pressures and by creating extreme conditions of acidity or alkalinity (pH). They can also add chemical catalysts to reactions, but these, too, often work best under physical conditions far removed from those of cells, which live at relatively low temperatures, at atmospheric pressure, and at nearly neutral pH. By contrast, enzymes in cells are able to catalyze reactions under the mild conditions of life and do so with much greater efficiency than their inorganic counterparts. They may be thought of as highly complex and efficient molecular machines.

How do enzymes work? The answer has to do with their three-dimensional configurations, which give them the ability to bind with great specificity to other molecules—substrates—and accelerate their tendency to react. The binding takes place at a particular site on the enzyme, which is both geometrically and electronically complementary to a portion of the substrate. Many enzymes will bind only to one substrate and not to any other molecule, even a very close relative. Once bound to an enzyme, the substrate may find itself in physical proximity to another reactant or it may be forced into a new configuration that strains particular chemical bonds, making them more likely to break or reform in ways that favor a desired reaction. Enzymes have diverse mechanisms by which they cause chemical bonds of substrates to change. In practical terms, they function as ingenious machines that alter substrate molecules: cutting them apart, putting them together, snipping particular pieces off them, adding others back, all with astonishing precision and speed.

One very interesting class of enzymes binds to DNA itself in order to direct the step-by-step replication of genetic information and to ensure that it is error-free. For example, enzymes called endonucleases cleave DNA at specific sequences, while exonucleases can cut off the ends of single strands. (Names of enzymes always end in -*ase*.) DNA gyrase catalyzes the "unzipping" and unwinding of the double helix in order for transcription to begin. A family of enzymes called DNA polymerases then directs the assembly of the new strands.

The first DNA polymerase to be identified was polymerase I, discovered in *E. coli* bacteria, which are widely used in genetics research. Scientists assumed that this enzyme was the sole director of replication, but thirteen years after its discovery, a mutant strain of the bacteria was found that had almost no detectable polymerase I. Although it reproduced at a normal rate, suggesting the existence of another form of the enzyme, this strain was unusually susceptible to the damaging effects of UV radiation and chemical mutagens. This was the first piece of evidence that polymerase I, in addition to directing replication, plays a central role in repairing damaged DNA.

If I were to forget to take my hat when walking from my office to my car on a sunny day, my bald head would receive a dose of UV radiation. If the sun were high in the sky and it was summer, the UV rays would be more energetic and more numerous. In even a few minutes, many of them would penetrate into living cells beneath the epidermis of my scalp, and some of them would strike the nuclei of cells. Some of those strikes would hit DNA, and some of those might hit crucial points of the DNA molecule during the process of replication or transcription, altering a nucleotide in a way that caused it to bond abnormally to its neighbor. This change would result in a kink in one strand of the double helix, a genetic error. When you consider that of the 300 trillion cells in an average body, some ten million die and are replaced every second, you get an idea of the number of cells at risk even from very brief exposure to agents that can chemically alter DNA.

What happens in the nucleus of a skin cell whose DNA sustains this kind of injury from UV light? Very probably and almost immediately, an endonuclease would recognize the defect and snip the affected strand on one side of the injury. Then an exonuclease would snip the other side, cutting off the damaged end. Polymerase I would then fill in the gap with undamaged nucleotides, and finally, a DNA ligase would connect the broken ends. This is a very elaborate, molecular version of cut-and-paste. (As efficient and effective as this kind of healing is, it is not a substitute for wearing a hat as protection from the sun.)

If, during replication, polymerase I accidentally incorporates the wrong nucleotide into a growing strand, the enzyme can recognize the error, excise it, and restore the correct sequencing. Therefore, polymerase I actually proofreads its own work, editing mistakes as it directs the synthesis of new copies of DNA.

Many variations exist on these themes, with many different enzymes available for the healing of DNA from the myriad kinds of damage it is likely to sustain. We know the details of some of them; the details of others are obscure. One very elaborate system, the "SOS response," has been discovered in *E. coli*. Agents that damage DNA induce a complex of changes in these bacteria that stop cells from dividing and increase their ability to repair damaged DNA, probably by stepping up production of healing enzymes.

Here, then, are basic activities of the healing system, discernible at the level of macromolecules, which are an interface between living and nonliving matter. At this level there is no immune system, nor are there nerves to carry messages from the brain. We are far below the world of organs. Even without knowing more about the details of self-repair of DNA, it is possible to draw a few conclusions:

• Healing is an inherent capacity of life. DNA has within it all the information needed to manufacture enzymes to repair itself.

• The healing system operates continuously and is always on call.

• The healing system has a diagnostic capability; it can recognize damage.

• The healing system can remove damaged structure and replace it with normal structure.

• The healing system not only acts to neutralize the effects of serious injury (as in the SOS response in *E. coli*), it also directs the ordinary, moment-to-moment corrections that maintain normal structure and function (as in the proofreading and editing activity of DNA polymerase I).

• Healing is spontaneous. It is a natural tendency arising from the internal nature of DNA. The occurrence of a lesion (such as a kink created by misbonding as a result of a hit by UV radiation) automatically activates the process of its repair.

In larger patterns of biological organization in the human being these same characteristics obtain. As above, so below; as below, so above.

The next stop on our tour is at the single cell, in particular the membrane surrounding the cell, the *plasma membrane,* a boundary and interface with the extracellular environment. DNA is now far below us in a distant nucleus, and we are in a world of interactions between large surfaces.

When I took high-school biology thirty-five years ago, plasma membranes were thought of as passive containers that kept cells' contents from spilling out. By the time I was in college, membranes appeared to be more interesting. They had a distinctive layered structure composed of lipids (fats) and proteins, with the proteins embedded in and attached to a kind of flexible, fluid lipid matrix. When I got to medical school, researchers had recognized the dynamic, active nature of plasma membranes. They are sites of active transport of substances from outside the cell to inside the cell, with receptors on their outer surfaces, specialized protein structures designed to bind to particular hormones and nutrients. Moreover, it was discovered that membranes connect to vast systems of tiny channels within cells and that they help cells take in wanted, and expel unwanted, materials. New membrane is constantly being synthesized within the cell, and old membrane is constantly being absorbed.

One of the most dynamic aspects of membrane biology is a process called endocytosis—the pinching off or budding of plasma membrane within a cell to form hollow structures called vesicles. In recent years, investigators have clarified some of the details of endocytosis and in so doing have revealed—to me, at least—another aspect of the healing system.

The best studied example of endocytosis involves receptors for LDL—low-density lipoprotein—a carrier molecule that transports cholesterol from the bloodstream to cells. When bound to LDL in the bloodstream, cholesterol is in the "bad" form that tends to deposit in arterial walls, causing atherosclerosis and coronary heart disease. A high level of serum LDL cholesterol is a risk factor for heart attacks, but many cells are equipped with receptors to bind LDL and remove it from the circulation.

When an LDL receptor on the external surface of a cell membrane binds to an LDL molecule, the receptor moves to another special structure on the membrane, a depression lined with a distinctive protein coat, called a "coated pit." Once in the pit, the occupied receptor undergoes endocytosis and winds up inside the cell in a vesicle, which then merges with other, similar vesicles. The materials in the coalesced vesicles are then sorted and sent in different directions. Once inside cells, LDL cholesterol cannot do our arteries any harm; cells actually need some cholesterol in their metabolism and can dispose of any excess. In the sorting process, the LDL receptor is recycled back to the surface of the membrane, while LDL (and excess cholesterol) is sent for disposal to a structure called the lysosome. Lysosomes contain powerful enzymes that can chop up large molecules into small, disposable pieces.

On the outside surface of the plasma membrane, the recycled LDL receptor is ready to bind more LDL and take another trip through the interior of the cell. Studies show that LDL receptors recycle every ten to twenty minutes. Since their lifespan is ten to thirty hours, they can make many trips in and out of the cell, transporting many molecules of LDL. Then, at some point they wear out. When an LDL receptor's structure and function deteriorate, it, too, goes off to a lysosome for destruction, and its place is taken by a newly synthesized receptor.

As researchers clarify the ins and outs of endocytosis, a picture is emerging of plasma membranes that is dizzying. It appears that at many points on the cell surface, membrane is forever being sucked into the cell ("invaginated" is the technical term), examined, sorted, and recycled back up to the surface. One phase of this process is the recognition and elimination of defective membrane structures via lysosomes.

Here again, as at the level of DNA, we can see the operations of an inherent, spontaneous healing system, in continuous operation, capable of recognition (diagnosis) as well as removal and replacement (treatment) of defective structure and function. Here at the cellular level, we can also see a capacity for regeneration of structure that allows the healing system to perform moment-to-moment maintenance. Healing at the membrane level is especially important, because cell surfaces are subject to much abuse and are also the sites of communication between cells through the interaction of receptors with molecules produced elsewhere.

Let us jump to a higher level of organization. Aggregates of cells form tissues, tissues form organs, organs form systems. At the tissue level, healing becomes more complex but shows the same general characteristics. The process of wound healing is well known and well studied; even so, many of us fail to see its larger significance. Suppose you cut your finger with a knife. Your immediate concerns are pain and bleeding. The pain will subside quickly; it is how you perceive the activity of peripheral nerves notifying your brain of the injury. Unless you have a clotting disorder, the bleeding will also stop soon with the formation of a clot that will harden to a protective scab. If you are attentive, you will notice the appearance of inflammation around the edges of the wound beginning within twenty-four hours of the cut: slight but definite tenderness, redness, swelling, and warmth. This is an immune response, caused by the migration of white blood cells to the area to defend against the entrance of germs as well as to clear the area of dead and dying cells.

The first wave of immune cells to invade the area are neutrophils, the most common white blood cells, which are the "infantry" of the body's defensive forces. They are soon followed by macrophages ("big eaters"), which can engulf and digest great quantities of cellular debris. Concurrent with this immune activity is the beginning of cellular proliferation from the normal surface (epithelial) cells at the edges of the wound. Spurs of these cells grow out from the edges under the clot to fuse in the midline, forming a thin but continuous layer of what will become new skin. Then a more vigorous proliferation of cells occurs with the appearance of a soft, pink, grainy tissue called granulation tissue. It will eventually fill the space of the wound. Under the microscope, granulation tissue shows itself to be full of fibroblasts, cells that synthesize the proteins that give our bodies architectural integrity, as well as newly forming blood vessels. The new vessels first appear as buds or sprouts on existing vessels at the margins of the cut. Finally, the immune cells recede, new skin develops and thickens, making the scab unnecessary, and, unless the wound was unusually deep, your finger will be as good as new.

Research into the mechanisms of the many steps of wound healing has demonstrated the important role of chemical regulators called growth factors. Growth factors are very small proteins (polypeptides) produced by cells or present in the bloodstream that either stimulate or inhibit cell growth. For example, a family of polypeptides called fibroblast growth factors (FGFs) not only stimulate fibroblasts but also induce all the steps necessary for new blood vessel formation. Epidermal growth factors (EGFs) stimulate cell division by binding to a special receptor on the cell membrane; when bound to their receptor, they somehow increase synthesis of both DNA and RNA in the cell nucleus. Transforming growth factor alpha (TGFα) binds to the same EGF receptor and stimulates cell growth, but its beta relative, TGFβ, has an opposite effect: it inhibits the growth of most types of cells.

The balance between these opposing factors is critical to health and healing, because unopposed pressure on cells in either direction would be calamitous. EGF and FGF, without antagonism, could produce wild growth of cells and perhaps transformation to cancer. (Uncontrolled proliferation of new blood vessels is a common feature of rapidly growing malignant tumors, for example.) Unopposed inhibition would thwart healing, leaving wounds unrepaired and vulnerable to infection or further injury.

So at this more complicated level of biological organization, in addition to all the features that we saw at the levels of DNA and plasma membranes, we can also see that *the healing system depends on a coordinated interaction of stimulating and inhibiting factors affecting the growth and proliferation of cells*. Furthermore, this kind of balance appears to underlie the normal life of healthy tissue, not just healing responses to injury. Once again the healing system is responsible for moment-to-moment maintenance of health in addition to its special functions required to manage injury and illness.

Another well-studied case of healing at the tissue level is the repair of a simple bone fracture. The healing system is so good at this that a radiologist may not be able to tell where a bone was broken once the process is complete. Following a fracture, the first steps of healing are similar to those we just reviewed. A blood clot fills and surrounds the fracture cleft, sealing it off and providing a loose framework on which fibroblasts and new blood vessels can grow. Eventually, the organized clot becomes a mass of tissue called a soft callus. Now, the healing system takes a different path from the repair of a surface wound. The beginnings of new cartilage and bone appear in the soft callus by the end of the first week, eventually converting it into a large, spindle-shaped provisional callus that acts as an effective splint. This reaches its greatest size two or three weeks after the injury, then becomes increasingly strong as bone construction intensifies.

The actual creation of new bone again involves mutually antagonistic forces, mediated both by growth factors and by special cells called osteoblasts and osteoclasts. The former build bone up while the latter tear it down, with muscle and weight-bearing stresses on the bone dictating the fluctuations in activity of the two phases. Assuming the fracture was well aligned when the healing process began, reconstruction is often perfect.

Scientists have elucidated the finer details of bone healing at the cellular level. Robert Becker, an orthopedic surgeon and researcher, spent many years proving that tiny electric currents generated by the injury cause cells at the edges of the fracture to *dedifferentiate*—that is, to revert from mature cells to primitive ones with high capacities for growth and regeneration. These primitive cells regain potentials that mature cells have lost; they resemble the cells of embryos, and are able to redifferentiate into all the cell types needed to make a perfect, new bone. Becker's work led to the development of electrical bone stimulators, appliances that encourage the healing of complicated skeletal injuries and bone infections, which are now widely used. It also led him to look beyond bones to other sorts of healing, such as the spectacular ability of salamanders to regenerate amputated limbs.

After conducting many experiments, Becker concluded that limb regeneration in salamanders is not fundamentally different from bone healing in humans. It, too, depends on tiny electric currents that make cells dedifferentiate and then redifferentiate into all the components of a new leg. His general conclusion was that, in theory, humans should have this same ability. That is, all the circuitry and machinery is there; the problem is simply to discover how to turn on the right switches to activate the process.

Regeneration of lost or damaged structure, which we have seen to be a capacity of the healing system at every level so far, is an everyday event in some tissues, especially those at surfaces exposed to constant irritation. Our bodies are forever shedding their outer layers of skin, and new skin is constantly being made by the layers below. The entire lining of the intestinal tract sloughs off and is renewed every day, a spectacular regenerative feat.

Even more impressive is the ability of the liver—the largest organ in the body and one of the most active—to regenerate lost tissue. You can cut away most of the liver—up to eighty percent of it—and the remaining portion will restore the lost substance in a matter of hours, as long as the tissue is normal. Similar restoration of structure and function can occur after partial destruction of liver cells by viral hepatitis and by chemical toxins.

Other organs of the body seem unable to regenerate. Heart muscle that is lost as a result of interruption of blood supply in a heart attack is not replaced by muscle. Healing occurs in the form of a fibrous scar, but there is no regeneration of the original tissue. The same is true of neurons in the brain. Heart muscle cells and nerve cells are so specialized in function—so differentiated—that they seem to have lost the capacity for new growth. Yet perhaps even in these vital cells there are switches waiting to be discovered that might turn on the appropriate sequences of DNA in the nucleus. If science begins to focus on the healing system, isolating and understanding its mechanisms, both electrical and chemical, for regulating cell growth and differentiation, it is not impossible that doctors will one day be able to spark the regeneration of damaged hearts and brains and severed spinal cords. That will truly be a new era of healing-oriented medicine.

If we look at the level of whole body systems, like the circulatory, digestive, and immune systems, healing appears no less prevalent or powerful but more diffuse and mysterious. When I was in medical school I was taught that atherosclerosis was irreversible. Once coronary and other arteries were stiffened and narrowed by cholesterol deposits, inflammation, and calcification, they could never improve, said the books and professors, only worsen. In fact, this pessimistic view was based on no experimental evidence, because no one had yet tried to reverse atherosclerosis.

Once, as a college newspaper editor, I interviewed an expert on rivers, long before ecology and environmental concerns were fashionable. His words made a great impression on me because they sounded right and resonated with my own experience. He told me that rivers are like living organisms in that they have many different mechanisms to keep themselves healthy. You can dump sludge into a river and, up to a point, the river can detoxify itself and remain in good health. For example, turbulence in a river mixes water with oxygen, a powerful purifier and germicide, as is ultraviolet light from the sun. Also, many of the plants that grow in rivers, both algae and higher plants, can remove contaminants from water. But if you keep dumping sludge, at some point you will exceed a critical level where natural purification mechanisms become overwhelmed and break down. Plants and beneficial microorganisms die, flow patterns change, the river becomes sick.

I was busily taking all of this down in my notebook for the story I was going to write. What I heard next so caught my attention that I stopped writing. The expert continued, saying that a river that appears hopelessly polluted is not beyond help. If you will simply stop putting bad substances into it, eventually the levels of contaminants will drop to a point where the natural healing mechanisms revive. Oxygenation increases, sunlight penetrates to deeper levels, beneficial organisms return, and the river cleans itself up.

Why shouldn't arterial systems behave the same way? In fact, we now have clear evidence that atherosclerosis *is* reversible, if you simply stop putting into your body the substances that cause it (mainly saturated fat) and stop obstructing the healing system with your mind (by cultivating anger or emotional isolation, for example). We do not yet know what mechanisms the system uses in this case, but we can observe regression of atherosclerotic plaques in coronary arteries, with corresponding increase of blood flow, in patients who follow programs to lower serum cholesterol greatly and learn to process stress and emotions differently. Moreover, the response to changes in lifestyle is rapid. Using sophisticated tests of cardiac perfusion (like thallium scanning), doctors can demonstrate increased flow through coronary arteries in some patients within a month of starting a program of lifestyle change.

I have seen equally rapid and dramatic responses in patients with many kinds of illnesses who stopped living in ways that promoted disease and switched to lifestyles that supported natural healing. I am not a medical researcher. I am a medical practitioner. Researchers and practitioners have very different outlooks and goals. As a practitioner my chief concern is to keep healthy people healthy and help sick people to get well; I haven't focused equally on why people get better. Still, I am convinced that just because we have not yet discovered a mechanism does not mean that none exists. I am confident that mechanisms of healing at complex levels of biological organization will emerge when investigators begin to search for them.

I DO NOT WANT to end this discussion of the healing system without at least a cursory look at its operations in the realm of mind. Because we know so little of the mind and because our science is so ill equipped to approach it, there is no possibility of seeing mechanisms. Still, it is interesting to observe the process of healing of psychological injuries, using grief as a model. Grief over loss is a universal experience, and its quality is the same whether the loss is of a pet, a job, a relationship, a spouse, or a child. Each loss ties in to all loss; each death reminds us of our own death. Yet the forms of grieving vary greatly from person to person and depend also on the nature and symbolism of each particular loss. Grieving is a kind of work we are required to do, a process of coming to accept loss and reaching a new emotional equilibrium with changed circumstances. Grieving itself is a variety of healing, an operation of the healing system.

Therapists and counselors who work with grieving clients recognize different stages of the process, which may or may not occur sequentially; perhaps it would be better to call them facets of grief rather than stages. One, often the first, is shock and denial ("No, this can't be happening!"). Denial is a natural anesthetic, and while it has a bad reputation (and, of course, is unhealthy if it persists), it may be very useful as a temporary mechanism to permit a basic level of functioning when the full impact of grief would be devastating. Denial may be succeeded by or alternate with anger and rage ("How dare this happen to me?"), which I can't help likening to the inflammatory response that comes soon after the initial pain and bleeding of a wound subside. Anger may give way to a stage of wishful fantasy ("If only I had been a better mother [father, husband, wife, son, daughter, person], this wouldn't have happened"), which often gives way to depression ("I can't go on"). Although it may look like illness, depression is actually a progressive stage of the grieving process, because it represents unconscious acceptance of the loss and release of the fantasy of being able to recover it. When acceptance becomes conscious, grieving can end, the loss is assimilated (in some cases even perceived as a gift that opens a new phase of life), and emotional ease is again possible. By understanding the natural contours of emotional healing, therapists may be able to help clients through it, encouraging appropriate expressions of emotion to facilitate movement toward completion.

We might argue about where emotional healing fits into the subject at hand. Is it higher or lower than healing at the level of body systems? Is mind the highest expression of genetic information encoded in

DNA or a manifestation of a field of consciousness underlying matter, including DNA? As above, so below; as below, so above. It makes no difference. The point is: wherever we choose to look in the human organism, from DNA to the mind, healing processes are evident.

Are there limits to what the system can accomplish? Some of the reported cases of complex healing indicate potential for repair and regeneration that is far beyond ordinary experience. Here is one example, taken from the roster of miraculous cures at Lourdes and reported in an article that appeared in the *Canadian Medical Association Journal* in 1974. The author wrote:

> In order for a healing to be classified as miraculous, five criteria must be met. First, it must be proved that the illness existed, and a diagnosis established. Second, it must be shown that the prognosis, with or without treatment, was poor; third, that the illness was serious and incurable; fourth, that the cure happened without convalescence, that it was virtually instantaneous; and finally, that the cure was permanent. These criteria must be met by the Medical Bureau of Lourdes, the Church, and the diocese in which the "miraculée" lives.
>
> At Lourdes, each case presented is reviewed by three panels of physicians. Since 1947, only 75 cases have been accepted at the first level. Of these, 52 were accepted by the second level, and only 27 were pronounced as scientifically inexplicable by the third level. After the panels of physicians have made their decision concerning the miraculous healing, the Church then makes a judgment as to whether these inexplicable cases are the result of divine intervention. The case is then sent to the local diocese where the local bishop sets up a commission to examine the evidence. These commissions are frequently more stringent than the medical panel at Lourdes, since out of the 27 cases mentioned above, only 17 were pronounced as miracles by the local diocese.

The story of Vittorio Micheli, born February 6, 1940, is one of the seventeen cases of latter-day miraculous healing:

> Vittorio Micheli was inducted into the Italian army in November 1961, being pronounced physically fit, albeit he had noticed minor pains in March of that year. In April 1962 he presented to the Verona military hospital complaining of pains in the region of the

left ischium [the bone of the pelvic girdle that supports weight in sitting] and haunch. Extensive clinical examination, X-ray investigations and biopsies led to the diagnosis of sarcoma [primary bone cancer] of the left pelvis.

By June the condition had worsened and X-rays in August showed "almost complete destruction of the left pelvis," according to army records. Micheli was put in a hip-to-toe cast, with which he was able to stand and move around. In August the army medical service sent him for radiological treatment but after three days concluded the case was not treatable by irradiation. The treatment was switched to chemotherapy but after two months no improvement was discerned and it was discontinued. In November X-rays showed luxation of the femoral head and by January the femur had lost connection with the pelvis.

The following May Micheli decided to go to Lourdes. His cast was exchanged for a stronger one and examination then showed the left hip to be deformed. The patient had totally lost control of his left leg. Pain was severe and continuous, requiring analgesics. He could no longer stand. The patient also suffered loss of appetite and digestive problems.

At Lourdes Micheli, still wearing his cast, was plunged into the baths. Immediately he felt hungry, a characteristic of Lourdes cures. His pains disappeared and he said later, under intensive examination, that he had the feeling his left leg had reattached itself to the pelvis. He felt well.

But he didn't jump straight out of the bath and run off to the grotto. His cast was still enclosing him. Indeed, although Micheli believed he had received a cure, the army doctors didn't. They kept the cast on him. But within a month Micheli was walking, still with the cast. In August radiographs showed the sarcoma had regressed and the bone of the pelvis was regenerating. The improvement continued and today [in 1974], although there is some distortion, the sarcoma has disappeared. Micheli works in a factory, standing for eight to ten hours a day. Articulation of his left hip and leg is "the same as normal" according to bureau records.

If this kind of healing can happen in one human being, I believe it can happen in all. All the circuitry and machinery is there. The challenge is to discover how to turn on the right switches to activate the process.

THE FACES OF HEALING:
OLIVER

AT EIGHTY-SIX Oliver Walston of Pemberville, Ohio, is still in good health. He walks with a limp, a residue of the rheumatoid arthritis that plagued him for much of his adult life, but it has been a long time—twenty-two years—since his arthritis was active, and he now has no pain. Oliver is a retired farmer and businessman who was the director of an insurance company, a constable, and the president of a school board. He says that until now, doctors have shown no interest in the story of how he lost his arthritis.

Oliver's joints began to bother him in his mid-thirties. "I first noticed it in my feet," he says. "Then my knees began to swell and ache badly, and soon after that it settled in my fingers, elbows, shoulders, neck, and spine. In the winter I could not purchase gloves large enough for my swollen hands, so I had to settle for big mittens. I also had to wear shoes two sizes larger than I used to."

Oliver tried all kinds of medication, both prescription and over-the-counter, but nothing gave him consistent or lasting relief. He also tried heat treatments and various topical remedies with no success. At the time of this story, when he was sixty-four, he was resigned to his condition and was managing the pain by taking twelve buffered aspirin tablets a day, six extra-strength and six regular strength. Here is what happened, in Oliver's words:

"On this particular day, my wife had washed my pajamas and hung them on the clothesline to dry. When dry, they were folded and put on the bed. I retired at 10 p.m. and put them on. About 1:30 a.m. I got up to go the bathroom and felt a sting on the inside of my left knee. I slapped it hard, shook my leg, and out fell a honeybee. Two days later the bee sting was still swollen and sore, but the arthritis swelling in that knee began to go down. The next day, the pain from the sting subsided, and I stopped taking the extra-strength aspirin, because the pain and swelling in all my joints began to recede. Two weeks later I stopped all the medication. Within five or six weeks, the swelling and inflammation were gone from all the joints. I've never been bothered by arthritis since, and I even went back to my old shoe size."

I asked Oliver Walston what he thought had happened. "I don't know," he replied. "Mother Nature does some wonderful things. I don't want to encourage people with arthritis to go out and get stung by bees. Maybe it will help some people, but it might make others worse."

In fact, bee-sting therapy has a long history of use for rheumatoid arthritis and other inflammatory and autoimmune disorders. Even some doctors practice it, usually under the name apitherapy or bee-venom therapy. Bee venom is a mixture of very powerful bioactive compounds, some of which have remarkable anti-inflammatory effects. For example, both adolapin and mellitin are more potent than common steroids, and another compound, apamin, currently under investigation in France, shows great promise as a new treatment for multiple sclerosis, another disease with a prominent autoimmune component. Purified bee venom is available for injection under the skin, but many apitherapists prefer to apply living honeybees to the patient, holding them with tweezers to the sites to be stung. They say the risk of this procedure is very slight, even when many stings are applied. Commonly, bee-sting therapy is repeated at frequent intervals.

But Oliver Walston did not really undergo apitherapy. He got one isolated sting, and somehow that changed the dynamics of an autoimmune problem of long standing, activating a complete and permanent healing response. He has some limitation of mobility in joints where extensive destruction of cartilage occurred, but there has been no active inflammation or progression of arthritis in the past two decades.

"Haven't any of the doctors you've seen over the years looked into the cause of your cure?" I asked him.

"No," was his succinct reply. "I think some of them were sorry I was no longer buying all the medicines."

6

THE ROLE OF THE MIND
IN HEALING

"I'M GOING TO fight this thing!"

How often I have heard patients declare their resolve to struggle against a life-threatening illness. They are supported in this stance by conventional wisdom and by societal norms. We are very comfortable with the symbolism and imagery of warfare in our approaches to disease. We fight wars against cancer and drug abuse. We look to medical scientists to develop new weapons against germs and other agents of disease. Doctors commonly refer to the pharmacopeia as the "therapeutic arsenal." It is not surprising that individual patients try to regain health by assuming warrior roles.

Over the years that I have been interviewing men and women who have experienced healing, I have come to feel that "fighting this thing" may not be the best way to obtain the desired result. Although there is no one state of mind that correlates exactly with activation of the healing system, a consistent theme in the interviews is acceptance of illness rather than struggle. Acceptance of illness is often part of a larger acceptance of self that represents a significant mental shift, a shift that can initiate transformation of personality and with it the healing of disease.

I find it difficult to talk to medical scientists about this possibility, because of the great gulf that exists between scientific understanding of mind/body interactions and public perceptions of the subject. Just recently I received a letter from a woman who attended a talk I gave on the future of medicine. She writes:

I am a medical technologist and after working in the hospital environment for a number of years, I became disillusioned with the traditional medical model. It just seemed to me that medicine as it is currently practiced is completely one-dimensional. I became interested in mind-body aspects of healing, and I continue to pursue learning everything I possibly can about the mind-body connection. I have since expanded my concept of True Health to include mind, body, and spirit. I really believe that we will, as a society, make a quantum leap in our true healing potentials once this mind-body-spirit complement is accepted and understood by all.

The writer speaks for many people today in her enthusiasm for mind/body medicine. There has been an enormous surge of books, magazine articles, and television shows on the subject, many of them featuring doctors and researchers who are dedicated to advancing knowledge of the mind's role in health and illness. What the public does not understand is that these visible efforts are not representative of medicine and science in general. In fact, relatively few in the medical establishment take the field of mind/body medicine seriously; and the most prestigious researchers, those who set priorities and influence funding, are contemptuous of colleagues who work in it. What research there is is often of poor quality. Mind/body medicine is not taught in medical schools, except occasionally as an elective course. Meanwhile, proponents of the biomedical model are rejoicing about what they see as imminent conquest of the final frontier: human consciousness. There is increasing consensus in establishment science that mind is merely the product of the brain's circuitry and biochemistry, which we are on the verge of clarifying to the last detail. From this perspective, where mind is always an effect rather than a cause, scientists are unlikely to come up with ideas for studying how the mind might affect the body.

From my vantage point as a medical school faculty member, I see movement backward, away from some of the progressive approaches of the recent past, and, as a result, a widening division between professional attitudes and public expectations. For example, when I was a student in the late 1960s, the entire medical community acknowledged four diseases to be psychosomatic (literally, "mind/body") in origin: bronchial asthma, rheumatoid arthritis, peptic ulcer, and ulcerative colitis. Today, that short list has been whittled down to two—asthma and rheumatoid arthritis—with researchers busily challenging those assumptions as well.

Nine years ago, I saw an unusual and difficult patient, a man in his early fifties who worked as a wholesale produce manager. Except for mild hypertension that had not required medication, he had been in good health—until he quit smoking. He had been a two-pack-a-day cigarette smoker for most of his adult life, but, increasingly, his family had put pressure on him to stop. Finally, he did. "It wasn't that hard," he told me. "I just put my mind to it and only really suffered for the first three days." But two months after he stopped, he developed ulcerative colitis "out of the blue," never having had any digestive problems. He went to a gastroenterologist, who started him on medication, told him not to drink milk, and sent him on his way. The medication did not control the patient's cramping and diarrhea and produced unpleasant side effects. After a month, he decided to follow his intuition that if he resumed smoking, his colitis would disappear. He did, and it did—very promptly. By the time he came to see me, he had repeated this pattern three times. Each time the colitis appeared faster after he quit smoking and took longer to disappear when he resumed. Now he feared he was going to be an addicted smoker with ulcerative colitis.

When I presented this patient to a group of second-year medical students at the University of Arizona, I was dismayed to find that they had learned nothing about the psychosomatic nature of ulcerative colitis. They had learned many facts about cellular and biochemical abnormalities in the disease but nothing about any involvement of the mind in its origin and possible remission. Shortly afterward an article in the *New England Journal of Medicine* reported for the first time on an increased incidence of ulcerative colitis in ex-smokers, but not in current smokers. After reviewing the pathophysiology of the disease and the pharmacology of nicotine exhaustively, the authors concluded that they could find no mechanism to explain the correlation.

If you work from the premise that ulcerative colitis is psychosomatic, it does not take a great deal of intelligence to surmise that smoking is an effective outlet for stress and that if you shut that outlet, the stress is going to go somewhere else. Why in some people it goes to the colon, while in others it produces compulsive eating or nail biting, must be a matter of individual susceptibility. My advice to the patient was not to make another attempt to quit smoking until he had mastered techniques of stress management. I sent him to a biofeedback therapist and a hypnotherapist and also gave him a number of suggestions about improving his lifestyle. (He was a major consumer of coffee, which irritates the colon, and was not eating in a way to make his digestive system happy.)

In this way I learned that ulcerative colitis was no longer one of the classic psychosomatic ailments; that concept had gone out of fashion.

I was much more aware of the successful attempt to eliminate peptic ulcer from that category. It is fashionable today to regard ulcer as an infectious disease, due to the activity of a bacterium, *Helicobacter pylori*. The discovery of the ability of this organism to cause chronic irritation of the lining of the stomach and the duodenum has led many doctors to conclude that ulcers are unrelated to stress and to rely entirely on antibiotics to treat the disease. I have no doubt that *H. pylori* is a factor in gastritis and ulcer (and, almost certainly, stomach cancer), but that admission does not negate the influence of mind. Most people infected with this germ do not get ulcers or other symptoms, and some people with ulcers do not have the infection. Might not stress change the chemistry of the stomach in ways that allow the germ to follow an aggressive, invasive course? All of my experience with infections suggests that the mere presence of a bad germ is not the whole story. Variations in host resistance determine the behavior of microorganisms capable of causing disease, whether they live in balance with their hosts or injure them.

I remember listening to a radio report of dramatic increases in stress-related disorders among children in the war zones of Bosnia. Two of the diseases doctors there are seeing increasingly are hypertension and ulcer, both normally rare in this age group. Evidently, Bosnian doctors still cling to the old-fashioned view that ulcer is a stress-related disorder.

Actually, some of the indifference toward mind/body interactions that I complain about is peculiarly American. In other countries psychosomatic medicine is more viable (though still marginal), and investigators are working to expand the list of stress-related disorders rather than eliminate it. In Japan, more than twenty conditions are recognized as psychosomatic. I am delighted to see among them "autonomic nervous system imbalance," a disorder I recognize and diagnose frequently but one that does not officially exist in the United States. I diagnose it by taking a careful history and by simply feeling hands. Cold hands (in warm rooms) are the result of reduced circulation due to overactivity of the sympathetic nervous system, which causes small arteries in the extremities to constrict. People with chronically cold hands often have disturbances of digestion and other body functions rooted in internal tension; if it persists, this imbalance of autonomic nerves can lead to serious problems. It is best treated by mind/body approaches rather than by prescribing drugs to suppress symptoms.

A German colleague who works at a hospital devoted to psycho-somatic medicine surprised me recently by describing the success his institution has in treating tinnitus—ringing in the ears—a common symptom that can be quite debilitating. American medicine has no specific treatments for tinnitus, no understanding of its cause, and lit-tle success in alleviating it. My German friend thinks tinnitus results from chronic muscle tension in the head and neck, often associated with poor posture and stress. He prescribes yoga and relaxation training along with body work and says he is frequently able to help rid patients of it.

Because I am not a researcher I will not waste words speculating about mechanisms to explain the role of the mind in healing. I can see many possibilities, not only in the operations of the autonomic nervous system, but also in the panoply of interactions between receptors and the many neuropeptides' that we classify variously as neurotransmitters, hormones, and growth regulators. Candace Pert, one of the pioneer investigators of these regulatory substances, sug-gests that each one might be associated with a particular mood state and might affect behavior in addition to its actions on body func-tions. She notes that receptors for many of the neurotransmitters cluster in the gut and in the brain, especially in areas concerned with emotion. Endorphin receptors certainly have this distribution; they affect intestinal function as well as produce euphoria and tolerance for pain. This gives deep biochemical meaning to the commonly referred to "gut feelings." Perhaps our guts are also seats of emo-tion. What goes on in our guts might influence deep brain centers and vice versa.

Since cells of the immune system have receptors for many of these same peptide molecules, it is likely that our defenses are also part of this web or net that connects the nervous system and the endocrine system, suggesting mechanisms that explain how host resistance to infection varies with host state of mind. Pert writes: "Clearly, the conceptual division between the sciences of immunology, endocrinology, and psychology/neuroscience is a historical artifact; the existence of a communicating network of neuropeptides and their receptors provides a link among the body's cellular defense and repair mechanisms, glands, and brain." In short, the mechanisms are there to be discovered if researchers will look for them. In the meantime, practitioners should not be constrained by the lack of research.

Let me share with you a few experiences that have strengthened my own long-standing belief in mind/body interactions and have made me pay even closer attention to the mental and emotional lives of patients who consult me for physical problems.

In August 1991, when my wife, Sabine, was seven months pregnant with her fourth child (my first), we were in British Columbia, where I was teaching a workshop on health and healing. One of the participants was a friend and colleague, Marilyn Ream, a family-practice doctor from Spokane, Washington, who works in a women's health clinic. Marilyn was completing training in interactive guided imagery therapy, one of my favorite mind/body approaches. I wanted her to give a demonstration of the method, and Marilyn asked Sabine if she would consent to be a volunteer subject in front of the group. Sabine agreed.

My wife has a history of back trouble associated with pregnancy. Usually, around the seventh month her lower back goes out—two vertebrae move out of place—and she is in the habit of getting weekly chiropractic adjustment to help. On this occasion we had been traveling for several weeks, no one was available to adjust her, and she was living with steady pain. Marilyn asked her if she wanted to work on her back in a guided imagery session. Sabine said no; she thought it was a mechanical problem needing a mechanical solution. Instead she wanted to work on issues around the birth. She wanted the baby to come on time, because I was scheduled to leave the country a week after the due date and she wanted the labor to be quick, because she had had long and difficult labors with her previous pregnancies.

Marilyn asked Sabine to lie on the floor, loosen her clothing, and take a series of deep breaths. Interactive guided imagery uses the forms of hypnotherapy to induce a state of light trance and openness to the unconscious mind; but, more than standard hypnotherapy, it empowers patients by encouraging them to develop their own strategies for managing illness. It assumes that the unconscious mind comprehends the nature of disease processes and how to resolve them, an assumption consistent with the healing system's diagnostic capability. The problem is to make that information accessible to waking consciousness and to encourage patients to act on it. Marilyn began the process by asking Sabine to picture herself in a familiar place where she felt completely secure, then to describe it. Sabine described a site in the canyon country of southern Utah. Marilyn directed her to focus on small details, to try to hear sounds and smell scents as well as see the place. Sabine warmed to the task and quickly became very relaxed.

Marilyn then asked her to shift her focus to her uterus and to the baby inside it. Sabine was soon in contact with the baby. Marilyn guided her through a dialogue with the baby, in which Sabine asked her (we knew the sex by this time) to come on time (she agreed to do so) and to help make the labor quick and uneventful. In this dialogue, Sabine would speak the words she "heard" the baby use in reply to her questions. After a time, Sabine felt she had completed this work, and Marilyn told her to return to her spot in southern Utah.

"How do you feel?" Marilyn asked.

"Great. Very peaceful."

"Is there anything else you'd like to work on? How about your back?"

"Mmmm. Okay."

"Good. Then put your attention on the part of your back that hurts and tell me what you find there."

Sabine gave a little gasp.

"What is it?" Marilyn asked.

"It's . . . it's all black."

"Go to the blackness and see if it has anything to say to you," Marilyn suggested.

"It says it's really angry," Sabine answered, sounding surprised. "It's angry at *me*."

Sabine was quite unprepared for the intensity of her back's anger at her. With Marilyn's guidance she entered into a tentative conversation with it and discovered that it was angry at her for being angry at it, and for not taking care of it.

"Ask it what it wants." Marilyn directed.

"It says it wants me to put warm towels on it."

"Will you do that?"

"Yes, but I've been putting cold on it. I thought cold was better for it."

"Tell it you'll put warm towels on it and ask it if it will stop hurting."

"I did. It says it will stop."

"How does it feel now?" Marilyn asked.

"Better," Sabine replied. She moved around on the floor. "Definitely better. That's the first time in weeks it's been any better."

"Is it completely gone?"

"No."

"Ask it if it can go away entirely."

"It says it can."

"Ask it to please do so."

"Okay. I did. And I think it did."

"Now how does it feel?"

"My God, I think it's gone."

"Is it gone?"

Sabine moved this way and that. "Yes, it's really gone."

When Sabine returned to normal consciousness, the pain was still gone. It remained absent that night and the next day. (Nonetheless, Sabine kept her promise to put warm towels on her back.) In fact, the pain did not return for the remainder of the pregnancy, even though Sabine got no further chiropractic work. She had never before been free of back pain in the last two months of a pregnancy.

I will tell you what happened with the labor and delivery in a moment. Meanwhile, on the way home from British Columbia, I too had an interesting experience with this technique. Sabine and I drove back to Tucson, stopping first to visit a friend in Olympia, Washington, who had a hot tub. Usually I am quite discriminating about hot tubs: some I get into and some I don't. I had my doubts about this one but soaked in it anyway. Two days later, I had a skin infection. Hot-tub folliculitis is now a recognized disorder, a bacterial infection of hair follicles, caused by an organism called *Pseudomonas* that is notoriously resistant to treatment. In my case, it produced several painful red lesions on the left lower leg and knee. I could not take proper care of myself on the drive, but each morning and evening I would put hot compresses on these sites of infection, try to squeeze material out of them, and sop them with hydrogen peroxide. They looked as if they contained pus, but nothing came out. Then new lesions appeared on my thigh and left arm.

As the infection progressed upward, I became more anxious about it. By the time we arrived home a week later, it had spread to my face, and I began to feel generally unwell. I was contemplating going to a doctor the next day, when Sabine, still flushed with enthusiasm about her pain-free back, said, "Why don't you call Marilyn and have her do a guided imagery session with you on the phone?"

"Oh, come on," I said. "This is a bacterial infection." Sabine looked at me in a knowing way. "My back was a mechanical problem," she reminded me.

I called Marilyn, more for Sabine's sake than for mine. Marilyn said she had never worked over the phone but was willing to try. I curled up on a couch with the phone cradled by my right ear and under Marilyn's guidance went to a favorite spot in New Mexico's Gila Wilderness. After I was settled in, Marilyn asked me to pick the one lesion that was bothering me the most. I picked the one on my face.

"Put yourself there," Marilyn directed, "and tell me what you see." I saw a mass of swirling, trapped, angry, red energy.

"Listen to see if it has anything to say to you." I put my attention on the spot and "listened." Immediately words popped into my mind.

"It says it can't leave my body by going outward," I reported excitedly. "I've been wanting it to go out, but it can't. The only way it can leave is by going inward and being absorbed."

"If that's the case, what should you be doing?" Marilyn asked.

My conscious mind supplied the answer. "Well, I suppose I should stop squeezing these things. Soaking them with compresses is all right, but I should be resting more."

"Does it have anything else to tell you?"

"I don't get anything else, except a thought that I should be eating hot peppers to stimulate my circulation."

"Then let's go back to that wilderness place you started off in."

When I hung up the phone, Sabine said she could see a difference in the lesions. "They don't look as purple," she told me. I could not see any difference, but I went to bed relaxed and confident that my body could take care of itself. The next morning, without my having eaten peppers or done anything else, I could see that the problem had clearly begun to diminish. Within twenty-four hours, all of the sites of infection were obviously on the mend, much to my delight.

If a pure mind/body approach like interactive guided imagery can cure back pain associated with misaligned vertebrae and a bacterial skin infection, why shouldn't it be able to turn around anything? These experiences left me convinced that no body problem is beyond the reach of mental intervention, especially since mind/body techniques are very time- and cost-effective and are unlikely to cause harm.

Three weeks before Sabine's due date I asked a friend and colleague, Dr. Steve Gurgevich, who practices hypnotherapy, to do a session with her, again in the interest of a timely, quick, uncomplicated birth. The baby was in a posterior presentation at this time, which worried us. Sabine's last baby had been posterior, causing long, painful labor. Steve did an hour-long session with her at the end of an afternoon, encouraging Sabine to talk with the baby, asking her to turn around before the beginning of labor and help make the labor quick. When he brought Sabine out of her reverie, she looked supremely relaxed. After Steve left, Sabine and I went to the kitchen to start dinner. Suddenly, she clutched her belly and bent over.

"What is it?" I asked.

"I think the baby's turning," she said, amazed.

It happened that our midwife was coming for dinner that night. She examined Sabine and reported that the baby was now in an anterior presentation, having turned within twenty minutes of being asked to do so. The baby came right on her due date, October 4. Labor lasted a mere two hours and six minutes, which was, if anything, a little too brief in that we barely had time to prepare. Needless to say, Sabine and I are both true believers in the effectiveness of mind/body approaches, and when we hear doctors and researchers dismissing the role of the mind in health and healing, we exchange knowing smiles.

In taking a history from a new patient, I ask many questions about lifestyle, about relationships, hobbies, ways of relaxing, patterns of eating and exercising, sex, and spiritual interests. In a formal history, all of these questions are grouped in a section called the "social history"; many practitioners omit it, because they consider it unimportant. The first time a medical student sits down with a patient to take a history, the process takes over an hour. Students follow a prescribed form, ask questions by rote, then painstakingly write up the lengthy answers. By the third year of medical school, under the pressures of the wards, students learn that they must speed up the process in order to get their work done. By internship and residency, histories become streamlined, mostly by eliminating questions. Unfortunately, the social history gets jettisoned first, since doctors put higher priority on questions about symptoms, past health problems, and current medications. I call it unfortunate because in my experience the social history most frequently contains clues to the origins of patients' problems as well as possibilities for their solution.

I am convinced that stress is a primary cause or aggravating factor in many conditions that bring patients to doctors. Suppose a patient comes in complaining of frequent headaches, and physical examination and blood tests are normal. If I want to determine whether the headaches are stress-related, I can usually do so by asking one simple question, namely, "What happens to the headaches when you go on vacation?" Symptoms that disappear on vacations are likely to arise from stressful circumstances in a person's workaday life. To determine which of the circumstances is the problem—job, marriage, children, lack of relationships, or something else—requires a bit more probing.

Because I take extensive social histories and work from a model of health and healing predicated on mind/body interaction, I am keenly aware of correlations between mental/emotional events and healing responses. These correlations are important, because they suggest ways that people can keep their healing systems in good working order and can use their minds to promote healing rather than obstruct it. I present this information in detail in Part Two of this book.

First, some caveats. Healing sometimes just happens in the absence of any profound change of heart or mind. Some scoundrels are healed of serious illnesses, while some saints die agonizing deaths. At the level of DNA repair by enzymes, the influence of mind on the healing process may be negligible, as it may be at other levels. Nonetheless, I see a clear role of the mind in healing, visible in correlations of healing responses with mental and emotional changes.

For example, a healing response may immediately follow the resolution of some intolerable situation, such as ending a bad marriage or quitting a miserable job or making peace with an estranged family member. A colleague wrote me that the most dramatic case of healing he has seen was "a bank president with chronic hypertension, whose blood pressure normalized one day after his wife filed for divorce. It dropped to 120/80 and stayed there."

Another correlation is disappearance of a serious medical problem with falling in love. I have seen this with autoimmunity—rheumatoid arthritis and lupus particularly—and also with chronic musculoskeletal pain and chronic fatigue. I wish I could arrange for patients to fall in love more often. If I could figure out how to do that, I would be a very successful practitioner indeed.

I have also seen healing mobilized by expressions of anger. New Age therapists who teach people to rid themselves of negative emotions may not like to hear this, but facts are facts. One example is a patient I worked with over a long period, a man in his thirties with chronic autoimmune disease that attacked his blood platelets and red blood cells. Through a complete reworking of lifestyle and the use of several mind/body approaches, including visualization, he was able to get off the steroids and other suppressive drugs he had been taking for years. Becoming aware of and then expressing anger toward doctors and hospitals was part of the change. Finally, his health improved so much that he felt able to fulfill a long-standing desire to make an adventurous trip through Australia and New Zealand. One day I received an emergency call from down under. My patient had been thrown from a horse and had cracked two vertebrae (weakened in the recent past from long-term steroid use); the shock had set off an episode of autoimmune destruction of blood cells, and he was being air-evacuated to a hospital in Arizona.

Despite the accident and the reactivation of the disease process, he looked better than I had ever seen him, and he said that he had enjoyed a year of unprecedented good health. As he checked into the hospital, I told him not to be discouraged, that setbacks were to be expected. The goal, I said, was to make the relapses less and less frequent and get through them faster with less drastic intervention. The patient was started on steroids, but his blood counts fell so low that the hospital doctors wanted to give him transfusions. He refused, and I supported him in his refusal. In the past, he had been able to turn falling blood counts around by working with his emotions and by visualizing his white blood cells protecting his platelets and red cells from immune attack. The doctors put ever greater pressure on him to take the transfusions. Finally, one night, as he lay sleepless in the hospital, he felt a surge of rage at his predicament and his dependence once again on hospital medicine. He experienced this as a body sensation as well as an emotional wave that he directed at the whole attending staff. Within hours, his platelet and red cell counts started to climb, making transfusions unnecessary, and he was discharged from the hospital within days. He also ended his steroid use following this episode faster than he ever had in the past. I have no doubt that appropriate, focused expressions of anger can sometimes activate the healing system, New Age therapists notwithstanding.

Belief in the healing power of some person, place, or thing can also be a key to success. This is the realm of placebo responses and miracle shrines. We do not seem to be able to will healing responses to occur, because our will does not connect directly to the autonomic nervous system and other controlling mechanisms of the healing system. Yet we can circumvent that obstacle by projecting belief in healing onto something external and interacting with it. I have already noted that if physicians understood this process and were better trained to work with projected belief, they would better fulfill their roles as shaman/priests and be much more effective at helping sick people get well.

Finally, the most common correlation I observe between mind and healing in people with chronic illness is total acceptance of the circumstances of one's life, including illness. This change allows profound internal relaxation, so that people need no longer feel compelled to maintain a defensive stance toward life. Often, it occurs as part of a spiritual awakening and submission to a higher power.

I will summarize one case history as an example. A Japanese friend of mine, Shin-ichiro Terayama, who is an executive director of the Japan Holistic Medical Society, is a cancer survivor. By training Shin is a solid-state physicist and management consultant. Now fifty-eight and radiantly healthy, he is an international networker for the cause of holistic medicine, an accomplished cellist, and a counselor of the sick, especially those with cancer. I do not think I would have liked him if we had met ten years ago, before he was diagnosed with cancer. In photographs from that time he appears pinched and unpleasant, nothing like the warmhearted, spiritually awake man I know.

Back then he was a workaholic, on call twenty-four hours a day. He slept little, drank between ten and twenty cups of coffee a day, was much enamored of beefsteaks and sweets, and had no time for music in his life. In the fall of 1983 he had a fever lasting a month and could not stand or walk, but medical tests were normal. In those days, Shin says, he had complete faith in doctors and hospitals. A few months later he had three episodes of blood in his urine and became very tired. A friend who was a lay practitioner of Oriental medicine and macrobiotics told him something was wrong with his kidney, a diagnosis he based on observation and a check of the acupuncture meridians. He recommended a radical change of diet, but Shin was not interested, and the doctors still told him nothing was wrong.

Early in the fall of 1984, Shin's fatigue increased so markedly that he could not work. He wanted only to rest. When he returned to a clinic for additional tests, an abdominal mass was discovered, and a subsequent sonogram revealed the right kidney to be enlarged by thirty percent. Still, Shin did nothing. In November 1984, at the urging of his wife, a physician, Shin went to a hospital. X-rays revealed a tumor, and the doctors pressed him to consent to surgical removal of the kidney. Shin asked if the tumor was benign or malignant and was told it was "something in between." In fact it was renal cell carcinoma—kidney cancer—and had already metastasized to his lungs.

In Japan, the diagnosis of cancer is still routinely withheld from patients lest it depress them unduly. This leads inevitably to subterfuge. After the surgery, Shin's doctor said that he wanted to give him a series of injections as a "preventive measure." In fact, the treatment was cisplatinum, a strong chemotherapy agent, but Shin did not know it. He did know that the shots made him vomit, turned his beard white, and caused his hair to fall out, and he refused to complete the series. His doctor next ordered "ray treatments" to the kidney area, which he said were like "artificial sunlight." After the first few of these, Shin became very tired, lost his appetite, and had to remain in bed all day. One night he had a powerful dream about attending his own funeral, which made him feel for the first time that he was very sick and might die and had been deluded about the real nature of his illness. He also developed an unusual symptom, a hyperacute sense of smell.

"I was on the second floor of the hospital," he recalls, "but I could smell food being prepared on the fourth floor. I could smell the body odors of all the nurses. I was in a ward with six patients, and the smells became intolerable. I had to get away from them; they reminded me of death." Shin waited until after dark, got out of bed unseen, and followed his nose to safety. The only place that smelled all right to him was the roof of the hospital, where he drank fresh air into his lungs. Meanwhile, a nurse discovered him missing from his bed and raised an alarm. When a search party found him on the roof, their immediate thought was that he was about to commit suicide, which would bring the hospital bad publicity. Eventually five nurses came and carried him bodily back to his room. Next morning his doctor scolded him, saying, "You caused a big commotion last night. If you want to stay here, you must follow the rules; otherwise you can go home." This was music to Shin's ears. He promptly signed out of the hospital and went home. He then consulted his macrobiotic friend, who urged him to adopt a strict brown rice diet. "I couldn't imagine it," said Shin.

When Shin awoke the next day, he was amazed to find himself alive. The morning seemed to him unbearably beautiful, and he was aware of a great desire to watch the sun rise. He went to the eighth-floor rooftop of his apartment house, where he could look over the skyline of Tokyo. He recited Buddhist mantras and poems, put his hands together to pray, and awaited the sun. When it rose, he felt a ray enter his chest, sending energy through his body. "I felt something wonderful was going to happen, and I started to cry," he says. "I was just so happy to be alive. I saw the sun as God. When I came back down to my apartment, I saw auras around all my family members. I thought everyone was God."

During the next few weeks Shin observed the strict diet and performed daily the important ritual of watching the sun rise from his roof—the one thing he looked forward to each day. His condition fluctuated. His doctor tried to warn him off the macrobiotic diet, urging him to eat more meat and fish, and also tried to get him to take oral chemotherapy. Shin refused. He then checked into a new healing retreat a friend had opened in the Japan Alps, with hot spring baths and excellent natural food. He rested, took daily walks in the forests and mountains, and began to play the cello, something he had not done for years.

"The clean air and water invigorated me," he recalls, "and I became aware of the natural healing power that was in me and around me. Gradually, I began to realize that I had created my own cancer. I had created it by my behavior. And as I came to that realization, I saw that I had to love my cancer, not attack it as an enemy. It was part of me, and I had to love my whole self."

Today Shin Terayama is not merely a cancer survivor. He is a transformed being, who neither looks, acts, nor thinks like his old self. I have been privileged to hike with him in the mountains of Japan and America, sit with him in hot springs, attend his concerts and lectures, and listen to him counsel dozens of newly diagnosed cancer patients. "You must love your cancer," he always tells his clients. "Your cancer is a gift. It is the way to your transformation and new life."

Many doctors might not agree that Shin's is a case of spontaneous healing. After all, he underwent all three standard treatments for cancer: surgery, chemotherapy, and radiation, even if he did not complete the latter two. Renal cell carcinoma is fascinating: for kidney cancer with lung metastases, the five-year survival rate is only five percent, yet it is one of the types of cancer most strongly associated with spontaneous remission. The feature of Shin's story that I find most impressive is his psychospiritual transformation, symbolized by the sun ray penetrating his chest on a rooftop in Tokyo, and summed up in his statement "I saw that I had to love my cancer, not attack it as an enemy." That is true self-acceptance.

Most people do not go through life in an accepting mode. Instead they are in a state of perpetual confrontation, trying by the imposition of will to shape events and control situations. According to Lao-tzu, the ancient Chinese philosopher, such an attitude is directly opposed to the way of life (the Tao), and those who cling to it are doomed:

> *As the soft yield of water cleaves obstinate stone,*
> *So to yield with life solves the insoluble.*
>
> *It is said, "There's a way where there's a will,"*
> *But let life ripen and then fall,*
> *Will is not the way at all:*
> *Deny the way of life and you are dead.*

Acceptance, submission, surrender—whatever one chooses to call it, this mental shift may be the master key that unlocks healing.

THE FACES OF HEALING:
MARI JEAN

IN 1978 Mari Jean Ferguson, then thirty-eight, was diagnosed with hypertension—high blood pressure. She had just given birth to her first child after a difficult pregnancy, during which she had experienced irregular heartbeats and bad respiratory allergies. Her doctors wanted to medicate her for all three conditions, but she refused.

"My then father-in-law was a pharmacologist who had worked for a drug firm," she says, "and I never took medications without first checking with him. In this case, he told me the drugs they wanted me to take were pretty heavy-duty and advised against them. He told me to wait a year and see what happened. I did continue with allergy shots, which I'd been taking for some time. Allergists had made a lot of money off me since I was a teenager, and being allergic was still my biggest medical problem. By using stress-management techniques and breathing exercises and by controlling my weight I was able to keep my blood pressure in the high-normal range for several years without drugs."

Mari Jean needed all the help with stress management she could get. Her career was in doubt, since she was up for tenure review as a professor at a prominent midwestern university. Having a child at age thirty-eight was frowned upon by the tenure committee, and eventually she was turned down. Also, her marriage was on the rocks. Following her daughter's birth her husband became "overtly abusive," disclaiming responsibility for the child on the grounds that it was not his.

It was Mari Jean's second marriage. Her first had ended in divorce when her husband fell into a pattern of binge drinking and psychiatric hospitalizations. That was in Berkeley, California, where Mari Jean had earned her Ph.D. in sociology in the late 1960s. She had come a long way from her home in northern Alberta, "where I wasted a lot of time in rebellion against my family. I was into a lot of truancy in high school, went to business college, got married early, and was always doing the wrong thing. My brother was the family hero and got all the approval." In 1970, her father died of cancer at age sixty, leaving her mother distraught.

When Mari Jean lost her academic job in 1981, she enrolled in a program to become a family therapist and went through therapy herself for two years. "I began to realize how dysfunctional my family had been, and I began to grow, but, ironically, that created more problems in my second marriage, because my husband stayed in place. Then out of the blue, he filed for divorce and cleared out all of the money."

Another blow came in 1984, when her brother died suddenly of myocarditis, a viral infection of the heart. Her mother, brokenhearted, had a series of strokes that required Mari Jean to make frequent trips to Alberta to care for her until she died in 1986. Mari Jean's blood pressure crept up until it was no longer manageable without medication; she started on the drugs just before her mother's death. Mari Jean, who was overweight and smoked cigarettes, now became clinically depressed. She took antidepressant drugs for a time and got back into psychotherapy. In 1989 she moved to Pittsburgh to start a new life, having accepted a job as an associate professor of sociology at a small college.

"I was very overqualified for this place," she says, "and I knew I didn't fit in, but I decided to keep my mouth shut and try." She now came under the medical care of Dr. Amy Stine, who maintained her on a combination of two antihypertensive drugs. "Despite my best intentions, I found myself getting into trouble again," Mari Jean recalls. "My department chairman is on a vendetta to get rid of me when I come up for contract renewal, and I've had to get a lawyer."

In October 1993, Mari Jean saw Dr. Stine for a checkup. Dr. Stine was surprised to find her patient's blood pressure way down: 90/60. "You're overmedicated," she told her, and eliminated one of the drugs. When Mari Jean visited Dr. Stine again, early in 1994, her pressure was still 90/60. "What are you doing?" Dr. Stine asked. Mari Jean paid little attention. "I've learned over the years that most doctors aren't that interested in you," she says. Dr. Stine took her off medication completely.

At the next visit, Mari Jean's blood pressure remained 90/60, an unusually low value. This time Dr. Stine demanded an explanation. "You haven't lost weight. You haven't changed your diet. You haven't stopped smoking. You haven't increased your activity. You haven't done any of the things people are supposed to do to get their blood pressure down. What did you do?"

"Do you really want to know?" Mari Jean asked. "I'll give you the short version. I saw myself repeating the same patterns I've done all my life, always putting myself before God, always saying, '*I'm* going to do this, *I'm* going to do that.' Last fall, for the first time in my life I said, 'Just let go—let whatever happens happen.' And that's it."

Dr. Stine says she has never seen anything like this case. Mari Jean Ferguson's blood pressure is still low normal and stable. "I'm awed that my mind alone could do this," Mari Jean says.

7

THE TAO OF HEALING

If the body is so good at healing, why do we get sick?

The healing system is always there, always operative, always ready to work to restore balance when balance is lost; but at any given moment its capacity to restore may be inadequate for a required task. Consider the example of DNA injury by ultraviolet light. If only one strand of the double helix is damaged, repair by enzymes is the norm. In the process of repair, polymerase I uses the intact strand as a guide to replace the damaged nucleotides. But what if both strands are injured? If two rays of UV happen to strike both strands in the same place, the injury will be beyond the repairing capacity of polymerase I. The change becomes fixed in replicating DNA—a mutation, and much more likely than not to have deleterious effects.

Or consider LDL cholesterol and the body's ability to remove it from the bloodstream by the activity of LDL receptors on the surface of cell membranes. As long as output of cholesterol by the liver remains below a certain level, serum LDL cholesterol will stay within safe limits, but if the owner of the liver eats a steady diet of bacon cheeseburgers, production of cholesterol will likely exceed the capacity of the system, and serum LDL cholesterol will rise to levels where arterial damage occurs.

Also, some people do not have enough LDL receptors. In one well-studied, inherited disorder of cholesterol metabolism, LDL receptors are lacking, and serum cholesterol remains dangerously high regardless of dietary manipulations. Unless they take cholesterol-lowering drugs, people with this problem will develop cardiovascular disease at very young ages.

In other cases, the activities of the healing system may be frustrated by complicating circumstances. Wound healing cannot be completed if a foreign body remains in the wound or if infection develops. If you are malnourished or have an abnormally low metabolism or are weakened by chronic illness, the healing system may not have enough available energy to deal with wounds and broken bones.

Some years ago I saw a young woman who complained of fatigue and inability to concentrate. Doctors had found nothing wrong with her, and she had embarked on a fruitless round of consultations with alternative practitioners. She had tried various homeopathic remedies to no avail. On the advice of a naturopath she had eliminated all sugars from her diet. Acupuncturists and herbalists had worked on her without success. She had spent a small fortune on psychotherapy but could not discover an emotional reason for lack of energy. When I saw her, she appeared droopy, listless, and depressed, frequently becoming tearful as she told me about her symptoms and her failure to find someone to treat them effectively. Her symptoms included disturbances of digestion and menstruation as well as a marked deterioration of her ability to heal. A year before the visit she had suffered a broken leg in a car accident. Despite proper treatment, the broken bone failed to heal; the medical term for what happened is a *nonunion* of the fracture. She showed me her right big toe, which was discolored, black and blue. "It's been that way since I stubbed it four months ago," she told me. "Cuts and bruises just don't heal the way they used to."

This woman had severe hypothyroidism, which doctors had failed to detect because her thyroid function tests were normal. Thyroid function tests are not always reliable, especially in young women. I suspected this patient's immune system was making antibodies to thyroid hormone, neutralizing it before it could exert its effects. As a result, her metabolism was greatly slowed, even though blood tests showed her thyroid functioning properly. Her healing system simply did not have enough metabolic energy available to it to do the required work. When she began to take supplemental thyroid hormone, her metabolism slowly normalized, as did her ability to heal.

So the short answer to the question "Why do we get sick?" is that the capacity of the healing system to restore balance can be exceeded by the forces or circumstances of imbalance. A longer answer would have to address the issue of why forces of imbalance exist, and that would take us deep into the realms of philosophical inquiry. My belief is that health and sickness are complementary opposites, that we cannot have one without the other, any more than good and evil can stand alone. The challenge is to use sickness as an opportunity for transformation.

Does healing necessarily mean complete disappearance of disease on the physical level?

No. The literal meaning of "healing" is "becoming whole." It is possible to have an inner sense of wholeness, perfection, balance, and peace even if the physical body is not perfect. I have known persons with missing limbs who seemed to me more whole than some persons with all their limbs. (See the story of Jan on page 115 for another example.) Of course, it is desirable to restore physical wholeness, and the healing system will do it if it can, but when physical disease is fixed and immovable, healing can occur in other ways, including adaptation to and compensation for any loss of structure or function.

Is it possible to die in a healed condition?

Why not? Death and healing are not opposites. To die as a healed person would mean being able to view one's life as complete and accept the disintegration of the physical body. There are many reliable accounts of the last days of sages, especially from Buddhist traditions and extending up to the present day, that illustrate the possibility of healing into death. They bear little resemblance to what goes on in modern hospitals, where doctors often see death as the ultimate enemy to be fought with all the weapons of modern medical technology. Trapped on this battleground, patients usually have no opportunity for final healing, nor do people in our culture have ready access to practical information about using life to prepare for death.

In other cultures and other times, the "art of dying" was a popular theme of books and discourse. I would like to see it revived.

What is the relationship between treatment and healing? If I want to pursue healing, should I forgo treatment?

Suppose I come down with bacterial pneumonia, a serious, possibly life-threatening infection of the lungs. I go to a hospital, receive intravenous antibiotics, recover, and am discharged, cured. What caused the cure? Most people, doctors and patients alike, would say it was the treatment. But I want you to consider a different interpretation. Antibiotics reduce numbers of invading germs to a point where the immune system can take over and finish the job. The real cause of the cure is the immune system, which may be unable to end an infection because it is overwhelmed by sheer numbers of bacteria and whatever toxic products they might make. Of course, the immune system is itself a component of the healing system.

I maintain that the final common cause of all cures is the healing system, whether or not treatment is applied. When treatments work, they do so by activating innate healing mechanisms. Treatment—including drugs and surgery—can facilitate healing and remove obstacles to it, but treatment is not the same as healing. Treatment originates outside you; healing comes from within. Nonetheless, to refuse treatment while waiting for healing can be foolish.

I am reminded of the story of a religious man caught in a flood. As the waters rise around his house, he resorts to prayer, confident that the Lord will save him. Eventually he is forced to go to the roof of his house, but he continues to pray. Two men in a rowboat pass the deluged house and call out to him, offering rescue. The man declines. "The Lord will save me," he says. Later, with the water swirling about his knees, a motorboat comes by with another offer of help. "No thanks," the man replies, "I trust in the Lord to save me." Finally, a National Guard helicopter flies over and drops a rope ladder. Although the water is now up to his neck, the man waves the chopper on. "The Lord will save me," he calls up to the guardsmen. But moments later the water closes over his head, and after a brief struggle, he drowns. The next thing he knows, he is in heaven, standing before his Maker. "Why didn't you save me, Lord? My faith in you never wavered. How could you let me down?" he asks. "Let you down?" thunders the Lord. "I sent you a rowboat. I sent you a motorboat. And then I sent you a helicopter. What were you waiting for?"

How do I know when treatment is appropriate?

You must learn what medicine can and cannot accomplish, which diseases respond to conventional treatments and which do not. It may be better to rely on the healing system than on medicine. Consider infectious disease, for example. The greatest medical advance of the twentieth century has been the reduction of infectious disease by means of improved public sanitation, immunization, and antibiotics. In the early part of this century, infectious disease was a common killer of children and young adults. In the latter part of the century, chronic degenerative disease, mostly in older people, has replaced infectious disease as the category of illness doctors are called upon to treat most often. With this shift, people in our society have become quite complacent about infectious disease, at least about bacterial infections, believing that antibiotics—"wonder drugs"—give us total protection.

This view is not shared by infectious-disease specialists, who are witnessing a relentless rise of organisms resistant to our strongest drugs. Diseases thought to be conquered, like tuberculosis, are resurgent. Organisms thought to be incapable of resistance, like the one that causes gonorrhea, are now resistant. Worse, the rate of development of resistance is increasing, as is the speed of its transmission. A new antibiotic might work for only a few months now before germs learn how to neutralize it; and once resistant strains appear in Chicago, they turn up in Beijing within weeks. The hard fact is that we are losing the arms race with bacteria.

These alarming developments raise an important question. Is it better to put our faith in weapons against external agents of disease or in internal resources that can make us less vulnerable? Experience with antibiotics and bacteria suggests that exclusive reliance on weapons, however effective they may appear to be at first, gets us into worse trouble down the road. The weapons themselves influence the evolution of bacteria in the direction of greater virulence, making them more dangerous adversaries. On the other hand, if we concentrate on improving host resistance, the germs stay as they are, and we are protected. So it is probably wiser to rely on the healing system than on drugs and doctors.

If I fail to get better, is it my fault?

I have always found it interesting to ask people why they think they got sick. When I was a medical student I asked that question of a number of older women with breast cancer, women of my grandmother's generation. The answers all had to do with past injuries: "Twenty years ago, I fell against a table and badly bruised my breast." "When I was in my early forties, I was in an accident, and my breast got hurt." When I pose the same question to patients today, there is no mention of injury. Instead they say things like, "I bottled up my anger at my husband for all those years," or "I never expressed the grief I felt," or "I've never been in touch with my feelings." Clearly, this is a significant change, but what does it signify?

Our cultural fascination with mind/body interactions, along with the popularity of self-help books and New Age philosophies, has fostered a sense of personal responsibility for illness. We make ourselves sick by certain habits of mind, by failing to discharge negative emotions, by not leading spiritual lives. People who promote these ideas are well intentioned. They want us to be more responsible for our own well-being and to recognize that we can use our minds to help the healing process, all of which is fine. But an unintended result of their message is to create a great deal of guilt. "I gave myself cancer." "If I don't get better, I must be a bad person." Guilt about illness is destructive; it cannot possibly help the healing system.

The once-popular idea that breast cancer results from an old injury has no scientific validity. It may be that the new formulations about bottled-up feelings are just as wrong. I think breast cancer results from a complex interaction of genetic and environmental factors, in which lifestyle choices, such as diet, use of alcohol, and exposure to estrogenic toxins, may have much more influence than emotions. I do believe that grief and depression may suppress immunity, giving malignant cells the chance to grow into perceptible tumors; but I reject the idea that people give themselves cancer by failing to express anger and other emotions. And I emphatically reject the notion that failure to heal represents any kind of judgment about a person's state of mind or spirituality. Dr. Larry Dossey, one of the few doctors who has looked into the relationship between prayer and healing, has compiled an impressive catalog of saints, both Eastern and Western, who have died of cancer, so many that cancer seems almost to be an occupational hazard of sainthood. Keep this in mind if you are tempted to believe that healing depends on enlightenment and transcendence of negative emotions.

Is spontaneous remission of cancer the best example of the activity of the healing system?

Because they are rare and dramatic occurrences, and because cancer is a feared disease that resists most attempts to cure it, spontaneous remissions attract attention and make good stories for the media. In my view they are not the best examples of healing responses. Cancer is a special case, unlike other diseases (see Chapter 19), and these cases distract us from the healing system's less glamorous but much more important work. Spontaneous remissions of cancer represent extraordinary activity of the system. The system's ordinary activity is really more remarkable.

Zen Buddhism urges practitioners to experience the extraordinariness of the ordinary, to discard the gray filters of habitual perception and see the miraculous nature of everyday experience. Beginners at meditation often imagine the goal to be attainment of unusual states of consciousness: out-of-body experiences, visions, celestial choirs heard with the mind's ear, psychic powers, and so forth. Zen masters teach that such experiences are irrelevant to the process of spiritual development and should not be given special attention if they occur. Instead, they direct students simply to sit and pay attention to the most ordinary aspects of existence, such as the rising and falling of the breath.

We hardly notice—let alone appreciate—the ordinary activities of the human body's healing system. Given all of the potential agents of injury and illness that surround us, all of the changes that occur within and around us from moment to moment, it is amazing that we survive at all. Think for a moment of all that can go wrong: constant bombardment with radiation that can damage DNA; millions of cell divisions each second, any one of which could result in a genetic accident; countless molecules of irritants and toxins that get into our systems through every possible point of entry; forces of wear and tear that abrade our tissues; pressures of aging; the sea of viruses, bacteria, and other potential agents of disease in which we live; not to mention emotional assaults that stress our nerves and threaten mind/body equilibrium. To make it from one day to the next without serious incident is nothing short of miraculous.

Each day in which we enjoy relatively normal health testifies to the activity of the healing system. Its inestimable value lies not in its ability to produce remissions of disease but rather in the maintenance of health through the vicissitudes of daily life. Here is a real opportunity to appreciate the extraordinariness of the ordinary.

Is it possible to enhance the activity of the healing system in order to protect health?

Yes. How to do that is the subject of the next part of this book.

THE FACES OF HEALING: JAN

JAN BARNETT HAS a big spleen, so big that it makes buying clothes difficult for her. "I look like I'm five months pregnant," she says with a laugh. Except for that, and occasional shortness of breath on exertion (a symptom of anemia), she leads a normal life—better than normal, actually, because she considers herself a very happy, lucky woman. "If I were to die today, I'd have no regrets," she told me. "It's been a full, wonderful life, and I have a great sense of inner peace."

Ten years ago, when she was forty years old, Jan went to a doctor for a well-person checkup. The doctor felt the enlarged spleen, and the results of Jan's blood tests looked bad. The doctor recommended splenectomy, once a common operation, as the spleen was considered an expendable organ, and sent Jan to a surgeon. Fortunately, the surgeon's views were more up-to-date. "We don't do that anymore," he told the patient, "at least not till we find out the reason for the enlargement." He sent Jan to a hematologist.

It turned out that Jan Barnett has a rare, poorly understood disorder called primary myelofibrosis, or agnogenic myeloid metaplasia; removal of her spleen would have killed her. "Myeloid metaplasia" means that marrowlike tissue is growing in a different place from where it should be—in this case, in the spleen. "Agnogenic" is a choice word meaning "of unknown cause" (or, perhaps better, "We haven't a clue as to why you have this condition or what we can do to fix it"). The root problem is replacement of functioning marrow by fibroblasts, the cells that make connective tissue. In response to this life-threatening process, the spleen takes over the job of manufacturing blood cells; its enlargement is a compensatory—or healing—response to the disease, which is why splenectomy would be disastrous.

The prognosis in primary myelofibrosis is uncertain. Most people who acquire it are older than Jan, often in their sixties or seventies, and they may die of other causes. In some people, the marrow disorder turns into leukemia. "They told me it was rare in my age group and that the average life expectancy was ten years," Jan recalls. "But they gave me some other statistics that were more hopeful, like twenty-five percent of people had no further problems. I thought, 'That's not so bad. I can be in that twenty-five percent.' " No treatment was offered or recommended. "I'm actually grateful for that," Jan says. "Since there were no drugs or surgery to help me, it left me to do all the work on my own." She was told to have regular blood counts to determine whether the condition was progressing.

In the few months after diagnosis, Jan made a number of changes in her life. "My eating was always healthy, so my diet didn't have to change much, but I began a committed exercise program that has become an important part of my life. Originally, I swam; now I do power walking. Exercise gave me an unanticipated, wonderful benefit in addition to the ones you'd expect. It gave me time to begin doing psychological work, to think about my inner life."

Jan says the most significant changes were psychological. "First of all, I gave myself permission to take care of myself. I resolved never to apologize for nurturing myself. I dropped out of an overtaxing school program in nursing and went instead for a master's degree in experiential education. (My experience was living with this diagnosis and coming to a holistic philosophy of health.) I made sure I always got plenty of rest and sleep. And I began to look at my inner turmoil.

"I grew up in an awfully dysfunctional family. My mother became mentally ill with manic depression when I was nine, and my stepfather was alcoholic. I remember seeing a doctor at the Mayo Clinic for a second opinion about the diagnosis of primary myelofibrosis. He asked me if I had ever had any exposure to toxins that might explain my getting this unusual disease, and I laughed, because what flashed into my mind was all the emotional toxicity of my family life. Most of it was centered around my mother. I didn't want to see her at all. Just saying or thinking the word 'mother' triggered a storm inside me. I didn't know that healing this attitude would be the key to moving toward wholeness.

"About five months after the diagnosis, I came to understand that the only way my relationship with my mother could change was for me to see her with different eyes. I remember the exact moment when I achieved this. It was like a rebirth, the beginning of my being a well person. You have no idea what life can be like when that kind of toxicity is removed. Ever since then I've lived with inner peace instead of inner turmoil, and I really don't worry about the physical condition. My family has been incredibly supportive; we've all grown from this. We're all aware of the preciousness of each day and the need to work out issues as they come up. We have our problems, but we work on them."

Jan works today as a bereavement coordinator for a hospice in Mankato, Minnesota. Her blood counts have been remarkably stable for the past ten years. The hematologists she has seen usually do not comment on her stability, but recently one did allow that she has "really done amazingly well." Jan says she gets out of breath if she climbs a lot of steps but otherwise has no limitations. "I get interesting feedback from my family," she says. "They tell me I'm just kind of different, that they feel a great sense of peacefulness around me."

THE FACES OF HEALING:
ETHAN

THE FIRST TIME Ethan Nadelmann had trouble with his back was in the summer of 1981, when he was twenty-four years old. There was no triggering episode, just severe lower back pain that seemed to appear out of nowhere. Ethan, who was physically fit and liked to play basketball, was suddenly disabled; in fact, he could barely walk. Ten days later, however, the pain slowly eased away, eventually disappearing as mysteriously as it had come.

Ethan is a political scientist, an internationally known expert on drug policy. In 1981, when he had his first experience of back pain, he was studying for general exams for his doctorate in government at Harvard, as well as contemplating entrance to Harvard Law School in the fall. Two years later, when he was under a great deal of stress from schoolwork—he was now in his second year of law school and third year of graduate school—Ethan had another episode of back pain, this one precipitated, he thinks, by working out with weights. Now the pain went into his right leg and was very severe, forcing Ethan to seek medical help from an orthopedic surgeon. A CT scan revealed a herniated disc in the lower lumbar spine. The doctor prescribed indomethacin (Indocin), a strong anti-inflammatory drug. The pain lingered for months. Finally, the orthopedist recommended that Ethan get a second opinion from another surgeon, who told him, "If you're not better in a month, you'll have to have surgery." Ethan got better in a month, eventually weaning himself off the Indocin. The experience left him shaken. "I became wary of playing basketball, stopped doing overhead presses on the weight machine, and generally became more cautious," he says.

For the next few years, Ethan's back caused him no major problems. "I had little flare-ups from basketball, racquetball, and heavy lifting," he recalls, "usually lasting a few days, maybe a week at most." He married in 1986, and became a father two years later. I first met him at that time, when he was leading an active, stressful academic life as an assistant professor at Princeton University.

In June 1991, when Ethan returned from a trip to Europe, his back was bothering him "a little," but the pain was omnipresent and increased throughout the summer. In late August, following a basketball game, the pain "got really bad and didn't go away." A week later, in early September, his condition deteriorated, and he sought help from massage therapists, including a shiatsu practitioner. She told him he would be uncomfortable after her treatments, and he was. A few days later, he woke up very early, which was unusual for him, and felt restless. He took a walk and shortly after returning home developed chills and a fever of 102 degrees. The next morning the fever and his back pain were gone, but instead there was right sciatic pain. He revisited the massage therapists.

Just at this time, he had to run an important, three-day meeting of a working group on drug policy reform. I happened to be a member of the group and was distressed to see Ethan in such obvious pain. On the second morning he told me he had awakened with severe pain in his right calf. The pain kept increasing. "I'm waking up in tears in the middle of the night," Ethan said. A few days later he went to the local hospital, where he received an injection of Demerol, which gave him one night of relief.

Massage therapy now gave only temporary relief, and Ethan went to the orthopedist for X-rays and an MRI scan. By now he could not even stand up straight. The MRI showed two ruptured discs, one of them "shattered into multiple fragments." The orthopedist recommended immediate surgery and prescribed oral narcotics and Valium.

Ethan called me for advice, but he was in such pain and on such high doses of narcotics and Valium that I found it hard to have a conversation with him. He himself says he does not remember some conversations from this period. I told him to get a second opinion before he consented to surgery. I also urged him to read a book, *Healing Back Pain,* by John Sarno, a New York doctor who makes a strong case that most back pain is the result of the mind's interference with normal functioning of nerves and blood circulation to muscles, a situation he calls tension myositis syndrome, or TMS. Ethan, through his drug-induced grogginess, made it clear that he did not want to hear anything about his problem being psychosomatic.

Shortly afterward, Ethan called to say he had obtained a second opinion and that it was the same as the first: immediate surgery to remove the shattered disc and relieve pressure on nerves. Again, I found it very difficult to talk to him. He said he was so disabled by pain that he was thinking of going in for the operation within the next few days. I told him to try to hold off, to see if he could get temporary relief from acupuncture or hypnotherapy, and to try to make an appointment to see Dr. Sarno.

I had several reasons for recommending Dr. Sarno's book. I had met a number of patients who had tried every imaginable treatment for back pain, then had gone to Dr. Sarno and been cured. The cure consisted simply of reading his book, going for an individual appointment, and attending evening lectures in which he explained how the mind produced pain in the back. This sounded too good to be true, but I remembered the one disabling episode of back pain I had had; it was clearly related to my emotional state—grief over the simultaneous loss of two close relationships—and it disappeared suddenly after three weeks. It never returned. Then I saw two cases of men with severe chronic back pain that disappeared as if by magic when the men fell in love. Finally, I had just attended an interesting professional conference of a group called the North American Academy of Musculoskeletal Pain, where I was invited to give a keynote address on the meaning of pain. The speaker after me gave a fascinating lecture on the lack of correlation between the subjective experience of back pain and objective measures of musculoskeletal dysfunction, such as X-rays and MRI scans. He showed X-rays and scans of patients that looked so awful you could not believe these people could stand or walk, yet they were free of pain and had normal mobility. In other cases, people were immobilized by pain, yet their spines looked normal. To my mind, all of this information was consistent with Dr. Sarno's philosophy.

Furthermore, I knew something of the extraordinary stress Ethan was under. In addition to all of the academic pressures, his marriage was strained badly, and his baby girl was at a demanding age. He seemed to me an ideal candidate for TMS.

Ethan did not visit a hypnotherapist, nor did he receive acupuncture; but he did read Dr. Sarno's book. He says he paid attention to it for several reasons. "First of all, I recognized that I was under a lot of stress. Second, the fact that the pain had suddenly jumped from my lower back to my leg seemed peculiar. Third, I remembered my experience in 1983, when an orthopedist told me I would get better in a month or have to have surgery, and I got better. And Dr. Sarno presented a very compelling analysis and argument."

Now the surgeon was pressing for an operation, and he was armed with MRI scans that showed a badly shattered disc. Ethan was worn down by pain and mentally clouded by opiates and Valium. Still, he managed to resist. "I saw another doctor, who gave me one cortisone shot. It gave only minor relief. Sometimes hot baths helped, but mostly the pain in the lower leg was agonizing." He read in Dr. Sarno's book that herniated discs by themselves do not cause pain. They can cause muscle weakness and other symptoms of nerve dysfunction, but not pain; the pain is TMS, caused by the mind, even though it might attach itself to an area of mechanical injury. Ethan made an appointment with Dr. Sarno and dragged himself to New York to keep it.

"Sarno wasn't very interested in the MRI," Ethan recalls, "only in the results of muscle testing in the leg, which showed no nerve dysfunction. He did a quick physical exam and told me it was a clear case of TMS, that I should get off the painkillers because I didn't need them. And he told me I would definitely get better and would be playing basketball again. All I had to do was accept his diagnosis. His evening lecture happened to be that evening, so I attended. There were maybe forty people there, mostly upper middle-class. I heard a lot of talk of people getting better. One guy talked about how his back pain had jumped into a finger. Anyway, as I was sitting there, listening to all this, my pain subsided. Afterward I went to dinner at a friend's. There was no pain.

"Sarno told me I shouldn't do any kind of physical therapy. He thinks any interventions directed at the back reinforce the mistaken idea that the pain originates there. Instead he wants you to figure out what kind of psychological pain is going to the body. Well, I wasn't completely ready to abandon physical approaches, so the next morning I kept an appointment I had made with an osteopath. He told me Sarno was partly right but that I should still get physical therapy. The pain started to come back a little that day. That night I dreamed about Sarno having an argument with the osteopath over the issue of physical therapy. When I woke up the pain was less, and I decided not to go to physical therapy. I had some mild opiate withdrawal when I stopped the painkillers."

Ethan says the pain then assumed a new pattern. "It would nudge me awake early in the morning, then fade and become insignificant later in the day. Over the next six weeks it disappeared entirely." He then began looking seriously at his marriage and the possibility of ending it, setting a time limit for trying to make it work.

One month later Ethan resumed exercise with weights and basketball without worries. One month after that, he had a "major personal breakthrough" that left him feeling highly invigorated and fitter than ever. A year later, he and his wife separated, and he felt satisfied to have come to a resolution. "It was the pain and my experience of healing that provided the impetus to do it," he recalls.

Ethan's brother, a doctor, does not accept Ethan's interpretation of events. "He tells me the cortisone shot did it. But, according to my reading, that should last three to six months at best, and I've now been pain free for almost three years, except for occasional muscle soreness related to exercise. Once I had a period of pain in my side, which made me worry briefly about an ulcer. Then I decided it was my mind looking for yet another physical focus for pain, and as soon as I did that, it went away. I've since met many other people who have had similar success with Sarno's approach, people of diverse backgrounds. He is a combination of a scientist and a faith healer. His intellectual arguments made great sense to me; they rang true. I also had little faith in surgical solutions, having seen too many people whose pain returned a few years after having back surgery."

I asked Ethan what he would tell others who suffer from back pain. "Read Sarno's book and see if it rings true for you," was his answer. "People seem to have a hard time accepting the theory until they've exhausted all other remedies or, like me, are facing the knife."

THE FACES OF HEALING: EVA

"IT'S BEEN FIFTEEN years," says Eva Forrester proudly. "Fifteen years. Look at me! If I can do it, you can do it." Eva works as a clerk in the largest health food store in Tucson, Arizona, and this is what she says to many of the customers who come to her for advice. Eva had breast cancer fourteen years ago. Today she is a healed woman, who tries to inspire others to overcome life-threatening diseases.

In 1979, at the age of fifty, Eva Forrester found a lump in her left breast. X-rays gave no cause for alarm, and the first doctor she saw told her the lump felt benign. When another doctor tried and failed to get a needle aspirate of the lump, a biopsy was scheduled. "Before the nurse said anything about the result, I knew," Eva recalls. "I knew it was cancer. They wanted to do a mastectomy. I refused. I panicked. I told them I wanted to wait, although I don't know what I thought I was waiting for. I liked my doctor, an osteopathic surgeon. He said, 'We have to do something.' I decided to consult with my family in Mexico."

Eva is Mexican-American, born in Chihuahua, the child of a Mexican mother and a Lebanese father. "My father was a dental surgeon, and my nephew is an M.D., so I come from a medical background. I have a real extended family; I'm very blessed in that way. When I told them the news, they were all scared. But I'm a Christian—I believe in God, and I've studied all other religions. I believe that what is supposed to be will be. So, finally, I consented to surgery." In 1980 Eva underwent a modified radical mastectomy. Her tumor was large, and had already spread to local lymph nodes, putting her in a high-risk category. She was sent to an oncologist at the University Medical Center, who wanted to start chemotherapy.

"I couldn't do it," Eva says. "Something in me said, 'No!' It was very sad how they treated me. First they sent a woman M.D. to try to persuade me. Next they said, 'You're going to be back here in no time at all and then we'll have to use higher doses on you.' Still, I said no. My own doctor finally agreed to respect my wishes. There would be no chemo, no radiation."

Instead, Eva embarked on a course of natural healing under the guidance of a chiropractor/naturopath. "I used all the herbs that were supposed to have anticancer properties, but I knew that what I really had to do was change my entire being, and I guess I'm still doing that. I changed my way of thinking, trying to see better things in others, getting closer to Christ, getting closer to the Indian way of life. (You know, I have some Aztec blood.) I worked to turn it all into a positive experience, and there have been many good results. I can relate to people much better than I used to, for example."

Seven years after the surgery, Eva went through a divorce. Her marriage, which had been strained at the time she discovered the lump, did not survive the mastectomy. "My husband could only see me as something less than a whole person," she says. "Some men just can't get beyond that. But I grew through that experience, too. I'm thankful to the Great Spirit for my journey, not bitter about it. I'm very close to my three children, all now in their early forties, and very close to my extended family."

I asked Eva if she had returned to the doctors for tests. "I've had some tests, but I don't go overboard," she answered. "I don't like X-rays, so I try to avoid them. The first few blood tests were kind of scary, but I just applied myself harder and used purely natural treatments. Now everything looks fine.

"Still, I have some hard days—you know how that is. But then I go to the store and the Great Spirit sends me a person who says, 'Eva, what you gave me is working,' and it's all worthwhile. So many young women have come into the store who have the same thing. They are so scared. I know many who have died—too many. It's very personal for me. I get involved with each one."

It is a fact of life in the America of the nineties that health food store clerks have replaced pharmacists as dispensers of practical advice to many sick people, especially those with difficult problems or ailments that do not respond well to conventional treatment. The change is another indicator of widespread disaffection with standard medicine. I have often watched Eva Forrester play this role behind the counter of the New Life Health Center. She stands in front of shelves of vitamins and supplements and engages clients with an open, nonjudgmental, comforting manner. She explains patiently the basics of natural healing, of helping the body rely on its own resources. And frequently, she leans closer to a client and says, "Look at me! Fifteen years! If I can do it, you can do it."

"I come from a culture that values healers," Eva explains. "Everyone knows how to find men and women who have this knowledge: *curanderos* and *curanderas*. That's the path I'm on. I want to become a very good *curandera*."

Part Two

Optimizing the Healing System

8

OPTIMIZING YOUR HEALING SYSTEM: AN OVERVIEW

HOW WOULD YOU experience optimal efficiency of your healing system? Very likely you would not be aware of it, because we tend to pay little attention to our health when it is good. You would recover speedily from illness and heal from injuries uneventfully. Ordinary stresses of everyday life might annoy you but would not derange your digestion or blood pressure. Sleep would be restful, sex enjoyable. Aging of your body would occur gradually, allowing you to moderate your activity appropriately and live out a normal life span without undue discomfort. You would not contract heart disease or cancer in middle age, be crippled by arthritis in later life, or lose your mind to premature senility.

This scenario is realistic and, I think, worth working for. Actually, the body wants to be healthy, because health represents efficient operation of all of its systems. A useful analogy is the engine of a car. When all components are doing what they should be doing in just the right way, efficiency is maximal, and operation is quiet, producing a "contented" purr that you rarely notice. An engine that calls attention to itself by sounding noisy and rough, knocking, and expelling black smoke is not efficient. Since efficiency is the ratio of work done to energy supplied, the sick engine is working harder to accomplish less. In a similar way it takes less energy to be a healthy person than to be a sick one, and just as a driver may not pay attention to the sound of a well-running engine, people may not be aware of the condition of good health until it breaks down. A program to boost the efficiency of the healing system will not necessarily produce immediately noticeable changes. It is a long-term investment in the future of the body. If you are seeking boundless energy, eternal happiness, an ageless body, or immortality, please look elsewhere. I will be writing only of real possibilities, consistent with the findings of medical science.

I propose to introduce this subject by asking you to consider obstacles to healing. If you understand the general kinds of problems that interfere with healing, you will know what kinds of preventive and corrective action you can take.

LACK OF ENERGY

Healing requires energy. Energy is supplied by metabolism, the process of conversion of caloric energy in food to chemical energy that the body can use for its various functions. Malnourished and starving people are not good candidates for spontaneous healing. Even people who eat enough may not metabolize well for one reason or another; despite their caloric intake, they may suffer deficits of energy that impede healing.

Recall the story I told of the young woman who came to me complaining of fatigue and who had suffered a nonunion of a broken bone in the leg (see page 108). Over the years, a number of (male) doctors had written her off as a complaining female, but to me the nonunion of a fractured bone and a persistent bruise on a big toe suggested a physical problem; and given her other symptoms and history, I suspected hypothyroidism even though her thyroid function tests were normal. The patient came from a distant city, and I found it very difficult to put her under the care of a physician who was willing to attempt thyroid hormone replacement. When she did start treatment, there was no change in her condition for quite some time. But finally, after ten weeks, her symptoms began to recede. Depression lifted, energy increased, and menstruation and digestion improved as metabolism slowly returned to normal. With these changes, her healing ability returned as well.

Hypothyroidism provides a clear illustration of the dependence of the healing system on the availability of energy from metabolism. More common reasons for insufficient metabolic energy are inadequate diets, impaired digestion, and improper breathing, all of which are within your control.

An adequate diet means one that provides not only enough calories but also all of the nutrients necessary for efficient metabolism without any excesses that promote disease. What constitutes a good diet is a matter of controversy, and much of the controversy is based on emotion rather than reason. In the next chapter I will summarize my views of leading-edge nutritional research to tell you how you can modify your diet in a manner that will increase your healing potential.

The term "impaired digestion" covers a wide range of ailments, from esophageal reflux to hemorrhoids, with a variety of stomach and intestinal complaints in between. But, until proved otherwise, most digestive problems should be assumed to be rooted in stress, because the mind has an unlimited capacity to interfere with normal operation of the gastrointestinal system by disturbing the balance of the autonomic (involuntary) nerves that regulate it. I will advise you how to neutralize stress and harmonize the functioning of the autonomic nervous system in order to avoid these problems.

When I say that improper breathing can lead to deficits of metabolic energy I have a picture in mind of an extreme example: a man I know in his late forties who suffers from emphysema and lifelong bronchitis and asthma. Despite a healthy appetite, he is no more than skin and bones, unable to store up reserves of metabolic energy simply because he cannot take in enough oxygen to burn the fuel he eats. Even in the absence of chronic lung disease, poor breathing can limit metabolism and the amount of energy available for healing. Poor breathing is correctable, and I will tell you how to change it.

Finally, I should mention that lack of energy can also result from immoderate expenditure of energy as a result of overwork, overexertion, lack of rest and sleep, and addictive use of stimulant drugs. Obviously, these problems are also correctable.

POOR CIRCULATION

The healing system depends on the circulation of blood to bring energy and materials to a malfunctioning or injured area. You can see graphic examples of impaired healing due to poor circulation in persons with diabetes whose arteries are subject to premature and rapid progression of atherosclerosis as a result of their altered metabolism. Diabetics must be careful not to cut or nick their feet, since even a slight break in the skin may turn into a large ulcer that refuses to heal. The body just cannot supply enough nourishment, oxygen, and immune activity to the area because of insufficient circulation.

You can maintain your circulatory system in good working order by following a healthy diet, by not smoking, and by exercising, and I will give you more specific suggestions in the following chapters.

RESTRICTED BREATHING

I have already mentioned that restricted breathing can reduce efficiency of the healing system through its dampening effect on metabolism, but I believe it can interfere in other ways as well. The operations of the brain and the nervous system depend on adequate exchange of oxygen and carbon dioxide, as do those of the heart and the circulatory system and all organs of the body. Breathing may be the master function of the body, affecting all others. Restrictions in breathing can be the result of past traumas, both physical and emotional. Most of us have never received instruction about breathing and how to take advantage of it as a harmonizer of mind and body. For that reason I devote a portion of Chapter 13 to the subject.

IMPAIRED DEFENSES

Spontaneous healing is unlikely to occur if the body's defenses are weak. Defense is the responsibility of the immune system, whose main job is to distinguish between self and not-self and take action against the latter. When immunity is crippled, as in AIDS, it is easy to see how much of a problem this creates for the healing system. When immunity is weakened in more subtle ways, impairment of healing may be less obvious.

There are three main categories of weakening influences on the immune system: (1) persistent or overwhelming infections; (2) toxic injury by certain forms of matter and energy; and (3) unhealthy mental states. You can protect yourself against all of these influences and, in addition, learn techniques to enhance immunity through adjustments in diet, exercise, and judicious use of vitamins, minerals, and herbs. You will find the information you need in this part of the book.

TOXINS

Toxic overload is one of the commonest reasons for diminished healing responses, but the subject is immensely complicated, emotionally charged, and highly political. We take toxins into our body with the food we eat, the water we drink, and the air we breathe, as well as in the form of drugs we use, whether we obtain them on medical prescription, buy them over the counter, or use them recreationally. I am concerned about toxic forms of energy as well as matter; electromagnetic pollution may be the most significant form of pollution human activity has produced in this century, all the more dangerous because it is invisible and insensible.

Whether energetic or material, toxins can damage DNA, which contains the information needed for spontaneous healing; disrupt the biological controls on which the healing system depends; weaken defenses; and promote the development of cancer and other diseases that already represent failures of healing by the time they make themselves known. Toxic overload may be a significant cause of allergy, autoimmune disease, and a variety of degenerative diseases (like Parkinson's disease and ALS [amyotrophic lateral sclerosis]), whose causes now seem obscure.

The medical profession and the scientific research community have been remarkably slow to pay attention to this issue, which I consider to be one of the greatest threats to health and well-being in the world today. You have probably read stories in the press about clusters of leukemia cases in neighborhoods near power lines, about the increasing incidence of lymphoma among farmers who use agricultural chemicals, and about a worldwide increase in asthma and bronchitis as air pollution gets worse. Recently, I have followed news stories about a mysterious cluster of lupus cases in the border town of Nogales, Arizona, not far from my home near Tucson. Systemic lupus erythematosus is a potentially serious autoimmune disease not known to be communicable or to have environmental causes. Yet the incidence in Nogales is many times the national average. In 1994 reporters found that a ranching operation on the Mexican side of the border had been dumping pesticides into streams and burning manure contaminated with pesticides because it could not afford to build a proper disposal facility. No causal link is yet established, but I predict one will be.

If you want to increase the likelihood of spontaneous healing, it is imperative that you learn to guard against toxic injury. That means limiting exposure, protecting your body from the effects of pollution, and helping your body eliminate any toxins that do get in.

AGE

We assume that age is an obstacle to healing, that old people do not heal as readily as young people and have lowered immunity and resistance in general. Actually, there is little research to support those assumptions, but observation suggests that they are true. It is impressive to watch how quickly children heal from simple surgeries, like hernia repairs and appendectomies. This is not to say that old people are incapable of spontaneous healing, just that it may take more time. Moreover, methods may exist to protect the healing system from the effects of aging as well as to stimulate general resistance and vitality in the elderly.

Traditional Chinese medicine has identified a number of natural substances that act as tonics of this sort. As a group they appear to be nontoxic and effective. Some of them are now available in this country. I have reviewed the literature on these substances, have tried some of them myself, and with patients, and will give you suggestions for how to use them. You cannot stop the changes of time, but you can modify lifestyle and activity as you age, and it is good to know that help is available to maintain the efficiency of your healing system.

OBSTRUCTION BY THE MIND

After reading Part One of this book and looking over the case histories presented throughout, you should have a firm conviction that the mind is a major influence on healing, for better or worse. Spontaneous healing can be triggered by mental events; it can also be frustrated by habitual ways of using the mind. I have already noted that the mind can depress the immune system and can unbalance the autonomic nervous system, leading to disturbances in digestion, circulation, and all other internal functions. You must know how to use the mind in the service of healing.

SPIRITUAL PROBLEMS

During my travels throughout the world I have met many healers who believe that the primary causes of health and illness are not physical but spiritual. They direct their attention toward an invisible world assumed to exist beyond the ordinary world of the senses. In this realm they search for reasons for illness and ways to cure it. Some of these people believe in karmic causes of illness (actions in the past or in past lives); others, in the ability of deceased ancestors to affect one's life and health; others, in possession by spirits; and still others, in the possibility of psychic attack by malevolent shamans. It is impossible to talk to most scientists about an invisible world, since scientific materialism looks only for physical causes of physical events. I have learned not to try to discuss the possibility of non-physical causation of physical events with most doctors, but I do discuss it with some patients and think about it a lot. Therefore, I would not consider this part of the book complete without some information about the spiritual dimension of healing and what you can do to make sure all is well on that level.

This completes my inventory of obstacles to spontaneous healing and identifies those subjects about which I need to give you information. Let's begin with diet.

9

A Healing Diet

AT A RECENT workshop I taught on natural health a man was wearing a T-shirt that said, "Eat Right, Exercise, Die Anyway." There is truth in that motto. We will all die, and our life span may be genetically programmed. Nevertheless, our choices about how we live may interact with genetics to determine the quality of life we experience as we age. I believe that lifestyle significantly influences our risks of contracting common diseases and certainly affects our ability to heal. Of all the choices we make, those concerning food are particularly important, because we have great potential control over them. But, as you probably already know, there is great disagreement as to what constitutes a healthy diet.

I have seen too many people who have lived to ripe old ages on "bad" diets to believe that food is the sole or even chief determinant of good health. It is simply one influence, one that we can do something about. Books about diet and health appear with great frequency, many of them contradicting each other. Even on the Big Questions, such as the health hazards of dietary fat, major disagreements exist among experts. Some doctors extol a low-fat diet as the key to health and longevity, while others say that cutting fat in the diet may add at best a few weeks to one's life span. There is similar disagreement about the benefits of vegetarianism. Many surveys find that vegetarians have lower rates of heart disease and cancer, but doctors argue about the reasons for that, with some maintaining that vegetarians tend to be more health conscious and take better care of themselves in general, while others say animal foods are hazardous, and still others say that if nonvegetarians ate the same amount of fat (less) and fiber (more) as vegetarians, there would be no differences.

I do not have time or space to enter into these kinds of arguments, and I do not wish to add to your confusion. Instead I want to outline simple, practical suggestions for modifying diet in ways that I believe favor healing responses. You will have heard some of this before, but essential truths cannot be repeated often enough. I am not interested in nutritional fads and will concentrate only on what I see as key areas of consensus emerging from studies of diet and health. These findings concern (1) total calories, (2) fat, (3) protein sources, (4) fruits and vegetables, and (5) fiber.

TOTAL CALORIES

An unexpected research finding that may have great practical significance is that experimental animals live longer with much lower rates of disease when they consume less than the recommended daily allowance of calories. The health and longevity benefits of "undernutrition" are clearly established for laboratory rats and mice, but remain unproved for humans, although there is every reason to believe they apply. The finding is unexpected because we associate less-than-optimal nutrition with poor growth and health, and common sense tells us that we do better if we are well nourished. In fact, most of us may be overnourished, and too much of a good thing may be doing us harm.

If we all lived in controlled environments and had measured portions of monotonous food dispensed to us at regular intervals, none of us would be overweight, I am sure, and I suspect many of us would live longer and experience spontaneous healing more frequently than we do now. Fortunately or unfortunately, we live in a world that tempts us with a great variety and abundance of food, and many of us eat not to satisfy physical hunger but to allay anxiety, depression, and boredom, to provide a substitute for emotional nourishment, or to try to fill an inner void. Most of us are not voluntarily going to embark on programs of undernutrition; I wonder if there might be other ways to take advantage of the research findings.

Two possibilities occur to me. The first is to modify diet to lower caloric content without greatly reducing the amount or appeal of food we consume. The second to is restrict caloric intake, either by fasting or by eating a limited diet at regular intervals—say, one day a week. I have experimented with both of these techniques, and think both are useful.

The easiest way to reduce calories in dishes you like is to cut the fat content. Fat has almost twice as many calories per gram as protein and carbohydrate, so it is the major contributor of calories to our diets. It is remarkably easy to cut fat by one-half, three-quarters, or more in dishes you prepare at home, and it is getting easier all the time with the appearance of low-fat cookbooks and low-fat or fat-free versions of popular foods, like chips, mayonnaise, and sour cream. Of course, fat also contributes taste and pleasure to food, and you do not want to sacrifice those qualities totally. Nor do you want to eat such great quantities of lighter foods that you wind up taking in more calories than before. (I know people who formerly ate ice cream only occasionally but now eat large helpings of nonfat frozen yogurt every day. I think their caloric intake has increased rather than decreased as a result of the change; this and similar adjustments may explain why obesity in America continues to increase, even as total fat in the American diet declines.) In short, it is possible to reduce caloric intake and still eat plenty of satisfying foods by using less fat, which is one way to reap some of the health benefits of undernutrition.

At different times in my life I have experimented with fasting one day a week, usually on Mondays. When I fast, I consume nothing but water or herb tea, sometimes with lemon in it, and I find this to be a useful physical and psychological discipline. It feels healthy. If you are very skinny and sensitive to cold, I do not recommend fasting in this way. Instead you might want to try drinking fruit juice or clear liquids one day a week. Not only do these practices give your digestive system a rest, they decrease total caloric intake and, again, may provide benefits of undernutrition without forcing you to give up the pleasures of eating. There are many secondary benefits as well, such as greatly increased appreciation of food following a fast and greater ability to eat consciously rather than unconsciously.

In any case, watch for further research reports on the health benefits of undernutrition. If the findings hold up and continue to look applicable to humans, it will be worth trying to cut your intake of calories in order to realize more of your body's healing potential.

FAT

I will devote more time to a discussion of fat than to any other aspect of diet, because I believe the implications of research on how fat affects the body are vitally important. Eating too much of the wrong kinds of fat can seriously impair your healing abilities and may be the biggest dietary mistake you can make.

Fats are mixtures of fatty acids, which are chains of carbon atoms with hydrogen atoms attached and a distinctive acidic chemical group at one end. Fatty acids can be classified by the lengths of the chains and by whether all of the available chemical bonds of the carbon atoms are occupied or saturated with hydrogen atoms. Unsaturated fatty acids have one (mono-) or more (poly-) links in the chain consisting of double or triple bonds between adjacent carbons. Points of unsaturation alter the configuration of the molecule, and its physical and chemical characteristics.

Fats composed mainly of saturated fatty acids are solid at room temperature, and the greater the saturated fat content, the higher will be the temperature of melting. Animal fats are highly saturated, as are two vegetable fats: the oils of coconuts and palm kernels. At the opposite end of this chemical spectrum are the polyunsaturated vegetable oils, all of which stay liquid in colder temperatures. The lower the temperature at which solidification occurs, the greater the degree of unsaturation. Corn, soy, sesame, sunflower, and safflower oils are examples of polyunsaturated fats. In the middle of the spectrum are vegetable oils composed primarily of monounsaturated fatty acids, those with just one double or triple bond in the chain of carbon atoms; examples are olive, canola, peanut, and avocado oils.

At the moment, conventional medical doctors who are concerned about nutrition are giving us two general kinds of advice about dietary fat. They are telling us to cut way down on the total amount of fat we eat and also way down on the amount of saturated fat we eat. In my view, this is only part of the story.

Evidence for the health risks of saturated fat is overwhelming. In most people, a high percentage of saturated fat in the diet stimulates the liver to make LDL (bad) cholesterol in quantities greater than the body can remove from the circulation. The result is damage to arterial walls (atherosclerosis), impairment of the cardiovascular system, increased risk of premature death and disability from coronary heart disease, and reduction of healing capacity through restriction of blood flow.

Evidence for the health risks of total fat is much less convincing. Given the popular prejudice against fat in our society, many people would like to believe that very low-fat diets will make us live longer, prevent cancer, and boost our immunity, but we do not have hard data to support these ideas. Very low-fat diets—around ten percent of total calories from fat, as compared with forty in the average American diet—are of great therapeutic benefit to persons with established cardiovascular disease, but they are hard to adhere to and may not do much for the rest of us. I believe it is worth cutting fat to moderate levels—say, twenty to thirty percent of total calories—but that it is much more important to concentrate on reducing saturated fat and the other unhealthy fats that I will write about in a moment.

The main natural sources of saturated fat are beef, pork, lamb, unskinned chicken, duck, whole milk and products made from whole milk (especially cheese, butter, and cream), and processed foods made with tropical oils (palm and coconut). Of all of these, beef fat may be the greatest threat to health. In addition there are unnatural sources of saturated fat: margarine, solid vegetable shortening, and all processed foods made with partially hydrogenated oils. In these products, liquid vegetable oils have been artificially saturated with hydrogen to make them solid or semisolid at room temperature and increase their resistance to spoilage. No matter how good the oils are that go into this process, what comes out is saturated and hazardous to cardiovascular health.

Obviously, the easiest way to remove saturated fat from the diet is to cut way down on animal foods, especially meat and whole milk products—a strategy I recommend. In addition, you should eliminate sources of tropical oils and artificially solidified oils, which are dangerous for another reason, which I will explain below.

Not long ago, doctors recommended replacement of saturated fats like butter with polyunsaturated vegetable oils, like corn and safflower, in the belief that these oils would lower cholesterol and benefit the heart and arteries. During this period, margarine, whose only virtue in the early part of this century was its low cost, changed in the public mind from a cheap substitute for butter to a healthy alternative to it. Sales of safflower oil, the most unsaturated of all the vegetable oils, boomed. I hope this era has now come to an end. Polyunsaturated oils are bad for us in other ways. They are chemically unstable, owing to their content of fatty acids with energetic double and triple bonds that tend to react with oxygen, resulting in toxic compounds that can damage DNA and cell membranes, promoting cancer, inflammation, and degenerative changes in tissue. I strongly recommend eliminating them from the diet.

Moreover, when unsaturated fatty acids are heated or treated with chemical solvents and bleaches, they tend to deform from a natural, curved shape (called the *cis*-configuration) to an unnatural, jointed shape (called the *trans*-configuration). Trans-fatty acids, or TFAs, may be extremely toxic, even though medical scientists have been very slow to recognize the danger. Even now, as they are finally beginning to admit that margarine may be worse for the heart than butter, they are still focusing solely on margarine's content of saturated fat rather than on its abundance of TFAs. The body builds cell membranes out of cis-fatty acids and also uses them in synthetic pathways for hormones. We do not know what it does with TFAs; if it tries to use them in the same ways, the result might be defective membranes and hormones. I believe that TFAs in the diet damage the regulatory machinery of the body, significantly compromising the healing system. Remember that TFAs are never found in nature, only in fats that have been subjected to unusual chemical and physical treatment. Some researchers refer to them as "funny fats," but there is nothing funny about what they may do to us. You can avoid any danger by eliminating from the diet all margarine and solid vegetable shortening and products made with them, all products listing "partially hydrogenated" oil of any kind on the label, and all commercial brands of polyunsaturated vegetable oils (corn, soy, sesame, sunflower, safflower), since these have been extracted with heat and solvents that promote formation of TFAs. (I refuse even to consider cottonseed oil as a food. It has a high percentage of saturated fat, may contain naturally occurring toxins, and is likely to be contaminated with pesticide residues.)

What then *can* we eat? Vegetable oils that are predominantly monounsaturated—olive, canola, peanut, avocado—do not pose the cardiovascular risk of saturated fats or the cancer risks of polyunsaturates. The individual oils within this category differ significantly from one another, and it is important to know the advantages and disadvantages of each.

Olive oil appears to be the best and safest of all edible fats. The body seems to have an easier time handling its predominant fatty acid, oleic acid, than any other fatty acid. Replacing saturated fat in the diet with olive oil leads to a reduction of bad cholesterol (whereas replacement with polyunsaturated vegetable oils lowers good cholesterol as well). Olive oil is delicious and has been used as an edible oil for thousands of years. The best-quality, called extra-virgin, is extracted with gentle pressure rather than with heat or solvents; you can buy it in almost any supermarket for a reasonable price. Olive trees are extraordinarily long-lived and beautiful, inspiring reverence in cultures that cultivate them; they produce well without heavy applications of pesticides and agricultural chemicals. Moreover, in populations that use olive oil as their main cooking fat, rates of cardiovascular disease are lower than expected for the amount of total fat consumed, and rates of degenerative diseases and cancer are also lower than in many other populations. Olive oil is the outstanding element of the Mediterranean diet that has attracted so much research attention in the past few years. Mediterranean peoples eat plenty of fruits and vegetables, whole grain breads, substantial quantities of fish, and moderate amounts of animal foods, but when all of these factors are analyzed, olive oil has the highest correlation with better health.

As a result of my own research, I have come to rely on olive oil as the principal fat in my diet, using it for almost all cooking in which I use fat, for all salad dressing, and occasionally as a dip for bread (though I usually eat bread without anything on it). If you do not like the taste of olive oil, you can buy "light" varieties that lack the distinctive odor and flavor; although these might be useful in some dishes, like Oriental stir-fries and baked goods, they are probably less healthful because they have been processed. If the only change you make in your diet is to replace butter and margarine with olive oil, you will have made a tremendous step toward better health and healing.

Canola oil (the name is a contraction of "Canadian oil," because the product was developed in Canada) is a modern version of a traditional cooking oil of India and southern China extracted from rapeseed. Rape is a mustard relative, whose seed contains an oil with very little saturated fat and a high percentage of monounsaturated fatty acids. It also contains a toxic fatty acid, erucic acid. Modern growers have reduced the erucic acid content of rapeseed oil and improved it in other ways; but despite its current popularity—canola oil has eclipsed safflower oil as the darling of the health food industry—I am much less enthusiastic about it than I am about olive oil. We have no comparable epidemiological data for canola oil of the sort we have for olive oil to suggest that health is better in populations that use it. The canola oil you find in supermarkets has all been extracted in ways that deform fatty acids, and rape is heavily treated with pesticides that probably find their way into the oil. You can buy organic, expeller-pressed canola oil in health food stores at considerably higher cost, and this is the only kind I would use. I keep a bottle of it in my refrigerator for occasional recipes where I want a perfectly neutral-flavored oil, but I find that I use it up very slowly. In my opinion it is a distant runner-up to olive oil.

Peanut oil, once the preferred choice of Chinese cooks, has a much greater percentage of polyunsaturated fatty acids than olive oil and may also contain toxins, both natural and unnatural. I see no reason to use it. Avocado oil, available only in health food stores, is too expensive and has nothing to recommend it for use in the kitchen. Avocados are interesting additions to the diet but, given their fat content, should be used with great moderation. If you cannot give up the idea of spreading fat on your bread, try a little mashed, seasoned avocado instead; it is a way of replacing a highly saturated fat with a monounsaturated one.

There are three other oils in my refrigerator that I use in small quantities as flavorings: roasted (dark) sesame oil, walnut oil, and hazelnut oil. These are polyunsaturates that must be kept cold and not used in foods heated to high temperatures. They have strong odors and tastes that I like in soups, salad dressings, and marinades; in small amounts they are delicious and not unhealthy.

Before I leave the subject of fats, I want to mention one other category that seems to promote health and healing. These are the omega-3 fatty acids found in some fish and a few plants. Omega-3s are highly unsaturated fatty acids with special properties. They appear to reduce inflammatory changes in the body, protect against abnormal blood clotting, and, possibly, protect against cancer and degenerative changes in cells and tissues. A great deal of research suggests that optimal diets should include sources of these hard-to-find compounds. Here are your choices:

You can eat the fish that contain omega-3s in their fat, mostly oily fish from cold northern waters: sardines, herring, mackerel, bluefish, salmon, and, to a lesser extent, albacore tuna. (I will have more to say about fish in the next section of this chapter.) Or you can take omega-3 supplements as capsules of fish oils. Canola and soy oil provide tiny amounts, but two less common vegetable oils from flax and hemp are rich sources: the seeds of these plants have high concentrations of omega-3s. You can buy flax seeds, flax meal, and flax oil in health food stores. Hemp oil is becoming available in some health food stores. Finally, one wild green—purslane—is an omega-3 source. Mediterranean peoples use it in soups, and it is easily grown in the garden; in fact, it tends to be a persistent weed.

I do not recommend taking fish oil capsules. They may be contaminated with toxins and may not provide the same benefits as eating the right fish. My personal preference is to eat salmon, sardines, or herring two or three times a week. (Mackerel is harder to get, bluefish is often contaminated with mercury, and albacore tuna is not a rich enough source.) If you choose not to eat fish, your best bet is hemp oil or flax, since purslane is not easy to come by. Hemp oil is greenish and nutty, quite good mixed with olive oil in salad dressing. Flax oil is sweet and nutty when fresh, but it deteriorates quickly and often tastes unpleasantly like oil paint (for which it is used as a base) by the time it gets to the table. If you can find good-tasting flax oil and like it, by all means use it. Otherwise, I would recommend adding flax meal to the diet. My suggestion is to buy whole flax seeds, which are quite cheap, keep them in the refrigerator, and grind enough for a few days or a week at a time, using a coffee grinder or blender. You can sprinkle flax meal over cereal or salad or add it to breads and cookies. It tastes good. A tablespoon of hemp or flax oil a day or two tablespoons of flax meal will give you a good helping of precious omega-3 fatty acids.

Here, then, are my recommendations about dietary fats:

- *Cut total fat* by eliminating deep-fried foods, moderating consumption of chips, nuts, avocados, butter, cheese, and other high-fat foods, and learning to modify recipes to reduce fat content of favorite dishes. Read labels of products you buy to determine fat content, and try to keep your fat intake in the range of twenty to thirty percent of total calories.

• *Make a special effort to cut saturated fat in your diet* by cutting down substantially on meat, unskinned poultry, whole milk and whole milk products, butter, margarine, vegetable shortening, and all products made with tropical oils and partially hydrogenated oils.

• *Eliminate polyunsaturated vegetable oils from your diet* by avoiding safflower, sunflower, corn, soy, peanut, and cottonseed oils and products made from them.

• *Learn to rely on olive oil as your principal fat,* preferably a flavorful brand of extra-virgin olive oil.

• *Learn to identify and avoid all sources of hazardous transfatty acids:* margarine, solid vegetable shortening, and all products made with partially hydrogenated oils of any kind.

• *Increase consumption of omega-3 fatty acids* by eating the appropriate fish, hemp or flax oil, or flax meal regularly.

PROTEIN SOURCES

We need protein to make new tissue, to grow, and to maintain and repair our tissues. Proteins are complicated molecules, made up of a variety of amino acids, some of which are essential nutrients that the body is unable to manufacture and must receive in the diet. Protein deficiency results in stunted growth and dramatic impairment of healing ability; but in our society, protein deficiency is practically nonexistent. Instead, most people consume too much protein, which can also affect health adversely, and many of us get our protein from questionable sources.

Most people rely on animal foods for protein: meat, poultry, fish, milk, and milk products. Vegetable sources are beans, grains, and some nuts. An important difference between animal and vegetable sources is that the latter are less concentrated. For example, the protein in beans is diluted by edible starch and indigestible fiber, so that you have to eat a greater volume of a vegetable protein source to get the equivalent of a portion of an animal food.

When you eat more protein than your body needs to make and repair tissue, it will be used instead as an energy source, as fuel. But protein is not an ideal fuel for the body. Because protein molecules are big and complicated, their digestion and metabolism require more work than the digestion and metabolism of carbohydrates and fats. So proteins are less efficient fuels: the ratio of work in to energy out is not as favorable as for other nutrients. A practical consequence is that if you are eating a high-protein diet, your digestive system is doing a lot of work, and less energy may be available to you for healing.

There is another problem with protein as fuel: it does not burn clean. Carbohydrate and fat, being composed solely of carbon, hydrogen, and oxygen, burn to carbon dioxide and water. Protein contains nitrogen, and in the process of metabolism degrades to highly toxic nitrogenous residues. The burden of dealing with these falls on the liver, which processes them to urea, a simple compound that is also highly toxic. The kidneys must then take up the task of eliminating urea. Tying up liver and kidney function in this way reduces the contribution of those organs to the body's healing system. Furthermore, the nitrogenous-breakdown products of protein metabolism can also irritate the immune system, increasing the risk of allergy and autoimmunity, which represent derangement of body defenses. For all of these reasons, it is better not to consume too much protein. You want to give the body enough for growth, maintenance, and repair, but not so much that it becomes a significant source of metabolic energy.

How much protein is too much? Remarkably small amounts are enough to satisfy the minimal requirements of the average adult— perhaps two ounces, or sixty grams, of a protein food a day. Many people in our society eat much more than that at every meal. Certainly four ounces (less than 120 grams) is plenty. In general: if you have a protein meal once a day—that is, a meal organized around a main course of meat, chicken, fish, eggs, or tofu—that is probably enough. Try to design other meals around carbohydrates and vegetables: stir-fried vegetables with rice, say, or pasta and vegetables, or salads and bread. Cutting down on protein will free up energy, spare your digestive system and especially your liver and kidneys from extra work, and protect your immune system from irritation.

In addition to thinking about protein in general and how to cut down on it, you should consider the advantages and disadvantages of the common sources of dietary protein, another subject that I consider important. Your choices about what kind of protein you ingest may have great influence on your long-term health and capacity for healing.

One problem is that diets rich in animal protein put you high on the food chain, not a good place to be. The food chain is the pattern of dependence of higher organisms on lower organisms for energy. Plants make energy from the sun. Herbivorous animals get that same energy by eating the plants. Carnivorous animals get it further removed from the source by eating the flesh of herbivores. The bigger the organism and the more carnivorous it is, the higher it is said to be on the food chain. One consequence of eating high on the food chain is that you take in much larger doses of toxins, because environmental toxins concentrate as you move up from level to level. The fat of domestic animals often contains high concentrations of toxins that exist in much lower concentrations in grains, for example. An independent problem is that the methods we use for raising animal sources of protein further load them up with unhealthy substances.

Here is a quick review of sources of dietary protein:

Meat has several strikes against it. It is a major source of saturated fat in the diet, as well as a highly concentrated form of protein. Being high on the food chain, it accumulates environmental toxins. Unless it is raised organically, it is also full of added toxins: residues of growth-promoting hormones, antibiotics, and other chemicals used by all commercial ranchers and farmers. "White meat" is no better than red meat, except that veal has less fat than beef, and pork fat (lard) seems less hazardous for the human cardiovascular system than beef fat. Unless meat is cooked very well, it may transmit pathogenic viruses and bacteria to humans who eat it.

Chicken has one main advantage over meat: its fat is external to muscle tissue and can be removed with the skin. Otherwise, chicken presents the same toxic hazards as the flesh of cows, sheep, and pigs and may contain even more added hormones. Dangerous bacteria, particularly salmonella, often contaminate chicken and can sicken humans who eat it unless the chicken is well cooked.

Fish increasingly appears to be a very healthy source of protein. I am referring here to scale fish, not to shellfish. Populations that eat the most fish have the highest longevity and lowest disease rates, and within those populations, the healthiest individuals are those who eat the most fish. Why fish is good for us is not clear. Omega-3 fatty acids may be a part of the explanation, but they are in some fish only, and the answer may not have to do with any one component. Are fish eaters healthier because of the fish they eat or because of what they don't eat? Most of them eat much less animal flesh, for example. There are important cautions about fish today. Much of it is contaminated by toxins that have been dumped into rivers and oceans. Larger, more carnivorous fish and fish that live in coastal waters are most dangerous in this regard. I recommend against eating swordfish, marlin, and shark because their flesh is likely to contain toxins. Increasingly, fish are being farmed throughout the world, especially salmon, trout, and catfish. Farmed fish may not be as beneficial to health as their wild counterparts (farmed salmon have lower amounts of omega-3s) and may have residues of drugs used to control diseases in crowded conditions. But even with these drawbacks, fish are a good protein source.

Shellfish are much less attractive, because they are more likely to contain toxins. They live in coastal effluents and feed in ways that expose them to high concentrations of wastes. Raw shellfish can easily transmit diseases to humans.

Milk products tend to be very high in saturated fat, unless they are made from skim milk or low-fat milk. Many people cannot digest the sugar (lactose) in milk, and many more probably experience irritation of the immune system from the protein in milk. (This is a particular problem with cow's milk; goat's milk does not seem to bother the immune system nearly as much.) If you have allergies, autoimmune disease, sinus trouble, bronchitis, asthma, eczema, or gastrointestinal problems, it is worth eliminating all milk from the diet for at least two months to see what happens to the conditions. In very many cases, they will improve dramatically. Commercial dairy products are another source of environmental toxins, drugs, and hormones.

Eggs, at least the whites of eggs, are good sources of high-quality protein, but egg yolks contain fat and cholesterol that most of us should limit. Commercially raised eggs are produced under awful conditions, may contain toxic residues of drugs and hormones, and may be contaminated with salmonella. Avoid raw and undercooked eggs, and try to find eggs from free-ranging chickens raised without drugs and hormones.

Grains and beans contain carbohydrate and fiber along with protein, so you can eat more of them without suffering a protein overload. Since they are often treated with a variety of agricultural chemicals, I recommend looking for organically produced varieties.

Nuts and seeds, like almonds and sunflower seeds, are sources of vegetable protein, but their high content of fat (mostly polyunsaturated) argues for moderation in their consumption.

Soybeans have much more protein than other beans, along with significant amounts of polyunsaturated fat. Soy protein can be isolated and transformed into an astonishing variety of forms, including facsimiles of animal foods. You will find most of these in the refrigerator cases of health food stores, but also look in Oriental grocery stores. Many forms of tofu and tempeh are now available, along with better and better burgers, wieners, and lunch meats, including some excellent low- and nonfat versions. There may be great health benefits to soy foods that are just coming to light. They contain a group of chemicals called phytoestrogens that may offer significant protection against prostate cancer in men and estrogenically driven diseases in women, including breast cancer, endometriosis, fibrocystic breast disease, and uterine fibroids, as well as the discomforts of menopause. Low incidence of these conditions among Japanese women may be due to their high consumption of soy foods, especially tofu. Two of the best-known soy phytoestrogens—genistein and daidzein—are now being explored for their ability to moderate human hormonal imbalances.

Having reviewed the major sources of dietary protein, I will now give you my simplest recommendations for taking advantage of this information to change your diet in a direction that favors spontaneous healing:

• *Eat less protein.* Learn to recognize sources of protein in your diet and to cut down on them. Practice making meals that do not revolve around large servings of dense protein foods.

• *Begin to replace animal protein in the diet with fish and soy protein.* By doing so you will both reduce your exposure to toxins and other harmful elements in meats, poultry, and milk and gain the benefits of health-promoting components of fish and soybeans.

FRUITS AND VEGETABLES

Our mothers were right to tell us to eat our vegetables. Vegetables and fruits appear to offer significant protection against cancer, heart disease, and other common ailments as well as to help immunity and healing. Besides, perfectly ripe fruits and good-quality vegetables are some of the greatest delights of the table. What is better than slicing into an aromatic melon or a peach running with juice and flavor, or a creamy-ripe mango? How about a colorful bowl of mixed salad greens dressed with olive oil and balsamic vinegar; barely cooked, crisp sugar snap peas; or perfect ears of sweet corn? Many people miss out on these pleasures because commercial growers plant varieties chosen for resistance to shipping rather than for flavor, or because the crops are harvested before they are ready to eat, or because they have suffered in transit to stores. Other people think they do not like vegetables because they do not know how to cook them and have never tasted them properly prepared. Fresh fruits and vegetables probably deliver more health benefits than canned, frozen, or dried versions.

As researchers identify more and more protective compounds in fruits and vegetables, there is a tendency in our society to isolate the compounds and use them in the form of supplements. I am not sure this is a good idea. Beta carotene, for example, the water-soluble precursor of vitamin A (that is, the body makes vitamin A from it), is now used in capsule form by millions of people, who have heard that it is an antioxidant and may prevent cancer. There *is* strong evidence that beta carotene helps prevent cancer when we eat it in our food; evidence for its effectiveness as an isolated supplement is much less solid. Beta carotene is one member of a large family of carotenes, yellow and orange pigments found in many fruits (peaches, melons, mangoes) and vegetables (sweet potatoes, squash, pumpkin, tomatoes, and dark, leafy greens). Other carotenes, like alpha carotene and lycopene (in tomatoes), may be even more important contributors to the cancer-protective effect of these foods, or they may act synergistically with beta carotene. Until a mixed-carotene supplement appears on the market, people whose diets are low in fruits and vegetables may be wise to take supplemental beta carotene, but they would be wiser still to increase their consumption of carotene-rich foods.

Reductionism—the belief that properties of wholes can be reduced to effects of single components—is a common proclivity of Western science and medicine. When we find a plant in nature that has interesting biological effects, we want to identify and isolate the "active principle" of the plant and give it to patients in pure form. Traditional Chinese doctors think very differently. They do not object to scientific analysis of healing plants, but they do not believe in using isolated components. In their view the desirable effects of herbal medicine result from synergistic interactions of all components of each plant and of all the plants (often a dozen or more) used in a typical prescription.

Recently, scientists identified a compound in broccoli, sulphoraphane, that may be partly responsible for that vegetable's powerful cancer-protective effect. Should you eat broccoli or wait for capsules of sulphoraphane to appear in health food stores? I say broccoli, because parts are not equal to wholes. If you think you do not like it, try it cooked in new ways. Here is a simple way of preparing broccoli that is so delicious I cannot get enough of it:

Trim the end off a large bunch of broccoli, cut off the main stem, peel it beneath the fibrous layer, and cut into edible chunks. Separate the head of broccoli into bite-size pieces and peel a bit of the skin from the stems to make them more tender. Wash the broccoli and place it in a pot with ¼ cup cold water, 1 tablespoon of extra-virgin olive oil, salt to taste, and several cloves of chopped or mashed garlic. Bring to a boil, cover tightly, and let steam until the broccoli is bright green and very crunchy-tender, no more than five minutes. Remove the lid and boil off most of the remaining liquid. Serve at once. You can mix this with cooked pasta (penne or rigatoni), season it with red pepper flakes and parmesan cheese, or eat it as is. It is beautiful to look at, utterly delicious, low in fat, rich in vitamins and minerals, and filled with sulphoraphane too!

If you would like to try a more exotic preparation of broccoli, here is a modified version of a Chinese dish with black bean sauce, without all the fat (often cottonseed oil) used in many Chinese restaurants:

Prepare the vegetable as in the previous recipe. Put it in a pot with the following ingredients: 2 tablespoons of salted black beans (available in Chinese grocery stores) that have been washed in cold water and drained; 2 large cloves of garlic, mashed; 2 teaspoons of finely chopped fresh ginger root; 1 tablespoon of dark sesame oil; 2 tablespoons of soy sauce; 2 teaspoons of sugar; 1 teaspoon of red pepper flakes, 2 tablespoons of chopped scallions; and ¼ cup dry sherry. Bring to a boil, cover, and steam, as in the previous recipe, until the broccoli is just crunchy-tender. Uncover to evaporate most of the liquid and toss broccoli well in the black bean sauce before serving (over rice, if you wish).

Of course, there is a caution about supermarket produce: it may be contaminated with toxins, put there not by nature but by agribusiness. I discuss this subject in detail in the next chapter and will tell you how to protect yourself. It is important to try to find chemical-free produce and to know which crops are the most likely to be contaminated.

FIBER

Fiber is the indigestible residue in plants that we eat, made up of carbohydrates too complex chemically for our digestive systems. Adequate fiber in the diet promotes digestive health, allowing us to have regular bowel movements and improving the biochemical environment of the large bowel. Some forms of fiber also benefit the cardiovascular system by helping the body eliminate cholesterol. Populations that have very low intakes of fiber have high rates of colon cancer and vice-versa. If you do not eat enough fiber, your digestive system will not function at peak efficiency, which can compromise healing ability in several ways.

The main sources of dietary fiber are fruits, vegetables, and whole grains. Insoluble fiber, such as in wheat bran, is an important bowel regulator. Soluble fiber, such as in oat bran, helps eliminate cholesterol. Some people who require fiber to regulate the bowels take it in supplementary form as bran or psyllium (a seed with a fibrous husk). I think it is easier to eat more fruits and vegetables, whole grains, and cereals and breads made from whole grains, which may have other benefits as well.

.   .   .

HERE IS A BRIEF summary of my recommendations for a healing diet:

- *Try to eat fewer calories* by eliminating high-fat foods and modifying recipes for favorite dishes by cutting fat content. Also experiment with periodic fasting or restricted dieting.

- *Cut down appreciably on saturated fat* by eating fewer foods of animal origin and none containing palm or coconut oils, margarine, vegetable shortening, or partially hydrogenated oils.

- *Do not use polyunsaturated vegetable oils for cooking. Use only good-quality olive oil.*

- *Learn to recognize and avoid sources of trans-fatty acids* (margarine, vegetable shortening, partially hydrogenated oils, and common brands of liquid vegetable oils).

- *Increase consumption of omega-3 fatty acids* by eating more of the right kinds of fish or adding hemp oil or flax products to the diet.

- *Eat less protein of all kinds.*

- *Try to replace animal protein foods with fish and soyfoods.*

- *Eat more fruits and vegetables of all kinds.*

- *Eat more whole grains and products made from whole grains.*

These recommendations are practical, sensible, and probably familiar to you. They are also important enough to repeat because they are the bare essentials of a healthy diet. They do not require you to become a food faddist or to give up everything you like. And, based on my knowledge and experience, I can assure you that they will help your healing system work more efficiently.

10

Protecting Yourself from Toxins

Spontaneous healing depends on the unobstructed, efficient operation of all components of the healing system. If any of those components are injured or preoccupied with other tasks, the process of healing will be impaired. One of the greatest threats to the system is toxic overload from the multitude of harmful substances in today's environment. The word "toxin" comes from the Greek word for "bow," as in "bow and arrow." Untold numbers of poisoned arrows must have pierced the bodies of Greek warriors for the word to take on its present meaning, and images of war are not inappropriate to this discussion, for in a sense our bodies are under attack.

Medical scientists, especially those in the employ of government and industry, have been very slow to recognize the threat to public health posed by toxic residues; instead they often downplay it. The following quotation from a review article on organic food that appeared in a journal of food science and nutrition is typical of the official response to consumer fears about toxic chemicals used on produce.

> The substitution of "organic" for "chemical" fertilizers during the growth of plants produces no change in the nutritional or chemical properties of foods. All foods are made of "chemicals." Traces of pesticides have been reported to be present in about 20 to 30% of both "organic" and conventional foods. These traces are usually within the official tolerance levels. Such levels are set low enough to protect consumers adequately. Indeed, there is no record of a single

case of injury to a consumer resulting from the application of pesticides to food crops at permitted levels.

Not long ago a full-page color advertisement for a leading manufacturer of agricultural chemicals appeared in national magazines, showing an orange with a long label affixed to it; printed on the label were hundreds of names of chemical compounds. The caption read, "Mother Nature Is Lucky—She Doesn't Have to Label Her Products," and the text of the ad went on to inform us that since all fruits and vegetables are composed of myriad chemicals, there is no reason to worry about the addition of a few more. Recently, a more insidious argument has begun to circulate: namely, that natural toxins—contained in many crops—pose a greater threat to health than manmade ones.

Proponents of these arguments assume that the main concern is "injury," some immediately identifiable, acute response to the ingestion of pesticides. In fact, such cases do occur:

Aldicarb in watermelon, 1985. Aldicarb is an extremely toxic systemic carbamate pesticide. Its illegal use on watermelon led to the largest reported North American epidemic of food-borne pesticide poisoning. Active surveillance ascertained reports of 638 probable cases and 344 possible cases. Another 333 probable and 149 possible cases were reported from other western states and provinces of Canada. Illness ranged from mild gastrointestinal upset to severe cholinergic poisoning [an effect similar to that of nerve gas]. Levels in the melons that caused illness ranged from 0.07 to 3 ppm [parts per million] of aldicarb sulfoxide. The epidemic ceased after melons in distribution chains were destroyed, an embargo was imposed, and an inspection program was instituted.

But my concern about pesticides and other environmental toxins has not so much to do with the possibility of acute injury as with long-term compromise of the healing system and increased risks of cancer, immune dysfunction, and a variety of chronic ailments (like Parkinson's disease) in which cause-and-effect relationships with toxins have not been adequately investigated. Such effects could result from cumulative exposure over time to toxins from various sources.

And of course it is nonsense to say that the existence of harmful compounds in nature in any way excuses adding more of them to the environment. It is true that black pepper, basil, tarragon, alfalfa sprouts, celery, peanuts, potatoes, tomatoes, and white button mushrooms contain naturally occurring toxic compounds, but our bodies have evolved along with those species and probably have a better ability to defend against any injurious agents they contain. Moreover, if our healing system is already occupied with the neutralization of natural toxins, it will have a reduced ability to deal with an added load of artificial ones. Similarly, certain locations on earth have high background radiation due to high altitude or emissions of radioactivity by surface rocks, but this does not mean we should be complacent about exposure to X-rays or to nuclear waste. Cancer risks from radiation correlate with cumulative totals over a lifetime; the harmful effects of exposure to manmade radiation added to those received from natural sources can easily overwhelm the body's defensive capabilities.

In short, do not believe people who try to allay your concerns about toxic exposures. This is a real threat, and you must learn to take protective measures. Your body's ability to eliminate unwanted substances depends on the healthy functioning of four systems: the urinary system, the gastrointestinal system, the respiratory system, and the skin; it can discharge wastes through urine, feces, exhaled air, and sweat. The liver processes most foreign chemical compounds, detoxifying them if possible or breaking them down to simpler compounds that can leave the body by one of those four routes. In order to maintain your eliminative capacity, those four systems must be in good working order. You can ensure they are by drinking enough pure water to help the kidneys maintain a good output of urine, by eating enough fiber to ensure regular bowel function, by exercising your respiratory system regularly, and by periodically increasing output of sweat through aerobic exercise or exposure to heat (as by taking saunas or steam baths).

Some people sustain most of their exposure to toxins in the workplace. If you work in a chemically hazardous occupation (such as the manufacture of plastics, rubber, leather, textiles, dyes, poisons, or paper, or in a mine or dry-cleaning facility, or on a farm that uses agrichemicals), you should inform yourself about the dangers of products you come in contact with (by contacting the Environmental Protection Agency or consumer groups concerned with environmental toxins, for example) and take all precautions to minimize exposure. The rest of us are most likely to contact toxins in the air we breathe, the water we drink, and the food we eat, as well as from a few other sources. Let me review those sources, giving suggestions for self-defense.

AIR POLLUTION

Truly clean air has become a rarity as the twentieth century ends. Even in the Arctic, haze from industrial pollution now darkens the atmosphere, and many of us have had the experience of watching air quality deteriorate in places we have lived in over time. When I was working as a medical intern in San Francisco in 1968–69, I never saw smog in that city. From my apartment on a hill, I could see smog over Oakland, across the bay, where it was held by prevailing westerly winds. Ten years later, pollution increased to a point where it overwhelmed the atmosphere of the whole region, and today heavy smog in San Francisco is a common occurrence. In some locations, pollution is so much the rule that people's standards of air quality have changed: I was recently in Los Angeles on a day following high winds when pollution was low and heard radio commentators describe conditions as "smog free."

Some air pollution does come from volcanoes, forest fires, and dust storms, but to that background human activity has added an immense amount of industrial waste and automobile exhaust. Many of the compounds in smog are irritating to the respiratory tract; I have no doubt that worsening air pollution is the major cause of worldwide increases in asthma and bronchitis as well as a contributing cause to the rising incidence of chronic sinusitis, respiratory allergies, emphysema, and lung cancer. Some components of smog are known to be carcinogenic, while others probably damage cell membranes and other structures that make up the body's healing system. Researchers are also busily documenting the health hazards of secondhand tobacco smoke, which is a major problem in offices, shops, trains, planes, and restaurants.

It is much harder to protect yourself from pollutants in the air than from contaminated food and water. If you live in a city that is subject to bad smog, moving elsewhere may seem too drastic a remedy; however, you might consider moving to a less polluted district of your city, as there are usually microclimatic variations in any region that cause smog to concentrate more in some areas than others. In the most polluted cities of the world—Mexico City being the worst example—it is not uncommon for people to experience chest pain and breathing difficulty on bad days and for city governments to cancel school and issue warnings to keep very young and very old people indoors. If this is a preview of the future of our cities, it is a most unsettling one; but even if you live in a city with dirty air, you can protect yourself significantly by paying frequent visits to parks and groves of trees. Trees have a marvelous capacity to purify air; you can sense it even in the middle of the worst urban sprawls. When I visit Japan, which I do frequently, I usually have to spend a few days in Tokyo; I always seek refuge in the Meiji Shrine, a forested oasis in a desert of steel and concrete. Within a few moments of stepping inside the great *torii,* the wooden gates that mark the boundary of sacred space, I notice a change in the air: it feels purer, healthier, more breathable, and even an hour's walk within the park recharges me and enables me to cope with Tokyo's irritating smog. Remember this strategy if you find yourself caught in a city at a time of bad pollution: seek out parks and trees.

Indoors, you should make every effort to remove sources of pollution, such as all chemical products that give off volatile fumes; move them outside. Gas appliances, like stoves and water heaters, can contribute to indoor air pollution (newer gas stoves have automatic sparkers that eliminate pilot lights and reduce this threat), as can aerosol sprays. The medical profession increasingly recognizes environmental illness, such as "tight building syndrome" or "sick building syndrome," in which persons working in sealed buildings with recirculated air suffer a variety of symptoms that may be due to inhaled toxins. A common culprit is new carpet; chemicals used in carpet adhesives may trigger immune depression in some sensitive people. Commercial airliners also provide unhealthy indoor environments, especially now that companies are adding less fresh air to cabins in an effort to conserve fuel (and most international flights still permit smoking).

You can protect yourself from particulate air pollution with filters installed in your home's ventilation system or placed in whatever room of your house you spend the most time in. High-efficiency particulate air (HEPA) filters are readily available and reasonably priced;

you can get information on them from heating and ventilation contractors. Because they can do wonders for people with respiratory ailments, I recommend them frequently to patients. You should definitely get one if you live in a heavily polluted area or are forced to live or work with people who smoke.

You can also help your body neutralize inhaled pollutants by taking protective antioxidants, nutrients that protect tissues by blocking the chemical reactions by which many toxins cause harm. Increasing consumption of fresh fruits and vegetables is the simplest way to go about this. You can also take antioxidants in supplement form, the most effective and safest ones being vitamin C, vitamin E, selenium, and beta carotene.

Here is a simple daily antioxidant formula that I use and recommend to my patients:

Take between 1,000 and 2,000 milligrams of vitamin C two or three times a day. Your body may absorb this vitamin more easily in a soluble powder form rather than as a large, compressed tablet. I take a dose of vitamin C with breakfast, another with dinner, and, if I remember, a third before bed. I know it is more difficult to take anything three times a day rather than twice, so I do not insist on the bedtime dose, but I do urge you to take vitamin C more than once a day. (If you take it only twice, use the higher dose.) Plain ascorbic acid may irritate a sensitive stomach, so you should take it with food or look for a buffered or nonacidic form. If you experience flatulence or loose stools, take less; people vary greatly in their bowel tolerance to vitamin C. Eating plenty of fresh fruits and vegetables will satisfy your basic requirement for this important vitamin; however, larger amounts will give added protection against toxic overloads, and since ascorbic acid is itself nontoxic, there is every reason to supplement the diet with it. For people who cannot eat ample amounts of fresh fruits and vegetables, supplemental vitamin C is essential.

Vitamin E is a second powerful, nontoxic antioxidant. Although it is naturally present in grains and seeds, it is impossible to get large enough amounts from dietary sources to give the kind of protection needed against the toxins we breathe and take into our bodies in other ways. People under forty should take 400 international units (IU) of vitamin E a day; people over forty, 800 IU. Since vitamin E is fat-soluble, it must be taken with a meal to be absorbed. Also, natural vitamin E (d-alpha-tocopherol) is much better than synthetic (dl-alpha-tocopherol), especially when it is combined with the other tocopherols normally present in plant sources. You can easily find natural vitamin E with mixed tocopherols in health food stores. I usually take this supplement with lunch.

Selenium is a trace mineral with antioxidant and anticancer properties. Selenium and vitamin E facilitate each other's absorption, so the two should be taken together, whereas vitamin C may interfere with the absorption of some forms of selenium and should be taken separately. (This is a problem with many antioxidant formulas I see in drug and health food stores; they combine selenium with vitamins C and E in the same capsule.) I used to recommend daily doses of 50–100 micrograms of selenium, but ongoing research on its cancer-protective value suggests that higher doses are more effective. I now recommend 200–300 micrograms of selenium a day, the higher amount for those with any increased cancer risks. Doses above 400 micrograms a day may not be healthy. You can buy selenium supplements in any drugstore. I take mine with vitamin E at lunchtime.

I mentioned beta carotene in the previous chapter with regard to possible differences between consuming protective nutrients in the form of whole foods and taking them as isolated supplements. I hope that we will soon be able to buy supplements of mixed natural carotenes, as these would probably work much better than isolated beta carotene. In the meantime, try to add yellow and orange fruits and vegetables, tomatoes, and dark, leafy greens to your diet. I also take 25,000 IU of beta carotene as a supplement with my breakfast. I recommend a natural form, such as that obtained from marine algae, over synthetic forms; you will probably most easily find it in a health food store.

In summary, then, here is a simple formula that will not cost you too much trouble or money and will definitely help your body neutralize the harmful effects of toxins, however you ingest them.

> At breakfast: Take 1,000–2,000 milligrams of vitamin C and 25,000 IU of natural beta carotene.
>
> At lunch: Take 400–800 IU of natural vitamin E and 200–300 micrograms of selenium.
>
> At dinner: Take 1,000–2,000 milligrams of vitamin C.

At bedtime (if convenient): Take another 1,000–2,000 milligrams of vitamin C.

CONTAMINATED WATER

We have much greater control over the water we drink than over the air we breathe; bottled water is available everywhere, as are inexpensive water filters for the home. Public health agencies concentrate on disinfecting water to protect us from infectious diseases; they largely ignore the problem of toxic contaminants, one of which is the very chlorine commonly used for disinfection. Toxins get into drinking water from many sources, including waste runoffs from industry, acid rain, leaching of agricultural chemicals into water tables, and the dissolution of metals and plastics from pipes. It is important to know where your drinking water comes from and what it might contain. You can have water tested to get this information, but will probably have to take samples to a private lab, because government laboratories will only test for bacterial content and a few of the major inorganic toxins like lead and arsenic.

Bottled water may or may not be an improvement over tap water, depending on where it comes from and how it is handled. If you are going to buy bottled water, ask to see an analysis of it, and do not use any brands that do not taste delicious. Only buy bottled water in glass or hard (clear) plastic containers; soft (translucent) plastic bottles commonly give the water an off taste that represents dissolved plastic.

Filtering water is much more economical than buying bottled water, because you can install a filtration system for a reasonable price. The best, by far, is steam distillation, but home distillers are expensive and use power. The next-best system is reverse osmosis, in which water is forced through a semipermeable membrane that acts as a barrier to contaminant molecules. Reverse osmosis systems are one-fifth the cost of distillers; they remove more foreign substances from drinking water than activated carbon filters, but they require adequate water pressure and produce a fair amount of waste water. They can be installed under the sink or on the countertop. When shopping for a reverse osmosis system, find out how often the filters must be changed and how convenient and costly it will be to change them.

Activated carbon filters remove unpleasant odors, colors, and tastes from drinking water but not dissolved minerals. They are convenient for the elimination of chlorine, which I believe to be a major health hazard. As a strong oxidizing agent, chlorine is highly reactive, tending to combine with organic contaminants in water to form carcinogens. Chlorine in drinking water may also contribute to heart disease and long-term damage to components of the healing system. Try to avoid drinking water that has an obvious taste of chlorine. You can buy inexpensive, portable carbon filters to take with you when you travel. I use them in hotels and restaurants to filter chlorinated water by the glass.

My advice about drinking water is simple and concise:

- *Inform yourself about the source of your drinking water* and what contaminants it might contain.

- *Install a reverse osmosis filtration system in your kitchen.*

- *If you use bottled water,* buy only brands in glass or clear plastic containers from bottlers who are able to provide an analysis or certification of purity.

- *Do not drink water that tastes of chlorine.* When you travel, order bottled water or take a portable carbon filter with you.

You should not become paranoid about contaminated water, but you should exercise sensible precautions. Remember also that by eating fruits and vegetables, taking antioxidant supplements, and keeping your body's systems of elimination in good working order, you will be able to neutralize or discharge toxins you do consume.

TOXINS IN FOOD

Obtaining food that is free of toxic contamination is much more difficult than obtaining pure water—an indictment of our agricultural practices. Again, I do not want you to become unreasonably fearful. Eating is a major source of pleasure in life and should be indulged in without anxiety. But I do want you to be informed about real hazards and know what steps you can take to protect yourself.

I will repeat my warning in the previous chapter that eating high on the food chain exposes you to greater risk of concentrated doses of environmental toxins. If you eat meat or poultry, shop for brands certified to be free of added drugs and hormones. If you eat fish, try to avoid very large, carnivorous species (swordfish, marlin) and species that live mostly near coastal effluents (like shellfish). Here is one aspect of the problem:

DDT in fish, 1985. The findings on DDT in ocean fish in southern California are an example of the long-term implications of using persistent pesticides. For several years, a local DDT manufacturer had used the sanitary sewer for discharge of some of its industrial waste which contained DDT. A few million pounds of DDT were deposited on the ocean bottom around the sewage outfall. This waste discharge was halted many years ago but recent analyses of fish from this area have shown elevated levels of DDT (to over 1 ppm) in the edible flesh. In addition, some DDT was also dumped into the ocean by use of ocean dumping barges but the exact location is not known. Evidence indicates that the DDT levels are decreasing over time, but the levels found raise a health concern because DDT is considered a potential human carcinogen. The FDA [Food and Drug Administration] action level of 5 ppm for DDT in fish was set long ago and did not consider the carcinogenic risk associated with DDT exposure.

When you eat lower on the food chain, you minimize these risks but still have to worry about toxins in produce. I have already referred to the naturally occurring toxins. The best defense against this class of compounds is to cut consumption of foods with the highest content (black pepper, peanuts, celery, alfalfa sprouts, for example) while eating a highly varied diet. Eating a varied diet offers two advantages. It ensures that you will get all of the nutrients that you need, and it reduces the risk of getting too much of any unhealthy elements.

Manmade toxins are another matter. Fruits and vegetables are treated with a great variety of agrichemicals: pesticides, fungicides, ripening agents, fumigants, and so forth, all within regulated guidelines for "acceptable" levels of residues. Many of these chemicals cannot be removed by washing, because they adhere tightly to vegetable tissue or because they are applied in ways that carry them inside the products. I cannot emphasize too strongly that residues of toxic chemicals in foods we eat are major health hazards, affecting us in ways that current medical science and governmental policy often fail to recognize. Let me recount two stories that illustrate my concern.

During my travels to Japan I have been struck by the very high incidence there of atopic dermatitis—eczema. As many as fifty percent of Japanese babies are afflicted with this disease, and cases among adolescents and young adults are much more severe and extensive than in this country. Eczema is a discomforting and disfiguring disease, both physically and emotionally, since it produces itching and red skin eruptions, often on the face and hands. In Japan I commonly see patients with eczema over most of their bodies. Conventional medical treatment is inadequate, to say the least, since it relies on topical and systemic corticosteroids to suppress the dermatitis without curing it, and patients become dependent on this medication with all of its associated toxicity. The epidemic of atopic dermatitis in Japan is a recent phenomenon. What has changed in the Japanese population that might account for it? Not genetics, certainly. Eczema has an inherited component—it often runs in families—but no significant genetic change can have occurred among Japanese in the past fifty years. What has changed is diet. Japanese now eat much more meat and many more dairy products than they did in the past. These animal-protein foods may directly irritate the immune system, creating a predisposition to allergic reactions like eczema. They also contain more added toxins than the plant and fish-based foods of the traditional Japanese diet. In addition, the use of agrichemicals and additives to processed foods has increased enormously in postwar Japan. A Japanese friend who is an internist has seen dramatic cures of eczema in people who switch to organic foods; she reports that some of her patients are eventually able to discontinue steroid treatment. To me this suggests that allergy, as well as other sorts of immune dysfunction, may be one consequence of toxic overload produced by eating chemically contaminated food.

A young woman patient of mine who suffers from severe asthma, chronic sinusitis, and multiple inhalant and food allergies has also found that chemical-free food makes a great difference. She is so sensitive and so aware of her body's reactions that she can often tell within hours of a meal which foods cause her respiratory difficulty and which do not. She has learned that buying organically produced fruits and vegetables is necessary for her health.

Because organic fruits and vegetables are more expensive and not as easily available as conventional produce, it is worth knowing the crops that are most likely to contain residues of harmful compounds. For example, by any standards of measurement, apples top the list of most contaminated foods; knowing that, I no longer buy them unless they come from certified organic producers. The next-most-hazardous fruit crops are peaches, grapes (and raisins and wine made from them), oranges, and strawberries. Most heavily contaminated vegetable crops include potatoes, carrots, lettuce, green beans, peanuts, and wheat. I strongly advise you to seek out certified organic versions of these foods and products made from them (including products made from wheat flour).

The good news is that the organic agriculture movement is flourishing, entirely the result of rapid growth of markets for organic produce as consumers become more knowledgeable about toxins in food. Not long ago, agricultural experts insisted it was not feasible to use organic methods on a commercial scale; you could do it in home gardens, they maintained, but not on large farms. Now, inspired by market demand, producers can grow fruits and vegetables organically on any scale; moreover, they can do so more profitably than they ever imagined, both because they do not have to buy expensive agrichemicals and also because certified organic produce commands higher prices. Fully half of the producers in California have now converted or are in the process of converting to organic methods, a boon to consumers as well as to the earth. It will be easier to find organic produce in ordinary stores in the near future, and the cost will be more competitive. This is a consumer-driven trend; you can help accelerate it by letting store managers know what you want.

Additives used in processed foods comprise another category of toxins. Two kinds that I recommend avoiding are chemical dyes (identified on labels as "certified color," "artificial color," or by a specific name like "red no. 3") and artificial sweeteners, including saccharin and aspartame. In general, processed foods contain more fat and more salt than you might otherwise eat, as well as a host of preservatives, flavor enhancers, and other additives that may interfere with spontaneous healing. Therefore, it is wise to reduce the percentage of processed foods in your diet and to choose only products made without artificial additives.

In summary, here are my suggestions for minimizing exposure to toxins in foods:

- *Reduce consumption of animal products and buy only meat and poultry certified to be free of drugs and hormones.*

- *Minimize consumption of foods known to contain natural toxins,* such as black pepper, celery, alfalfa sprouts, peanuts, and white button mushrooms.

- *Eat a varied diet* rather than eating the same items every day.

- *Always wash fruits and vegetables* (even though that will not remove many contaminants).

- *Peel fruits and vegetables if possible,* especially if they are not organically produced.

- *Try to buy only organically produced* apples, peaches, grapes, raisins, oranges, strawberries, lettuce, celery, carrots, green beans, potatoes, and wheat flour.

- *Look for sources of organic produce, join cooperatives and buying clubs that distribute it, and let store managers know that you want it.*

- *Reduce consumption of processed foods and try to avoid those containing chemical dyes and artificial sweeteners.*

DRUGS, COSMETICS, AND OTHER SOURCES OF TOXINS

I consider drug toxicity to be a subcategory of chemical pollution. People take drugs for medical reasons and for social/recreational reasons, obtaining them on prescription, over the counter, or illegally. It is important to understand that no fundamental difference exists between drugs and poisons except dosage. All drugs become toxic in high enough dosage, and some poisons become useful drugs in low enough dosage. I have no objection to the use of medical drugs when they are the best treatments for diseases, but I also encourage both doctors and patients to explore alternative treatments that reduce or eliminate the possibility of drug toxicity, which is the most common sin of commission of conventional medicine today. Herbal medicines are dilute forms of natural drugs. Being dilute, they deliver lower doses of potential toxins but still should not be consumed thoughtlessly or without good reason. In whatever form and for whatever reason you take drugs, you are increasing the workload on your liver, since it is the task of the liver to metabolize most foreign substances. You can help your liver deal with other toxins by not also burdening it with drugs.

Of the recreational drugs in use in our society, alcohol and tobacco are the most toxic. Alcohol is directly toxic to liver and nerve cells; it is also a strong irritant of the lining of the upper digestive tract. It has beneficial effects as well, particularly as a relaxant (and promoter of social interchange), as a tonic to the cardiovascular system, and as a stimulant to production of HDL (good) cholesterol. Assessment of the influence of alcohol on health must, therefore, involve a risk-benefit analysis of the patterns of use of each individual. In persons with healthy livers, stomachs, and nervous systems, *moderate* consumption of alcohol may promote health and healing. In those with ailing organs, even moderate drinking may be harmful, and heavy consumption for anyone may be incompatible with optimal health.

The case of tobacco is less equivocal. Although tobacco may facilitate concentration and relaxation, nicotine is highly addictive, especially when inhaled deeply; it is also a very strong stimulant that constricts arteries throughout the body, interfering with blood circulation and thus with healing. In addition, addiction to nicotine exposes the user to the harmful effects of other elements of tobacco smoke, including many carcinogenic compounds. Inhaling smoke compromises respiration, which, as I have noted, is one of the main functional components of the healing system. If you are one of the lucky few who can use tobacco nonaddictively, I will not try to argue you out of it, as long as you do not expose me to your secondhand smoke. Otherwise, I urge you to make all possible efforts to quit.

Medical drugs, in addition to their main constituents, are often dyed with the same synthetics used to color food. If you consume a substantial quantity of brightly colored pills and capsules, they can be a significant source of those chemicals that cannot do you any good; here is another reason to look for alternative treatments. Another source, less commonly thought of, is cosmetics, especially shampoos, hair conditioners, and lotions that can be absorbed through the skin. I recommend avoiding all cosmetic products containing chemical dyes (read labels!); it is not that difficult to find brands that are colorless, white, or tinted with vegetable extracts, although you may have to shop for them in salons or health food stores.

Poisons of all sorts, especially pesticides and herbicides, are among the most hazardous toxins in the environment. Try not to handle these materials, do not keep them in the home, and try not to use them in or around your home. Be equally cautious about all dyes, solvents, and other chemical products that give off fumes and have strong odors. If you are exposed to any of these substances, wash yourself well, breathe plenty of fresh air, drink lots of water, sit in a sauna or steam bath, and don't forget to take your antioxidants!

TOXIC FORMS OF ENERGY

It is clear that life evolved on earth in spite of certain frequencies of radiation that can damage DNA. To the natural radiation that bombards us from outer space, from the sun, and from the earth itself, human activity has added a great deal of electromagnetic pollution whose long-term biological effects are not well understood. Despite the lack of information, it is worth taking sensible precautions.

One end of the electromagnetic spectrum includes short-wavelength (high-energy) forms of radiation, such as nuclear energy and X-rays, that can knock electrons out of their orbits around atomic nuclei, creating charged particles (ions). The dangers of ionizing radiation are well known: it can kill in high dosage and by causing mutations in DNA promotes damage to the immune system and the development of cancers that may not manifest themselves until years after exposure. You can protect yourself from ionizing radiation by not working in an occupation that exposes you to it (uranium mining, nuclear power plant maintenance, radiology); by not living near a source of it, either natural or manmade (such as a nuclear waste disposal site); and by not letting doctors and dentists X-ray you without good reason. Remember that there is no such thing as a safe dose of ionizing radiation, since every bit adds to the cumulative total you receive over your lifetime, and it is that cumulative total that correlates with damage to DNA. Another reason to eat fruits and vegetables and take antioxidant supplements is that they can block chemical reactions that mediate radiation injury to genes.

Ultraviolet (UV) radiation from the sun is not ionizing; its waves are longer and less energetic, just beyond the highest-energy (violet) form of electromagnetic energy that we can see as visible light. Still, UV radiation is powerful enough to damage DNA in skin cells, making it the major cause of skin cancer, the incidence of which is increasing at an alarming rate. One possible reason for the increase is weakening of the earth's protective ozone layer as a result of atmospheric pollution so that the intensity of solar radiation reaching the surface of the earth is greater now than in the recent past. This is all the more reason to protect yourself by staying out of the sun when it is at a high angle in the sky, by wearing protective clothing, using sunscreens, and not making the mistake of going to tanning parlors in the belief that they offer just the "healthful tanning variety of UV." *All* UV radiation is harmful; in addition to hurting the skin, it promotes the development of cataracts and macular degeneration, two common causes of loss of vision in older people. You can protect yourself from this hazard by wearing UV-protective eyeglasses when you are in the sun and by taking antioxidants.

Beyond the other (red) side of the visible light spectrum are still-longer wave forms such as microwave and ELF (extremely low frequency) radiation, much used for military communications. Microwaves can agitate molecules of plant and animal tissue, generating heat, which is the basis for their use in microwave ovens; but aside from the danger of being cooked if you stand in the path of a concentrated beam, microwave and ELF radiation have not been considered biologically hazardous. Now that view is changing, with a number of scientists warning that these forms of energy can disrupt delicate biological control systems involving small electrical currents and weak electrical fields. Earlier, I described the role of these systems in the healing of wounds and bone fractures (see page 80); they may be the basis of most forms of complex healing of tissues and organs.

Microwave ovens are not a problem, because they rarely leak radiation unless they are obviously damaged. (They can, however, alter the chemistry of protein-containing foods cooked in them for a long time and can also drive foreign molecules into food wrapped in plastic or cooked in plastic containers. Never microwave food in other than glass or ceramic containers, and never cover it with plastic wrap during cooking. Use these convenient appliances for rapid defrosting and heating of food rather than for long cooking of main dishes.) But it may be unhealthy to live near a microwave transmitter or in the path of military communications hardware.

In the home, a number of familiar appliances create electromagnetic hazards that may also interfere with healing. Electric blankets and heating pads are best avoided, since they generate large electrical fields and are used right next to the body. Electric clock radios are dangerous for the same reason. Do not keep one near your head while you sleep. If you work in front of a computer video display terminal, it is worth investing in a screen that eliminates any electromagnetic transmissions and fields; these are available from computer supply dealers.

IF ALL THIS SOUNDS discouraging, I am afraid it is also realistic. Toxins, both chemical and energetic, are more and more a fact of life in our industrial world, and you must know their dangers. My suggestions for self-defense are reasonable and practical; even if you implement only some of them, you will be protecting your healing system from harm. Fortunately, nature provides us with products that can strengthen our healing abilities and make our bodies more resilient and resistant. I discuss this more cheerful subject in the next chapter.

11

USING TONICS

ANYTHING THAT INCREASES the efficiency of the healing system or helps it neutralize harmful influences will increase the probability of spontaneous healing. Tonics are natural products that do just this, and they are one of my special interests. In the sense of a strengthening or invigorating medicine, the word "tonic" derives from a Greek word meaning "stretch." Tonics stretch or tone our systems in the way physical exercise tones our muscles. Working the body—subjecting it to graduated tension followed by relaxation—increases natural resilience, an essential quality of health, because it determines our responsiveness to environmental stress. The more resilient we are, the greater our ability to bounce back from any kind of stress or injury.

Tonic medicines are now in very low repute among most practitioners of conventional Western medicine. They conjure up images of snake-oil salesmen hawking nostrums from painted wagons, and antique posters advertising patent liquids containing opium and alcohol. Today's doctors prefer magic bullets—drugs that exert specific effects in specific diseases by known biochemical mechanisms. They do not like panaceas—remedies with very general effects, said to be good for whatever ails you, whose mechanisms of action are at best obscure. Attitudes are very different among practitioners of traditional medicine in the East, where tonics are held in high esteem and both doctors and patients are willing to pay large sums for natural products believed to augment internal resilience and resistance.

An outstanding example of such a product is ginseng, obtained from species in the genus *Panax,* whose name comes from the same root as "panacea," that is, "all-heal." (Panacea, incidentally, was another daughter of Asklepios, the god of medicine in Greek mythology.) Demand for ginseng has always greatly exceeded supply, with the result that many adulterated and imitation products are on the market while prices for the best qualities of authentic material are sensationally high. Many Asians esteem ginseng as an invigorating tonic; some say it should be reserved for old age. Used regularly, it increases energy, vitality, and sexual vigor, improves skin and muscle tone, and confers resistance to stress of all sorts. Since it is generally nontoxic, it meets all the requirements of a useful tonic. I often recommend it to chronically ill patients and to those who are debilitated or lacking in vitality.

I also use and recommend a number of other tonics, some of them more familiar than others. I will describe those I recommend most frequently, having selected them for effectiveness, safety, and availability. Even if you are not chronically ill, debilitated, or lacking in vitality, you might want to experiment with this interesting category of natural remedies. They cannot hurt you, and given the threat of environmental toxicity from so many different sources, it is worth knowing about substances that can enhance immunity and resistance, functions central to the efficient operation of the healing system. I begin with the familiar ones and move on to the exotics.

GARLIC

Garlic (*Allium cepa*), the most pungent member of the onion family, is a central flavoring ingredient in many of the world's cuisines. It is equally esteemed as a medicinal plant in many cultures, and recent research has documented some of the healing properties attributed to it in folk medicine. Garlic is a rich source of sulfur-containing compounds with biological activity; although a number of controlled experiments demonstrate the plant's health benefits, it is not yet known just which compounds are responsible. The effects of garlic are numerous and varied, affecting many systems of the body that participate in healing; in my view the breadth of garlic's actions justifies categorizing it as a true tonic.

Some of its most dramatic effects are on the cardiovascular system. It lowers blood pressure by more than one mechanism, mimicking some of the newest antihypertensive drugs without their tendency to cause impotence, headaches, and other toxic effects. I have known people who have controlled moderate hypertension just by eating garlic every day. In addition, garlic lowers cholesterol and blood fats (triglycerides) while increasing the protective (HDL) fraction of total cholesterol and reducing the susceptibility of LDL cholesterol to oxidize. (Oxidation of LDL cholesterol is the first step in the process by which it damages arterial walls.) Finally, garlic reduces the clotting tendency of the blood by inhibiting the readiness of platelets to aggregate—i.e., to clump together. Platelet aggregation on roughened walls of arteries damaged by atherosclerosis commonly initiates the formation of blood clots that lead to heart attacks and strokes. For all of these reasons garlic appears to offer significant protection from cardiovascular disease. (Epidemiologists think that its routine consumption in parts of Spain and Italy may contribute to lower-than-expected incidence of atherosclerotic disease in those regions.)

In unrelated activity, garlic also acts as a powerful antiseptic and antibiotic, counteracting the growth of many kinds of bacteria and fungi that cause disease in humans. Furthermore, it enhances activity of the immune system, increasing numbers of natural killer cells that check the spread of cancers. Several studies show garlic to be an anticancer agent, again suggesting several different mechanisms. In addition to stimulating immune activity, it appears to block the formation of some carcinogens in the gut and protect DNA from damage by other carcinogens. Miscellaneous effects of garlic include protecting liver and brain cells from degenerative changes (probably as a result of its content of antioxidant compounds) and lowering blood sugar.

You can get all of these benefits simply by adding garlic to your food in any form. You can also buy a variety of garlic supplements: oil-filled capsules, capsules of "deodorized" oil, or tablets. Although the safety of garlic as a culinary herb is clear, we have no data on the safety of long-term use of concentrated extracts. One caution is that they might lead to bleeding problems in persons being treated with anticoagulant drugs, including aspirin. The effectiveness of garlic supplements is also unknown; manufacturers make many claims and try to disparage competing products, but we really do not even know how many of garlic's health benefits depend on its odoriferous constituents, so it is difficult to say whether the deodorized products work well or not.

My personal recommendation is to eat more fresh garlic. Mash it raw into salad dressing, cook it lightly in olive oil to flavor pasta, and, in general, add it near the end of cooking to enjoy its flavor. I grow garlic in my garden, planting individual cloves in September and harvesting big bulbs in May that keep for many months. I cannot imagine life without garlic and consider it one of the best general tonics for the healing system.

GINGER

Like garlic, ginger (*Zingiber officinale*) is a familiar culinary spice that has long enjoyed a strong reputation as a medicinal plant. (The specific epithet *officinale* in a botanical name indicates the plant's official status in medicine of the past.) From ancient times doctors in both China and India regarded it as a superior medicine, adding it to combination remedies for its tonifying and spiritually uplifting properties. Today people in many different parts of the world value it for its warming effect and ability to stimulate digestion, settle upset stomachs, and relieve aches and pains. In recent years a great deal of medical research, much of it in Japan and Europe, has documented remarkable therapeutic effects of ginger and its components; American doctors tend to be unaware of these studies. The chemistry of ginger is quite complex, with more than four hundred compounds known to contribute to the plant's fragrance, taste, and biological activity. Much of the focus of research has been on two groups of these—gingerols and shogaols—that give ginger its pungent taste. In addition, the "root" (actually a rhizome) contains enzymes and antioxidants that are probably also key components.

The tonic effects of ginger on the digestive system are clear: it improves the digestion of proteins, is an effective treatment for nausea and motion sickness, strengthens the mucosal lining of the upper GI tract in a way that protects against formation of ulcers, and has a wide range of action against intestinal parasites. Chinese cooks use fresh ginger in most dishes because they believe it neutralizes undesirable qualities of other ingredients, especially fish and meat, that might produce indigestion.

Other well-studied actions of ginger affect the production and deployment of a group of biological response moderators called eicosanoids, which mediate healing and immunity. The body synthesizes these important compounds from essential fatty acids and uses them to regulate critical cellular functions. Three principal categories of eicosanoids—prostaglandins, thromboxanes, and leukotrienes—are much in the news as subjects of ongoing research. Imbalances in eicosanoid synthesis and release underlie many common illnesses, from arthritis and peptic ulcer to the increased platelet aggregation that can trigger heart attacks and strokes. Ginger modulates this system in ways that reduce abnormal inflammation and clotting. It may be as effective as some of the nonsteroidal anti-inflammatory drugs that are now so popular, but much less toxic because it protects the lining of the stomach instead of damaging it. It is as a modulator of eicosanoid synthesis that ginger may be most helpful to the healing system.

Additionally, ginger tones the circulatory system and has anticancer effects, blocking the tendency of some carcinogens to cause mutations in DNA.

You can take ginger in the form of the fresh rhizome or as candied slices, honey-based syrups, or encapsulated extracts. A simple and delightful preparation is ginger tea: for an individual serving, put one-half teaspoon of freshly grated rhizome into a cup of boiling water, cover the pot, and steep for ten to fifteen minutes. Strain, add honey to taste, and drink hot or iced. You can buy honey-based ginger syrups in health food stores and add them to hot or cold water for an instant beverage, or you can make your own by adding one part of fresh, grated ginger to three parts of raw honey; keep this in the refrigerator.

When ginger is dried, its chemistry changes; in particular, the gingerols, which are abundant in the fresh rhizome, convert to the more pungent shogaols. These two classes of compounds may have different properties, with shogaols having more powerful anti-inflammatory and analgesic effects. Therefore, it might be wise to use more than one form of ginger, and persons with arthritis and other inflammatory conditions might get more benefit from capsules of dried, powdered ginger, which are available in health food stores. Ginger is nontoxic, but you may experience heartburn if you take a large dose on an empty stomach. I suggest taking it with food.

GREEN TEA

Green tea, the national beverage of Japan, is made from the unfermented leaves of the tea plant, *Camellia sinensis*. In preparing more familiar black tea, leaves are piled up in heaps and "sweated," a natural fermentation process that darkens the leaves and changes their aroma and flavor. Recently, medical researchers have discovered a number of health benefits of green tea, having to do with its content of catechins, a group of compounds mostly destroyed in the fermentative conversion to black tea. (Oolong tea is somewhere in between. It is briefly sweated, resulting in a color, flavor, and catechin content intermediate between green and black tea.) Catechins lower cholesterol and generally improve lipid metabolism. They also have significant anticancer and antibacterial effects.

All tea contains theophylline, a close relative of caffeine; in high doses it can be quite stimulating, and people can become addicted to it just as they become addicted to coffee. In moderation, green tea, with its slightly bitter taste and delicate aroma, makes a pleasant and healthful addition to the diet. It is my favorite caffeinated beverage, one I associate with relaxation and good company. It seems silly to me to take green tea in the form of a supplement, but I see many tablets and products containing extracts of it in health food stores, all trying to take advantage of the publicity about protective effects of catechins against heart disease and cancer. There are even green tea underarm deodorants that rely on the herb's antibacterial properties.

One of my favorite varieties of green tea is *matcha*, a bright-green powder used in the Japanese tea ceremony and also served informally as a treat. It is prepared from very young, select tea leaves that are steamed, dried, and ground very fine. To prepare a beverage from it, you place a teaspoon of the powder in a ceramic tea bowl, add a small amount of boiling water, and whip the mixture to a froth with a bamboo whisk. *Matcha* is usually enjoyed with small sweets. It is definitely stimulating, having been used by Zen monks to maintain wakefulness during long periods of sitting meditation. You can buy *matcha* and ordinary green tea (*sencha*) at Japanese grocery stores; the latter is also now widely available in teabags in supermarkets.

If you are currently a drinker of coffee, black tea, or cola, you might consider switching to green tea. Not only is it a relatively benign form of caffeine, it offers impressive benefits as a general tonic.

MILK THISTLE

A most interesting tonic herb from the tradition of European folk medicine is milk thistle, *Silybum marianum.* The seeds of this plant yield an extract, silymarin, that enhances metabolism of liver cells and protects them from toxic injury. Although the pharmaceutical industry has produced many drugs that damage the liver, it offers nothing to match the protective effect of milk thistle, which is itself nontoxic.

Anyone who is a heavy user of alcohol should take milk thistle regularly, as should patients using pharmaceutical drugs that are hard on the liver, including cancer patients undergoing chemotherapy. I recommend this herb to all patients with chronic hepatitis and abnormal liver function, and have seen cases of normalization of liver function in persons who took it every day for several months and also worked to improve their diets and lifestyles. If you work with toxic chemicals or feel you have suffered toxic exposures from any source, take milk thistle. It will help your body recover from any harm.

You will find milk thistle products in all health food stores. My preference is to use standardized extracts in tablet or capsule form. Follow the suggested dosage on the product you buy, or take two tablets or capsules twice a day. You can stay on milk thistle indefinitely.

ASTRAGALUS

If you are Chinese you will recognize this tonic herb at once. Under the name *huangqi* it is widely sold both singly and in many combination formulas for the treatment of colds and flus. *Astragalus* is a large genus in the pea family, some species of which are toxic to livestock. (Locoweed of the American Southwest is an astragalus.) But the toxins are only in the above-ground parts, never in the roots, and it is the root of a nontoxic Chinese species, *Astragalus membranaceous,* that provides the herbal medicine. The plant is a perennial herb with long, fibrous roots, native to northern China and Inner Mongolia. Both wild and cultivated plants are sources of commercial astragalus, which is sold in bundles of thin slices that resemble wooden tongue depressors and have a sweet taste. Chinese herbalists recommend adding these slices to soups and removing them before serving because they are too tough to chew. You can buy dried astragalus in Chinese herb stores, or you can buy astragalus tinctures and capsules in health food stores. You will also find in health food stores many Chinese herbal products that contain astragalus as a principal ingredient.

Traditional Chinese doctors consider this plant a true tonic that can strengthen debilitated patients and increase resistance to disease in general. They also use it as a promoter of other herbs known to increase energy, aid digestion, and stimulate the production and circulation of blood. In contemporary Chinese medicine astragalus is also a chief component of *fu zheng* therapy, a combination herbal treatment to restore immune function in cancer patients undergoing chemotherapy and radiation. Research in China has demonstrated increased survival in patients receiving both herbal and Western therapies, as well as moderation of the immunosuppressive effects of the latter.

Pharmacological studies in the West confirm that astragalus enhances immune function. It increases activity of several kinds of white blood cells as well as production of antibodies and interferon. These properties have to do with the root's content of polysaccharides, large molecules composed of chains of sugar subunits. Polysaccharides are structural components of many organisms; until recently they did not excite much interest among Western pharmacologists, because they are not the types of molecules that act as magic bullets and because conventional wisdom holds that they cannot even be absorbed from the gastrointestinal tract. But polysaccharides are a common feature of many herbal medicines that enhance immunity, so we must not yet understand their properties.

I recommend astragalus to many patients, since I find it to be safe and effective. In particular, I suggest it for people with chronic infectious diseases, such as bronchitis, sinusitis, and AIDS. I also recommend it to many cancer patients, both those undergoing conventional treatment and those who have completed treatment. And I think taking astragalus regularly is beneficial for people who are debilitated, lacking in energy or vitality, or feeling vulnerable to stress. It is easy to find astragalus products in health food stores; follow dosages specified on the labels.

SIBERIAN GINSENG
(ELEUTHERO GINSENG, SPINY GINSENG)

The root of a large, spiny shrub native to northern China and Siberia, Siberian ginseng (*Eleutherococcus senticosus*) is now one of the most widely used tonic herbs in the world, so much in demand that authentic material may be difficult to obtain. *Eleutherococcus* is a genus in the ginseng family, different from *Panax*, the source of true ginseng. Soviet scientists discovered the remarkable "adaptogenic" (stress-protective) properties of this species in the course of searching for ginseng substitutes, and as news of its benefits spread, many Soviet athletes and military personnel began to use it to increase physical performance and endurance.

Much animal and human research has demonstrated the protective effects of Siberian ginseng as well as its ability to enhance immune function. Active components include polysaccharides and a distinctive group of compounds called eleutherosides. In buying Siberian ginseng products, look for alcohol extracts or dry extracts (in tablets or capsules) that have been standardized for eleutheroside content; this is your only assurance that you are buying genuine material.

Unlike most of the tonic herbs I will mention in this chapter, Siberian ginseng has no extensive historical use as a folk remedy; it is a recent discovery. Modern Chinese doctors have taken great interest in it and now prescribe it, usually as a single remedy, for many chronic illnesses. It is a reliable tonic with general restorative effects, especially useful for people who lack energy and vitality, and can be used safely over long periods of time. Take two capsules or tablets twice a day, unless the product you buy specifies otherwise.

GINSENG

Two species of *Panax* are the source of this most prized and famous tonic: *P. ginseng,* native to northeastern China, and *P. quinque-*

folium, native to northeastern North America. Both species are now widely cultivated for commerce, and both have similar restorative qualities, but Oriental ginseng is more of a stimulant and sexual energizer, while American ginseng may be more powerful as an adaptogen. The plants are very slow growing, and older roots are believed to have greater therapeutic benefit than younger ones. Ginseng fanciers pay dearly for old roots of wild plants, much less for young, cultivated roots. Many forms of ginseng are on the market, from whole dried roots to ginseng brandies, wines, teas, and candies, and a multitude of tableted and encapsulated extracts. Be warned: some of these products contain little or no ginseng. Whenever a medicinal plant is scarce and expensive, imitation and adulterated products will be sold. *Panax ginseng* owes its beneficial effects to an unusual group of compounds called ginsenosides that are not found in any other genus. If ginseng products are real, they must contain ginsenosides, the more the better, so unless you are buying whole roots (which are unmistakable once you have seen them), buy only products that are standardized for ginsenoside content.

Among Chinese and Koreans, ginseng is especially valued as a tonic for the elderly, because it can improve appetite and digestion, tone skin and muscles, and restore depleted sexual energy. Chinese men say that it is not for women, but it may be that men simply do not want to share a limited supply; however, ginseng may have estrogenic activity that would argue against its use by women with hormonal imbalances or those who have estrogen-dependent diseases like uterine fibroids, fibrocystic breast disease, and breast cancer. One Chinese man told me not to waste ginseng in my youth. Save it for old age, he advised. "Then you will see what it can do for you."

Ginseng is generally safe, but the Oriental variety can raise blood pressure in some individuals, as well as cause irritability. People who experience those side effects should lower the dose or switch to American ginseng (which is preferred by many Orientals). I recommend ginseng frequently to people who have low vitality or have been weakened by chronic illness or old age. Many people who take it tell me they are quite happy with its effects and plan to stay on it. Standardized ginseng extract, made by a Swiss method, is now available at drug stores throughout the world.

DONG QUAI (TANG KUEI)

The root of *Angelica sinensis,* a plant in the carrot family, dong quai is known in traditional Chinese medicine as a blood-building tonic that improves circulation. In this century it has come into common use in the West as a general tonic for women, and many Western herbalists and naturopaths prescribe it for disorders of the female reproductive system, especially for irregular or difficult menstruation. Chinese doctors recognize its ability to tone the uterus and balance female hormonal chemistry, but they think of it as beneficial to both sexes and often include it in tonic formulas for men, combining it with ginseng and ho shou wu (see below). In men it is supposed to help build muscle and blood.

Dong quai is nontoxic and does not have estrogenic activity, although many people think it does. I recommend it frequently to women experiencing menstrual problems or menopausal symptoms and women who lack energy, with good results. It is readily available in health food stores in tinctures and capsules, and since it is not a scarce or expensive herb, most products made from it are of good quality. If you want to experiment with it, try taking two capsules of the root twice a day or one dropperful of the tincture in a little water twice a day. Give it a six-to-eight-week trial to see what it does for you.

HO SHOU WU

The name of this tonic herb means "Mr. Ho has black hair," referring to its power as a rejuvenator and maintainer of youthfulness. The root of *Polygonum multiflorum,* ho shou wu is a very famous Chinese blood tonic, believed to clean the blood and increase energy, as well as to nourish the hair and teeth. It is widely believed to be a powerful sexual tonic when consumed regularly and to increase sperm production in men and fertility in women. Research in China has shown it to lower elevated cholesterol; there has been no research on it in the West, and it is usually available only from suppliers of Chinese herbal medicines.

One way to experience the benefits of this herb is to take it in a liquid formula known as shou wu chih, or Super Shou Wu, that combines it with other tonic herbs and flavors. This is a very dark liquid with a pleasant aromatic taste that should be diluted: two tablespoons to a cup of hot or cold water. Drink this amount once or twice a day for at least a month to see if it gives you increased energy and increased sexual energy. (To turn graying hair black, you would probably have to consume it every day for years, and I would like to see the before-and-after photographs.)

MAITAKE

Maitake is the Japanese name for an edible and delicious mushroom, *Grifola frondosa,* known to mushroom hunters in America as "hen-of-the-woods," because it grows in big clusters on the ground at the bases of trees or stumps, clusters that resemble the fluffed tailfeathers of a nesting hen. The Japanese name means "dancing mushroom," possibly because people danced with joy on finding this rare and prized species. Finding a big hen-of-the-woods—they can weigh up to a hundred pounds—can indeed be cause for celebration, not only because it is a huge quantity of a choice wild mushroom but also because it is an eminently salable commodity worth twenty dollars a pound or more. Italians love to cook it in sauces for pasta or pickle it in olive oil and vinegar marinades after parboiling. Unfortunately, maitake in the wild is uncommon, even though it will fruit in the same spot for many years.

In 1965 a master Japanese mushroom hunter wrote: "Top rank hunters are those who seek maitake. They go out to their own secret grounds to spend several days looking for maitake with a dream of fortune at a stroke. Maitake hunters are not supposed to let others know their secret spot. If he finds a spot where he can crop more than 10 kg (22 lbs) of maitake, he found a 'treasure island.' He would never tell anyone his secret location until he dies. He would only indicate the location in his will to his eldest son just before he dies. Some hunters are even willing to die without telling their own sons or families. . . ."

All this changed in the early 1980s, when Japanese scientists discovered how to cultivate maitake on sawdust; the cultivated form is now sold at reasonable prices in supermarkets throughout Japan.

Mushroom growers in this country are just beginning to experiment with it. In cultivation the mushroom looks like a floral bouquet in shades of gray and gray-brown, except, instead of flowers, it is made up of many overlapping, fan-shaped mushroom caps. The undersides are white, with tiny pores instead of gills. *Grifola* belongs to a family of mushrooms called polypores, distinguished by that kind of spore-bearing tissue. In general polypores are nontoxic, but only a few are edible; most are tough and woody, growing as brackets or shelves on dead or living trees. In the West, polypore mushrooms have mainly been of interest to forest pathologists, because they are important causes of heart rot in living trees and important decomposers of dead and dying trees; but in the Far East, many of them are highly esteemed as medicinal herbs, especially in the class of superior drugs, the tonics and panaceas that increase resistance and promote longevity.

Traditional Chinese doctors did not use maitake, but they did use many of its relatives, including a very close relative, *Polyporus umbellatus,* or zhu ling. Modern testing has shown zhu ling to have anti-cancer and immune-enhancing properties related to its content of polysaccharides. Now Japanese researchers have tested maitake for similar effects, with impressive results. In fact, extracts of maitake turn out to be more powerful anticancer and immune-enhancing agents than any of the other medicinal mushrooms tested so far. In combination with chemotherapy, they increase the effectiveness of lower doses of Western drugs, while protecting the immune system from toxic damage. Perhaps Chinese doctors will begin including this mushroom in their fu zheng therapy. Maitake extracts also show activity against HIV and hepatitis as well as an antihypertensive effect.

Until cultivated maitake turns up in supermarkets here—a likely prospect, because the mushroom is not difficult to grow, retains its freshness extremely well, and has a firm texture and good flavor— you will have to buy tablets and capsules of maitake extracts in health food stores. Several firms are now marketing these products, using material imported from Japan. Prices are high but should come down once cultivation catches on here.

I recommend supplements of maitake to people with cancer, AIDS, and other immune system problems as well as to those with chronic fatigue syndrome, chronic hepatitis, and environmental illnesses that may represent toxic overloads. As soon as fresh maitake becomes available, I will make it a regular addition to my diet.

CORDYCEPS

I will close this list of natural tonics with another mushroom, one that is stranger than maitake. *Cordyceps sinensis* grows not on trees but on the living bodies of certain moth larvae. The mushroom organism, in the form of fine threads, penetrates a larva, eventually killing and mummifying it. The mushroom then sends up its fruiting body: a slender stalk with a swollen end that will release spores. Cordyceps occurs in mountainous regions of China and Tibet and is now cultivated as well, because it is in great demand as a supertonic that builds physical stamina, mental energy, and sexual power. Chinese doctors say it is simultaneously invigorating and calming as well as life prolonging. Chinese people usually buy it in whole dried form, consisting of the mummified larva and attached fruiting body of the mushroom, which they add to soups and stews made from duck and chicken. In addition, extracts of cordyceps are included in many compound tonic formulas. Cordyceps is considered safe and gentle, indicated for both men and women of any age and state of health, even the most infirm.

This exotic remedy came to worldwide attention following the Chinese National Games of 1993, when a team of nine Chinese women runners broke nine world records, one by an unprecedented forty-two seconds. Charges of steroid use were leveled at the athletes, but their coach held a press conference to deny the accusations, holding up a box of the Chinese herbs he felt were responsible for his team's performance and a lab report stating that they were natural and safe. The main ingredient was cordyceps. The track world was unconvinced, with one American distance runner calling the broken records "tragic" and another saying the Chinese had set women's running back for years. In the words of one commentator:

> This suspicion was understandable. The improved performance of the Chinese distance runners had occurred suddenly and sensationally. The new 1,500-meter record-holder had been seventy-third at the same distance the previous year, and the forty-two-second improvement in the 10,000-meter race seemed impossible. And, as journalists and runners were aware, a number of East German coaches had moved to China after the fall of the Berlin Wall; their

former country had long been associated with steroid use. Furthermore, the Chinese success was only among women runners, who are more apt to benefit from steroid use.

But there was strong evidence that the records were untainted. The Chinese runners had passed the drug tests. They also showed no outward signs of steroid use, such as acne, deepened voices, or highly defined musculature. And there is no doubt that—although they are not alone in this—the Chinese provide their runners with stringent training. . . .*

In any case, interest in and sales of cordyceps boomed. If you do not wish to add mummified, fungal-infected caterpillars to your chicken soup, cordyceps is also available in the form of tinctures and extracts, either singly or combined with other Chinese herbs. Ask for these products in health food stores. For general weakness, take it once a day, following dosage advice on the product. For health maintenance, in the absence of specific problems, take it once a week.

MY INTENTION HAS not been to overwhelm you with information but rather to make you aware of substances that can help you resist the effects of toxins, stress, and aging on your healing system. Instead of despairing at the thought of all the harmful influences that exist, know that you can protect yourself and increase your healing potential through the use of products that are safe and effective. Let me quickly recap the information in this chapter:

- Eat more garlic and ginger; they taste good, and the list of their beneficial effects keeps growing.

- If you use caffeine, switch to green tea all or some of the time, since it is the most healthful of the caffeinated beverages.

- If you worry about exposure to toxins or feel you have a toxic overload, take milk thistle to help your body recover.

- If you are generally weak or lacking in vitality, experiment with Siberian ginseng or cordyceps.

---

* This controversy is not settled. The Chinese runners may have been on steroids as well as cordyceps.

• If you have depressed immunity and find that you get every bug going around, do a course of astragalus or maitake.

• If you feel debilitated as a result of age and lack sexual energy, experiment with ginseng and ho shou wu. Ginseng is a good general tonic for men, while dong quai is a good general tonic for women.

Tonic herbs have always been immensely popular in many countries of the world. I predict that as medical researchers document their safety and effectiveness, doctors here will begin to prescribe them more.

12

ACTIVITY AND REST

YOU CAN INCREASE the chance of experiencing spontaneous healing by giving your body appropriate exercise and sufficient rest.

Physical exercise benefits the healing system in many different ways. It improves circulation, making the heart a more efficient pump and maintaining the elasticity of arteries. At the same time it tones the respiratory system, increasing exchanges of oxygen and carbon dioxide, which helps the body eliminate metabolic wastes. It further aids elimination by promoting the flow of perspiration and movement of the intestines. By stimulating release of endorphins in the brain, it fights depression and improves mood. It regulates metabolism and the body's economy of energy. It neutralizes stress, allowing greater relaxation and sounder sleep. It even enhances immune function. Any program intended to optimize the body's healing potential must include regular exercise.

But what is the best and simplest way to get these benefits? A great many people in our society, both young and old, do not like to exercise at all. Others exercise fanatically, spending hours in aerobics classes and on exercise machines, often in attempts to control weight. Some become addicted to strenuous exercise because it gives them a "buzz," probably the result of endorphin release. Exercise physiologists and sports medicine doctors have made the whole subject of exercise very complicated. It seems to me that many of these people—the couch potatoes, the fanatics and addicts, and the experts—are all missing something.

Whenever I come home after visiting traditional cultures in the Americas, Africa, or Asia, I am struck by the oddity of our habits of exercise. In nonindustrial societies the demands of daily life give bodies all the work they need. Muscles have good tone because people lift and carry burdens, and they walk constantly. They walk to gather water and wood, they walk to their fields, they walk to markets, they walk to visit friends and relatives. Of all the technological inventions that have changed our patterns of activity for the worse, the automobile gets the prize. I believe it has compromised health significantly, not only because it has darkened the air of our cities with exhaust emissions, but especially because it has deprived us of opportunities to walk.

Human beings are meant to walk. We are bipedal, upright organisms with bodies designed for locomotion. Walking is a complex behavior that requires functional integration of a great deal of sensory and motor experience; it exercises our brains as well as our musculoskeletal systems. Consider balance, which is merely one component of walking. In order to maintain the body's balance unconsciously and effortlessly as it changes position and moves over uneven surfaces in a gravitational field, the brain needs a lot of information. It relies in part on a mechanism in the inner ear responsible for sensing orientation in three-dimensional space; if this mechanism fails, people cannot maintain equilibrium. But in addition to data from the ear, the brain depends on visual input and information from other senses to keep us in balance: from touch receptors that let it know what part of the body is in contact with the earth and from proprioceptors in muscles, tendons, and joints that keep it continually informed of the exact position of each part of the body in space. Interference on any of these channels can lead to wobbling and falling. In the brain all of this information is processed by the cerebellum, which uses it to coordinate responses of muscles to the everchanging requirements of locomotion.

When you walk, the movement of your limbs is cross-patterned: the right leg and the left arm move forward at the same time, then the left leg and the right arm. This type of movement generates electrical activity in the brain that has a harmonizing influence on the whole central nervous system—a special benefit of walking that you do not necessarily get from other kinds of exercise. Dr. Fulford, the old osteopath who first taught me the basic principles of healing, believed that cross-patterned movement was necessary for normal development and optimal functioning of the nervous system. When babies first start to crawl, this movement stimulates further brain development. I often heard Dr. Fulford instruct adult patients to crawl as a way of speeding recovery from injuries. "Go back to that simple movement, and you will help the nervous system move beyond any blocks," he would say. Dr. Fulford, a shining example of physical health in his nineties, does not go to aerobics classes or use exercise machines; he walks.

Many of the healthiest people I have met are dedicated walkers. Shin Terayama, the man who recovered completely from metastatic kidney cancer, takes a daily walk before breakfast whenever he can, always maintaining a brisk pace and always including uphill walking if possible. At a recent workshop I led in Montana, a seventy-six-year-old woman in the group greatly impressed me with her stamina on hikes in the mountains. She was in excellent health and looked much younger than her years. I was even more impressed when she told me that both of her parents had died in their fifties and that she had been in declining health in middle age until she started walking. She had also improved her diet, stopped taking medicines, and started using vitamins, but in her mind commitment to walking was the critical factor in her improvement. She walked at every opportunity and joined walking tours on vacations. "It's my life," she told me on top of a ridge along the Continental Divide, and I believed her.

So I am going to pare my advice and comments on exercise down to one word: Walk! In my opinion, walking is the most healthful form of physical activity, the one that has the greatest capacity to keep the healing system in good working order and increase the likelihood of spontaneous healing in case of illness.

The advantages of walking over all other forms of exercise are numerous. You do not have to learn how to do it. It does not require any equipment except a comfortable pair of shoes. It costs nothing, and you can do it anywhere: in cities, parks, even indoors in shopping malls if the weather is inclement. The chance of injuring yourself is small, in great contrast to running and competitive sports. It is much less boring than riding a stationary bike or running on a treadmill. You can walk outdoors and enjoy the beauty of nature. You can also walk with friends and enjoy their company.

Walking will satisfy all the body's needs for aerobic exercise if you do it in ways that increase heart rate and respiration sufficiently. For an ideal aerobic workout, your walks should last forty-five minutes, and you should be able to cover three miles in that time. If your heart and respiratory rate are not elevated at the end of a forty-five-minute walk, you should try walking faster part of the time or look for long, gradual hills to climb. But remember that you are not walking just to get aerobic exercise; you are also going for the neurological benefit of cross-patterned movement combined with visual, tactile, and proprioceptive stimulation. You can obtain this effect from short walks throughout the day as well as from long aerobic walks, and you can enhance it by accentuating your arm swing from time to time. Also try coordinating arm swing with breathing.

I have experimented with many forms of exercise in my life, and I keep coming back to walking as the best. As I get older, I think it will be the one I rely on to keep my body, mind, and healing system all in good shape.

ACTIVITY MUST BE balanced by rest. Everyone has experienced the adverse effects of fatigue and sleep deprivation; lack of good quality rest is one of the most common causes of susceptibility to illness, and a good night's rest is an effective healing technique that will abort many incipient illnesses. Therefore, improving the quality of rest and sleep should be another priority in a program aimed at enhancing your healing capacity.

Consider the common impediments to rest. Many people are unable to sleep because they are overstimulated, often by drugs they have ingested earlier in the day. Others cannot sleep because of noise or aches and pains. Others cannot turn off their minds. There are simple remedies for all of these problems.

Stimulant drugs that interfere with sleep include coffee, tea, cola, and other caffeinated beverages; ephedrine, the chief ingredient in many herbal diet and energy products sold over the counter in drug and health food stores; pseudoephedrine, a decongestant in over-the-counter cold remedies; and phenylpropanolamine, commonly used in appetite suppressants. Even when these drugs are taken early in the day, they can interfere with nighttime sleep patterns. If you have difficulty getting restful sleep, try to eliminate all of these substances from your life.

While we are on the subject of drugs, let me state my opinion that sedatives are not to be relied on except for short-term management of unusual stress. If you have a death in the family or have just lost a job, it may be appropriate to take sedative drugs for a few consecutive nights to help you sleep, but taking them every night is not wise. All sedatives depress function in the central nervous system, all are addictive, and all suppress rapid-eye-movement (REM) sleep, the phase of sleep in which dreaming occurs. Dreaming is necessary for the health and well-being of the brain and mind; if you are not doing it, you are not getting quality sleep, even though the quantity appears sufficient.

The safest sedative I know is valerian, a natural remedy obtained from the root of a European plant, *Valeriana officinalis.* You can buy tinctures of valerian root in health food stores—the dose is one teaspoon in a little warm water at bedtime. Still, this product is a depressant and should not be used long-term. Quite recently a nonaddictive, nondepressant regulator of sleep cycles has become available: melatonin, the hormone secreted by the pineal gland, which regulates the biological clock, especially in relation to day/night cycles. Melatonin comes in one- or three-milligram tablets and is sold in health food stores—the dose is one to two milligrams at bedtime. (Avoid animal-derived forms, which may contain dangerous contaminants; use only synthetic forms.) International travelers say melatonin is the first really effective treatment for jet lag, especially for west-to-east travel, which most people find harder. Melatonin also appears safe and effective for resetting wayward biological clocks. If you get bone tired at seven in the evening, then find yourself wide awake when you get into bed at ten or eleven, it might change your cycles of tiredness and wakefulness in just the right manner to allow you to enjoy full periods of restful sleep.

If you cannot get to sleep or stay asleep because of physical discomfort, I have several suggestions. One is to try a new mattress, since many different kinds are available, including futons and air mattresses whose firmness can be adjusted with the touch of a button. Another is to have a session or two of adjustment from an osteopathic physician who specializes in manipulation (or from a good chiropractor). This kind of therapy may allow you to find more comfortable positions to sleep in. You can also try soaking in a warm bath before bed and taking hops, an herbal muscle relaxant, which you will find in health food stores: two capsules at bedtime is the usual dose.

I find that noise is a major obstacle to sound sleep, everything from barking dogs in the country to the sounds of traffic in the city. A simple solution, better than ear plugs, is to buy a white-noise generator, an electronic device that produces restful sound. White noise contains a mixture of many different frequencies of sound waves, just as white light contains all frequencies of visible light. It sounds like water running from a shower head, and most units have variable controls that allow you to change the basic sound from that of a steady downpour to rhythmic ocean waves. White noise is soothing and masks offending sounds. A more exciting technology, soon to be on the market, actually eliminates noise by analyzing offending sound waves and producing mirror-image waves that cancel them out. Portable devices of this sort are already available as headsets to be worn on airplanes to eliminate engine noise.

No matter how comfortable my bed and how quiet the room, when my mind is overactive, I usually cannot fall asleep and may wake during the night. In the morning I am very aware that I have not had the rest I need. Learning to leave behind the worries of the day is not as easy as taking a pill or turning on a sound machine, but it is one of the most useful skills you can develop. I often read myself to sleep; there is no shortage of sleep-inducing books, and reading distracts me from pointless rumination. I also use a simple breathing exercise that I will describe in the next chapter, because I find that focusing attention on breathing is an effective way to withdraw attention from thoughts. Another possibility is to get out of the mind by attending to the body—for example, by tensing and relaxing groups of muscles. Here is a simple exercise that may help you get to sleep when your mind is racing: Lie on your back with your arms at your sides, close your eyes, and take five deep, slow breaths. Then squeeze your eyes shut and tense the muscles of your forehead for a few seconds. Relax for a few seconds. Then tense the muscles of your face and relax in the same way, then the chin and neck muscles, and so on, going down the arms and front of the body until you flex the feet and toes. Then go back to the head, pressing it against the bed for a few seconds and relaxing, and proceed down the back of the body, again reaching the feet, this time extending them. Finally, relax completely and take five deep, slow breaths. The whole exercise will take no more than a few minutes. It is an efficient relaxation technique, especially useful when mental turmoil threatens to keep you from falling asleep.

By the way, a major source of my own mental turmoil is the news. The percentage of stories in the news that make me feel good is very small; the percentage of stories that make me feel anxious or outraged is very large and increasing, as news media focus more and more on murder, mayhem, and misery. It is easy to forget that we have a choice as to whether we let this information into our minds and thoughts. I find it so useful to disengage myself from it that I recommend "news fasts" as part of the eight-week program to a more efficient healing system. I think you will find that these fasts will allow you to get better rest and sleep.

To summarize this chapter: Give your healing system a morning walk and a good night's rest, and it will be ready for whatever challenges may arise.

13

MIND AND SPIRIT

THE LOGO OF THE American Holistic Medical Association is a staff with a single snake coiled about it, on which are superimposed three interlocking circles. The staff with the snake is the staff of Asklepios, the symbol of the medical profession, while the circles are meant to symbolize body, mind, and spirit, the three components of the whole person. It is a common belief of holistic doctors that conventional medicine attends only to the physical body, neglecting mind and spirit. I have written that mind often holds the key to unlocking spontaneous healing, and I have alluded to cultural beliefs about spiritual causes of illness, but when it comes to the specifics of these interactions, our ignorance is vast. We know little about the mind and the ways it affects the physical body, less about spirit, if that is even knowable in the usual sense of the word. Science, with its present materialistic bias, is not of much help, because it denies the possibility of nonphysical causation of physical events. It is all very well to share a holistic philosophy of health and medicine, but what practical advice can a holistic doctor give to patients about optimizing healing potentials by mental and spiritual methods?

MIND

I would like you to consider four activities of the mind and ways they interact with the healing system. They are: belief, thought, mental imagery, and emotion.

Belief

Belief in healers, miracle shrines, and drugs is clearly the basis of placebo responses, which I regard as classic examples of spontaneous healing. Belief also strongly influences perception, determining what we see and what we do not see as we move through the world. Years ago I met a woman who was able to find four-leaf clovers in any clover patch. She liked to bet people that within a minute of being told to look, she could find a four-leaf clover, and she always won the bets. Never having found one, I was completely mystified by her ability. When I would look through patches of clover, I could search without success until my vision blurred, and whenever I thought I saw four leaves on one stem, they always turned out to belong to two different clovers. But after meeting this woman and watching her do it, something changed for me. I realized that the key to her success was her belief that in any clover patch there was a four-leaf clover waiting to be found. With that belief, there is a chance of finding it; without it there is none. After meeting her, I began to look again, and soon I started to find four-leaf clovers. Sometimes I found several in one patch, and sometimes I found five- and six-leaf clovers (though I do not know whether they bring any extra luck).

Recently I was teaching at a retreat center in Montana, an erstwhile hunting lodge with a large, clover-filled lawn. One afternoon when I had nothing to do I thought I would see what I could find. So I got down on the ground and began searching. A woman who was in the class came over and asked, "Did you lose something? Can I help you find it?"

"I'm looking for four-leaf clovers," I replied.

"Really?" she said. "I always thought they were just a story. Don't they just paste an extra leaf on the ones that come sealed in plastic?"

"No, they really exist," I told her. "I'm sure there's one here."

She joined me on the lawn, and we both started looking. "It takes some concentration," I explained, "but it's good training for the eyes and brain, and there are worse ways to spend time." Five minutes later, I found a six-leaf clover, then a four. My companion was amazed. "I've got a lot of clover on the lawn in front of my house," she said. "I'm going to look as soon as I get back home." She may start to find four-leaf clovers now that she believes they exist; before she would never even have looked.

Spontaneous healing is something like a four-leaf clover: lucky, mysterious, and sometimes elusive. If you do not believe it can occur, your chance of experiencing it will be small. I am interested in what people can do to increase belief in healing. One technique, recommended by many New Age therapists, is to repeat affirmations, such as "My body can heal itself," or "I am filled with healing energy," or "My gallstone is getting smaller and smaller." I do not recommend this technique, because I have no evidence that it works. It assumes that verbal repetition can produce a change in belief structure, but my experience is that the kind of belief that shapes perception and impacts the healing system—gut-level belief, if you will—is often at variance with what people say to themselves and others. I do not think I would have discovered my ability to find four-leaf clovers by repeating over and over, "I believe in four-leaf clovers." That discovery came about suddenly when I saw reality differently through the eyes of another person. Now I can provide that experience for others, as I did for the woman on the lawn in Montana. Therefore the strategy I recommend is to seek out people who have experienced healing so that their reality can become your reality.

I remember a patient who came to me with a large fibroid tumor of the uterus, almost the size of a grapefruit. She was forty-nine years old, the wife of a gynecologist. Her husband supported the opinion of her gynecologist (his colleague), who told her she had to have a hysterectomy. The fibroid was causing her considerable discomfort, painful periods, and heavy menstrual bleeding. She did not want to have her uterus removed and came to see me in the hope that I would alert her to an alternative to surgery. I told her that since she was near menopause, she could simply try to wait until her estrogen levels declined; uterine fibroids feed on estrogen and usually shrink at menopause, sometimes completely. I recommended an herbal remedy (blue cohosh, *Caulophyllum thallictroides*), dietary changes to minimize intake of foods with estrogenic activity, aerobic exercise to reduce estrogen levels, and visualization therapy to bring mental influence to bear on the tumor. She was willing to try this program, but I could tell that her belief in the possibility of the tumor's shrinking was not strong enough to counteract the message she got from the medical profession: that there was no way to avoid a hysterectomy.

Then I remembered that my next scheduled appointment was with a woman who had successfully dealt with an even larger—melon-sized—uterine fibroid a few years before. She had told me with great delight how she had proved her doctor wrong, avoided a hysterectomy, and now, having gone through menopause, was problem-free. I thought she would be willing to tell her story to the gynecologist's wife. With their permission, I introduced these two women to each other; but as it turned out, they already knew each other, since they were neighbors. My second patient, just by her presence, was able to do a much better job than I could to convince the first patient to refuse surgery. She did refuse the hysterectomy, followed the recommendations I gave her to control her symptoms, experienced menopause a year later, and now is symptom-free.

I can think of no better way to change belief in a manner that facilitates rather than obstructs healing than to seek out the company of persons who have experienced it. Four-leaf clovers did not exist in my reality until I met someone for whom they were an everyday occurrence. My world is now a bit richer for their presence. As more people come to believe in spontaneous healing, more people will experience it, and that will benefit everyone.

Thought

In Buddhist psychology, addiction to thought is seen as a major obstacle to enlightenment, because when our attention is focused on thought, we cannot experience reality. Thought takes us out of the here and now and into the past, into the future, and into fantasy—all unreal realms. On a practical level, thoughts are the major source of anxiety, guilt, fear, and sadness—emotions that probably obstruct healing and certainly cause us a great deal of anguish. It is not possible to stop thought, except perhaps in very advanced levels of mental training (hence the joke about a surefire way to make gold: put such-and-such ingredients into a pot, place it on a fire, and stir for thirty minutes while not thinking of the word "crocodile"), but it is possible to disengage attention from thought. One way to do that is to focus instead on sensations from the body. There is a great advantage to having bodies, according to Buddhist teaching, because they are anchored in the here and now while our minds are careering about the past and future. Whenever we pay attention to sensations in the body, attention is in present reality. In the last chapter I suggested a simple relaxation exercise before falling asleep based on alternately tensing and relaxing groups of muscles throughout the body. The reason it works to promote sleep when the mind is overactive is that it withdraws attention from thought and puts it into the here and now.

Another useful focus for attention is breath. I will have more to say about breathing in the latter part of this chapter. Here I will simply note that breath is the most natural object of meditation and generally a much safer focus for attention than thought. If you find yourself having disturbing thoughts, instead of trying to stop them, try simply moving your attention to your breath.

Besides withdrawing attention from thought in general, there is another strategy for managing unwanted thoughts: putting attention into their opposites. If you are plagued by recurrent, fearful thoughts of getting cancer, think about your immune system constantly weeding out abnormal cells, or when you eat broccoli or drink green tea or take antioxidant supplements, think about how you are strengthening your body's defenses against cancer. Contradictory thoughts will cancel each other out, much as mirror-image sound waves cancel each other out in the new technology of noise elimination.

Meditation is a technique to break addiction to thought; in essence it is directed concentration. By sitting and trying to maintain the focus of concentration on some object—the breath, body sensations, a visual image—you learn to control attention and keep it in one place. Meditation practice is both simple and difficult: simple because the method is nothing more than maintaining focused attention, difficult because it requires changing lifelong habits of letting the mind wander where it will, especially into thoughts. Even when you learn to sit motionless for a half-hour and mostly keep your attention on your chosen object of meditation, you may not be able to extend that successful calming and focusing into the rest of your life. The real goal of meditation practice is to do it constantly, to practice meditation in action as you move through the world. Even if you are not ready to undertake that sort of training, you can begin by trying to move your attention to your body or your breath whenever you remember to do so, especially when you notice that your mind has been led away from the here and now by the endlessly fascinating process of thought.

Mental Imagery

The mind's eye has a special relationship with the healing system. A great deal of the cerebral cortex is devoted to vision. Located at the back of the head, this part of the brain mostly occupies itself with processing of information from the retinas of the eyes, but when it disengages from that task and turns inward, one of the most important channels for mind/body communication becomes available.

All of us spend time watching images in the mind's eye, but few of us have had training in this process—for example, to make the images sharper, brighter, and more exact in detail—and society places no value on it. In daydreaming we mostly attend to internal visual imagery. Our outward-directed culture regards daydreaming as an escape: children caught daydreaming in school are ordered to pay attention. (They *are* paying attention—to inner visual reality instead of outer, consensus reality.) An elementary-school teacher once asked my advice about a problem child in her class, a boy who was the "worst" daydreamer she had ever encountered. "He's just not there much of the time," she told me. "But if I pester him too much to pay attention, he makes his temperature go up, and I have to send him to the school infirmary; from there he often gets sent home for the day even though nothing's wrong with him." She had not connected the facts that the worst daydreamer she had ever met was also the only child she knew who had voluntary control of body temperature and could create fever at will. My interpretation is that those talents go together, and I suggested she call the boy the "best" daydreamer she ever met, not the worst. When it is not occupied with processing information from the eyes, the visual cortex can connect mind and will with the controls of the autonomic nervous system. It can also elicit spontaneous healing.

Another occasion for focusing on mental imagery is sexual fantasy, also a powerful channel to the autonomic nervous system. Sexual fantasy involves an interplay of imagery, highly charged emotions, and body responses. If you have any doubts about the power of the mind to affect the body, pay attention to what happens to your body when you indulge in this experience! For most people, the pictorial content of sexual fantasy is intensely private; even longtime lovers may keep the details of this experience to themselves. Another quality is that it is quite fixed and resistant to change: the same movies play over and over, and it is very difficult to alter the content. I am sure that if we could take more control of this process and bring the same intensity of emotional charge to images of healing, we could activate the healing system at will and maybe access regenerative capacities that are latent in our genes.

Because most of the time we view mental images unconsciously and without purpose, I think it is useful to work with a therapist when trying to draw on their great potential power to elicit spontaneous healing, at least initially. Hypnotherapists, visualization therapists, and guided imagery therapists can help you learn methods to take advantage of the mind/body connection through the medium of visual imagination. Once you master a technique, you can then practice on your own. My experience is that images with emotional charge work best, as is the case in sexual fantasy. A good visualization therapist will explore with a client a range of possible images to discover which ones elicit the strongest emotional responses.

I have known many people to rid themselves of warts by visualizing their disappearance in one way or another. (Children are better at this than adults, and warts have high rates of spontaneous remission in children.) One man came to me with a large wart on his left hand. Doctors had burned it off more than once, but it had always regrown. I told him to try surrounding it with white light for a few minutes each day, once on falling asleep and again on waking. He did this faithfully for a month without any change in the wart. Then I sent him to a visualization therapist, who discovered in the initial interview that he had a great fascination with steam shovels. Steam shovels and other earth-moving equipment had thrilled him ever since he was a small child. She suggested that he visualize a steam shovel scraping away at the wart each morning and night, and when he made that change he got results in a week. After two weeks the wart had shrunk to almost nothing, and a short time later it was gone, never to return.

Earlier in this book (see page 99) I described the case of a young man whose immune system was destroying his red blood cells and platelets. He had been through years of suppressive therapy with prednisone and other immunosuppressive drugs and had undergone splenectomy as a method of symptomatic management, all without success. I was able to help him design a healthy lifestyle and guide him toward natural interventions that eventually allowed his autoimmunity to subside. One of the interventions was visualization therapy with a trained professional, but he had no success in working with her at first. "I like her," he told me when he called in from another city, "but she keeps giving me violent images that I have problems with, like asking me to use laser beams against the white cells that are causing the reactions. I feel I've had enough medical violence done to my body, and I need a more peaceful image." Eventually he came up with one that worked for him: he imagined other white cells (the suppressor T cells) as motorcycle policemen who escorted his red cells and platelets in sidecars to protect them from aggressive white cells as they moved through his bloodstream. This visualization exercise worked brilliantly for him and became a central part of a program that put his disease into long-term remission.

You can practice using mental imagery to influence your body by daydreaming more consciously and purposefully and by paying attention to the emotional responses that particular images elicit. Try using visualizations to speed up the healing of wounds, sore throats, and other common ailments. Then if you ever have to mobilize your healing resources to manage a serious illness, you will have a good headstart.

Emotions

Many counselors and advocates of meditation advise people to gain control of their emotions—to even out the ups and downs of mood swings and cultivate evenness of temperament. That advice may be useful for some people. When I see patients whose lives seem out of balance, whose energy levels fluctuate wildly, who eat erratically and have unstable relationships, I usually recommend breathing exercises and meditation as methods to restore balance. But when I look at the role of emotions in facilitating spontaneous healing, I think it may be more useful to encourage sick people to cultivate passion. I have mentioned healing responses that occur after falling in love or expressing anger. Whether the emotion felt is positive or negative seems not to matter; rather it is the intensity of the feeling that gives it power to affect body function. More than negative feelings, apathy may be the major emotional obstacle to spontaneous healing.

What about depression, which is now epidemic in our culture? I experience depression as a state of high potential energy, wound up and turned inward on itself. If that energy can be accessed and moved, it can be a catalyst for spontaneous healing. The psychiatric profession treats depression almost exclusively by prescribing drugs, especially a new class of antidepressants called serotonin reuptake inhibitors, of which Prozac is a prototype. The pharmaceutical industry markets these drugs aggressively and successfully, partly by convincing people that they cannot know their full human potential unless they use them. Recently a woman friend of mine in her early fifties went for a routine checkup to her gynecologist, also a woman. After the examination was over, the gynecologist asked her, "Well, do you want me to write you a prescription for Prozac?" "Why should I want to take Prozac?" my friend replied. "I'm not depressed." "How would you know?" asked the doctor.

People who take Prozac and its relatives often say they simply feel everything less intensely, including their depression. Drug treatment has its place as one option for treating severe mood disturbances, but I worry about such enthusiasm for drugs that damp down passion, because I see intensity of feeling as a key to activating the healing system. Moreover, our capacity to feel joy may be the same as our capacity to feel despair, so that a depressed person may be more capable of experiencing ecstasy than someone who is always on an even keel or someone on Prozac. One technique for managing the down periods is to pretend to feel otherwise. Rabbi Nachman of Bratislav, a great Jewish mystic of the late eighteenth and early nineteenth century, who regularly experienced ecstasy on solitary wanderings through forests, recommended it to his followers:

"Always be joyful, no matter what you are," he taught. "With happiness, you can give a person life." Every day, he further stressed, we must deliberately induce in ourselves a buoyant, exuberant attitude toward life; in this manner, we will gradually become receptive to the subtle mysteries around us. And, if no inspired moments seem to come, we should act as though we have them anyway, he advised. "If you have no enthusiasm, put on a front. Act enthusiastic, and the feeling will become genuine."

SPIRIT

Have you ever wondered why distilled alcoholic beverages are called "spirits"? The original usage was in the phrase "spirits of wine," an old name for brandy. ("Brandy"—a short form of "brandywine"— comes from a Dutch word meaning burnt or heated wine; it was the first distilled liquor.) In brandy, the alcoholic essence that gives fermented grape juice its intoxicating power has been concentrated, resulting in a much stronger drink. The original idea of Dutch distillers was to reduce the volume of wine to make it more easily transportable to colonies on other continents: you could seal brandy in barrels, then dilute it with water at the end of an ocean voyage to re-expand its volume. Of course, when people tasted the contents of the barrels, few bothered to add water, and a new, more powerful form of alcohol flooded the world. In the old name for this product and in the persistent use of the term "spirits" to describe all strong liquors is a clue to the nature of spiritual reality and its relationship to matter.

What is concentrated in brandy is the vital essence of wine, that which gives it power to alter consciousness. If you warm a snifter of brandy and hold it in your hand, you can inhale (and sometimes feel the effect of) the volatile fumes that rise from the glass. In this concentrated form the essence of wine behaves like a gas as well as a liquid; that is, it is less dense and more active than it was in the form of wine, as well as more powerful. Spirit is the source of life and power, without which material forms are nonliving husks. It interpenetrates matter but is itself nonmaterial.

Many mystics have looked within themselves and identified breath as the evidence of spirit in the body. Breath is nonmaterial, or, at least, it straddles the border between material and nonmaterial reality. It has inherent movement and rhythm and is the source of life and vitality. In many languages the words for spirit and breath are the same: Sanskrit, *prana;* Greek, *pneuma;* Hebrew, *ruach;* Latin, *spiritus.* And in many cultures life is thought to begin with the first breath and end with the last. Until the breath cycle begins, spirit and body are not connected; the fetus and the newborn baby have a vegetative life but are not invested with spirit. Some cultures believe that God allots each person a certain number of breaths and that one's lifetime ends when that number is used up—an argument for learning to breathe more slowly.

A few years ago, I wrote:

At the very center of our being is rhythmic movement, a cyclic expansion and contraction that is both in our body and outside it, that is both in our mind and in our body, that is both in our consciousness and not in it. Breath is the essence of being, and in all aspects of the universe we can see the same rhythmic pattern of expansion and contraction, whether in the cycles of day and night, waking and sleeping, high and low tides, or seasonal growth and decay. Oscillation between two phases exists at every level of reality, even up to the scale of the observable universe itself, which is presently in expansion but will surely at some point contract back to the original, unimaginable point that is everything and nothing, completing one cosmic breath.

If breath is the movement of spirit in the body—a central mystery that connects us to all creation—then working with breath is a form of spiritual practice. It is also one that impacts health and healing, because how we breathe both reflects the state of the nervous system and influences the state of the nervous system. You can learn to regulate heart rate, blood pressure, circulation, and digestion by consciously changing the rhythm and depth of breathing. You can tone the healing system in the same way. I am going to suggest some simple techniques for doing this kind of work. Although you can do each one in a very few minutes, you will not realize their potential power unless you practice them regularly, preferably every day.

1. *Observe the breath.* Sit in a comfortable position with your eyes closed, loosening any tight clothing. Focus your attention on your breathing without trying to influence it in any way. Follow the contours of the cycle through inhalation and exhalation and see if you can perceive the points at which one phase changes into the other. Do this for at least a few minutes. Your goal is simply to keep your attention on the breath cycle and observe. No matter how the breath changes, even if the excursions become very small, just continue to follow them. This is a basic form of meditation, a relaxation method, and a way to harmonize body, mind, and spirit.

2. *Start with exhalation.* Breathing is continuous, with no beginning or end, but we tend to think of one breath as beginning with an inhalation and ending with an exhalation. I want you to try to reverse this perception in the next exercise, which you can do either sitting or lying down. Again,

focus attention on the breath and let it come of its own accord without trying to change it, but now experience exhalation as the beginning of each new cycle. The reason for doing this is that you have more control over exhalation, because you can use the voluntary muscles between your ribs (the intercostal muscles) to squeeze air out of your lungs, and this musculature is much more powerful than that used for drawing air in. When you move more air out, you will automatically take more air in. It is desirable to deepen respiration; the easiest way to do that is to think of exhalation as the first part of the cycle and not worry at all about inhalation.

3. *Let yourself be breathed.* This exercise is best done while lying on your back, so you might want to try it while falling asleep or on waking. Close the eyes, let your arms rest alongside your body, and focus attention on the breath without trying to influence it. Now imagine that with each inhalation the universe is blowing breath into you and with each exhalation withdrawing it. You are the passive recipient of breath. As the universe breathes into you, let yourself feel the breath penetrating to every part of your body, even to the tips of your fingers and toes. Try to hold this perception for ten cycles of exhalation and inhalation.

You may do these first three exercises as often as you like, for as long as you like, up to a maximum of ten minutes, but do them every day.

The next two exercises are formal breathing techniques from *pranayama*, the ancient Indian science of breath control that forms a part of yoga. *Prana* is a term for universal energy, of which breath is the bodily expression, and *pranayama* practice is intended to harmonize body energies and attune them with cosmic energy. These two exercises are safe and very useful. They also take little time; but, again, to determine what they can do for you and your healing capacity, you must practice them regularly.

4. *Take a stimulating breath.* Sit comfortably with the back straight, eyes closed. Place the tongue in the yogic position: touch the tip of the tongue to the backs of the upper front teeth, then slide it just above the teeth until it rests on the

alveolar ridge, the soft tissue between the teeth and the roof of the mouth. Keep it there during the whole exercise. (Yoga philosophy says this contact closes an energy circuit in the body, preventing dissipation of *prana* during breathing practice.) Now breathe in and out rapidly through the nose, keeping the mouth lightly closed. Inhalation and exhalation should be equal and short, and you should feel muscular effort at the base of the neck just above the collarbones and at the diaphragm. (Try putting your hands on these spots to get a sense of the movement.) The action of the chest should be rapid and mechanical, like a bellows pumping air; in fact, the Sanskrit name of this exercise means "bellows breath." Breath should be audible on both inhalation and exhalation, as rapid as three cycles per second if you can do that comfortably.

The first time you try this exercise, do it for just fifteen seconds, then breathe normally. Each time you do it, increase the duration by five seconds until you get up to a full minute. This is real exercise, and you can expect to feel fatigue of the muscles you are using. You will also begin to feel something else: a subtle but definite movement of energy through the body when you return to normal breathing. I feel it as a vibration or tingling, especially in my arms, along with greater alertness and disappearance of fatigue. This is not hyperventilation (which produces physiological changes as a result of blowing off excess carbon dioxide) but a way of activating the central nervous system. Once you can do the bellows breath for a full minute, try using it instead of caffeine as a pick-me-up in the afternoon. I find it particularly useful if I start to feel sleepy while driving on a highway. The more you do it, the more you will become aware of the energy it creates.

5. *Take a relaxing breath.* You may do this sitting with the back straight, lying on the back, or even standing or walking. Place the tongue in the yogic position and keep it there during the whole exercise. Exhale completely through the mouth, making an audible sound. Then close the mouth and inhale quietly through the nose to a (silent) count of four. Then hold the

breath for a count of seven. Then exhale audibly through the mouth to a count of eight. Repeat for a total of four cycles, then breathe normally. If you have difficulty exhaling with your tongue in place, try pursing your lips; you will soon get the knack of how to do it. Note that the speed with which you do the exercise is unimportant. What is important is the ratio of four : seven : eight for inhalation, hold, and exhalation. You will be limited by how long you can comfortably hold the breath, so adjust your counting accordingly. As you practice this breath, you will be able to slow it down, which is desirable. Do it twice a day. After one month, if it agrees with you, increase to eight cycles twice a day.

I do these relaxing breaths in the morning before I meditate and in the evening when I am lying in bed just before falling asleep. I also try to remember to do it whenever I feel anxious or experience an emotional upset. I teach it to almost all patients I see, and I receive reports of remarkable benefits. It cures digestive problems, allows cardiac arrhythmias to subside, lowers high blood pressure, combats anxiety and insomnia, and more. I think of it as a tonic for the nervous system—a spiritual tonic rather than a material one—and cannot recommend it too highly.

These five exercises will get you started on a program of using breath to optimize your healing system. As I said earlier, this is genuine spiritual practice, not just a method of improving health. The science of conscious breathing is not taught in medical schools. Throughout history it has been an esoteric subject, mostly passed on as oral tradition, and even today remarkably few books about it are available.

The energy that you can feel in your body after doing the bellows breath is the energy that Chinese doctors call qi (chi), their term for universal life energy. Most people experience it as warmth or tingling or subtle vibration. With practice you can learn to feel it more, move it about the body, and even transmit it to another person. Many healing systems from both East and West make use of energy transmission, usually through the hands, with or without touch contact between giver and recipient. From China and Japan come systems like reiki, jin shin jyutsu, and johrei; from our own culture comes therapeutic touch, a form of energy healing mostly taught and practiced by nurses. It is useful to try to feel, send, and receive this subtle energy. Not only can this practice relieve pain and accelerate healing; it directs attention toward the spiritual pole of existence, away from the material pole. The more you can experience yourself as energy, the easier it is not to identify yourself with your physical body.

Mystics and spiritual adepts teach that it is possible to raise spiritual energy, to increase its rate of vibration. One way to do this is to put yourself in the vicinity of persons, places, or things that have high spiritual energy. Throughout the world millions of people make pilgrimages to sacred sites—mountains, groves, shrines, and temples—where they feel uplifted, renewed, recharged. You can join them or look in your own territory for places that make you feel good, turn your thoughts to higher purposes, and take you out of yourself. You can also read the writings or life stories of men and women of high spiritual attainment, and you can view great art or objects of special beauty or listen to great music, because beauty in any form has a salutary effect on spirit. A simple way to get this benefit is to have flowers in your living space, since most people find their natural beauty inspiring.

Finally, you can pay attention to how you feel in the presence of various friends and acquaintances. Do some people always make you feel happier and better and more positive? If so, spend more time in their company and less in the company of those with an opposite effect on you. In some way, our spiritual selves resonate with others; if the interaction is positive, human connectedness is a most powerful healer, capable of neutralizing many harmful influences on the material plane.

A much-publicized example is the story of the Italian-Americans of Roseto, Pennsylvania, with their lower-than-expected incidence of coronary heart disease. The town was populated by immigrants from two villages in northern Italy, who came to America in the 1930s seeking better lives. They were a very close-knit community comprising large extended families with strong social bonds. They also ate a lot of calories, meat, and fat, and many smoked tobacco; nonetheless, they had few heart attacks. But their children, now in their fifties and sixties and eating the same diets, have the same incidence of coronary heart disease as other Americans. What changed from the first to the second generation? Researchers who studied these people felt the most significant difference was the loss of extended family and community; the younger generation lives in typical nuclear families with all of the social isolation characteristic of modern life. Somehow the high level of connectedness in the first generation of immigrants protected them from the expected ill effects of high-fat diets and smoking. I classify that kind of beneficial interaction between human beings as a spiritual phenomenon, one that is lacking in the lives of many sick people I see as patients.

14

An Eight-Week Program for Optimal Healing Power

I HAVE TAKEN the information in the previous chapters and arranged it in the form of week-by-week suggestions to help you change your lifestyle in a way that favors spontaneous healing. Each week's suggestions build on what you have done in the previous week; after two months, you will have created the foundation of a healing lifestyle. Read over the program, then try to set a date when you can begin. When you finish, you can decide how many of the changes you want to incorporate into your lifestyle on a regular basis. If the program seems to move along too fast for you, do not hesitate to slow it down and go at your own pace.

WEEK ONE

Projects

• Go through your pantry and refrigerator and remove all oils other than olive oil. Get rid of any margarine, solid vegetable shortenings, and products made with them. Read labels of all food products so that you can dispose of any containing partially hydrogenated oils. If you do not have any extra-virgin olive oil on hand, buy a bottle and start using it. You might also want to buy a small bottle of organic, expeller-pressed canola oil.

Diet

• Start eating some fresh broccoli this week. If you do not have a favorite way of preparing it, try one of the recipes on pages 151–52.

• Eat salmon, sardines, or kippers at least once this week. If you do not like fish, buy some flax seeds at a health food store, grind them, and sprinkle them over your food.

Supplements

• Start taking vitamin C if you do not do so already: 1,000 to 2,000 milligrams with breakfast, another dose with dinner, and a third at bedtime, if convenient.

Exercise

• Try to walk ten minutes a day for five days of this week. If you are already on a program of aerobic exercise other than walking, do the walk in addition.

Mental/Spiritual

• Think about your own experiences of healing. Make a list of illnesses or injuries or problems you have recovered from in the past two years. Note down anything you did to speed the healing process.

• Practice breath observation (see page 204) for five minutes every day.

• Buy some flowers to keep in your home where you can enjoy them.

WEEK TWO

Projects

• Find out where your drinking water comes from if you do not know and what impurities it might contain. Stop drinking chlorinated water. Get information on a water purifying system for your home, if you do not have one. In the meantime, buy bottled water.

Diet

- Eat fish at least once this week.
- Go to a health food store and look through the frozen and refrigerated sections to familiarize yourself with the many different products made from soybeans. Select one to try.
- Buy some Japanese green tea and try it. If you drink coffee or black tea, try to substitute green tea for some or all of your usual beverage.

Supplements

- Start taking beta carotene, 25,000 IU a day with breakfast.

Exercise

- Increase your daily walk to fifteen minutes and try to do it five days of the week.

Mental/Spiritual

- Pay attention to your mental imagery and make a few notes on kinds of images that have strong emotional impact for you. Think about how you might adapt them to use in healing visualizations.
- Visit a park or some other favorite place in nature. Spend as much time as you can there, doing nothing in particular, just feeling the energy of the place.
- Try a one-day "news fast." Do not read, watch, or listen to any news for a day and see how you feel.
- Begin doing all of the breathing exercises described on pages 204–7.

WEEK THREE

Projects

• Find out where you can buy organic produce. Inquire in grocery stores, health food stores, or use the resource guide at the end of this book. Make a commitment to buy organically produced fruits and vegetables, especially the ones mentioned on page 165.

• If you use an electric blanket, stop. Pack it up and give it away. Remove electric clock radios from the vicinity of your bed. Buy a radiation shield for the video display of your computer. Buy a pair of UV-protective sunglasses if you do not have any.

Diet

• Make a conscious effort to eat an extra serving of fruits and vegetables with at least one meal this week.

• Start eating fish at least twice this week.

• Replace at least one serving of meat with a soy food of your choice.

Supplements

• With lunch or your largest meal take 400 to 800 IU of vitamin E and 200 to 300 milligrams of selenium.

Exercise

• Increase the daily walk to twenty minutes, five days of the week. If you do other aerobic exercise, consider cutting it down to two to three days and substituting an aerobic walk on the other days.

Mental/Spiritual

• Make a list of inspirational books you would like to read in the areas of spirituality, religion, self-help, poetry, biography, or any other category, and select one that you will begin this week.

• Make a list of friends and acquaintances in whose company you feel more alive, happier, more optimistic. Pick one whom you will spend some time with this week.

• Buy more flowers.

WEEK FOUR

Projects

• Check on your bed, mattress, and sleeping location. Is an uncomfortable bed or noisy bedroom interfering with restful sleep? If so, consider making changes, as suggested on pages 191–92.

• Find out about getting an air filter for your home or bedroom if you live in a polluted area.

Diet

• Begin eating some more garlic this week in any form that appeals to you.

• Try to replace another meal of animal protein with soy protein.

Exercise

• Increase your aerobic walk to twenty-five minutes, five days of the week.

Mental/Spiritual

• Try to do two days of news fasting this week.

• Continue to practice the breathing exercises. Make sure that you do the relaxing breath twice a day.

• Contact someone you know to have experienced healing or recovery from illness or injury. Ask for details of the experience.

WEEK FIVE

Projects

• Locate a steam bath or sauna that you can use. Use it for up to twenty minutes one day. It should be hot enough to make you sweat freely; be sure to drink plenty of pure water to replace lost fluid.

Diet

• Try a one-day fruit fast, eating as much fresh fruit as you like but nothing else except water and herbal tea. Take vitamin C but skip the other supplements on this day.

• Buy a piece of fresh ginger root and make yourself some ginger tea, as described on page 175. Also try some crystallized ginger to see if you like it.

Exercise

• Increase your aerobic walk to thirty minutes, five days of the week.

Mental/Spiritual

• See if you can extend your news fast to three days this week.

• Practice the breathing exercises every day.

• Listen to a piece of music that you find inspirational and uplifting.

• Bring more flowers into your home this week.

WEEK SIX

Projects

• Look over the information on tonics on pages 171–85. Decide which one is most appropriate for you and find out where to get it.

- See if you can uncover any other stories of healing in your circle of friends, acquaintances, and business associates.
- Take a steam bath or sauna twice this week.

Diet

- Try a one-day juice fast today: any amount of fruit and vegetable juices you care to drink, plus water and herbal tea. Take vitamin C but skip the other supplements on this day.
- Continue to eat fish twice this week and soy foods twice this week.
- Continue to eat broccoli at least twice.

Exercise

- Increase your aerobic walk to thirty-five minutes, five days this week.

Mental/Spiritual

- Extend your news fast to four days.
- Visit an art museum or try to view some work of art, sculpture, or architecture that you find beautiful and inspiring.
- Continue the breathing exercises every day.

WEEK SEVEN

Projects

- Think about some kind of service work that you could do this week, such as volunteering for a few hours at a hospital or charitable organization or helping someone you know who is disabled or shut in—any activity in which you give some of your time and energy to help others.
- Continue the steam baths or saunas, three times a week if possible.

Diet

• For your fast day this week, drink only fruit juice, water, and herbal tea. Take vitamin C but skip the other supplements on this day.

• On the other days, continue eating as above: at least two meals of fish and two of soy protein, generous servings of fruits, vegetables, whole grains, ginger, and garlic.

Exercise

• Increase the aerobic walk to forty minutes, five days of the week.

Mental/Spiritual

• Reach out to resume connection with someone from whom you are estranged.

• Make time for flowers, music, and art.

• Increase the relaxing breath to eight cycles, twice a day.

WEEK EIGHT

Projects

• Review the changes you have made in your lifestyle in the past eight weeks and think about how many of them you wish to make permanent. Develop a realistic plan that you can stick to over the next eight weeks.

Diet

• Try a one-day water fast this week. You can have herbal tea with lemon if you like, but nothing caloric. If this proves too difficult, drink some diluted fruit juice. Take vitamin C but skip the other supplements.

• Think about how you can continue the dietary changes of this program in coming weeks.

Supplements

• Start taking your tonic. Make a commitment to give it a two-month trial to see what it does for your energy level, resistance, and outlook.

Exercise

• Reach your goal of a forty-five-minute walk, five days of the week.

Mental/Spiritual

• Continue the breathing exercises. Start using the relaxing breath whenever you feel anxious or upset, and be sure to do it at least twice a day.

• Try to maintain your news fast for the whole week. At the end of the week, think about how much news you want to let back into your life in coming weeks.

• Think of people who have hurt you or made you angry. Try to bring yourself to understand their actions and forgive them. Can you express forgiveness to at least one of them?

• Reward yourself with especially beautiful flowers for completing this program, and buy some flowers for someone else.

Congratulations! I have asked you to do a lot in the past two months, some of it unfamiliar and challenging. Know that you have been very good to yourself and your healing system. As a result of the changes you have made, you have a greater chance of experiencing spontaneous healing if the need for it arises. Try to incorporate into your life as many of these steps as you can from now on.

PART THREE

IF YOU GET SICK

15

Making the Right Decisions

When you get sick, you must decide what course of action to take in order to recover your health. If you do not accept this responsibility, others will decide for you and will not necessarily make the best choices. The most important decision is whether visits to health professionals will help or hinder your own healing system. You will need to understand the nature of your illness and to know whether conventional medicine can do anything for it without reducing the possibility of spontaneous healing. You will also want to know whether any alternative treatments exist that might be of benefit.

A good place to start is with a review of what conventional medicine can do effectively and what it cannot. For example, it is very effective at managing trauma, so that if I were in a serious automobile accident, I would want to go directly to an urgent care facility in a modern hospital, not to a shaman, guided imagery therapist, or acupuncturist. (Once out of danger, I might use those other resources to speed up the natural healing process.) Conventional medicine is also very good at diagnosing and managing crises of all sorts: hemorrhages, heart attacks, pulmonary edema, acute congestive heart failure, acute bacterial infections, diabetic comas, bowel obstructions, acute appendicitis, and so forth. You must be able to recognize symptoms of potentially serious conditions, so that you will not waste time before getting needed treatment. In general, *symptoms that are unusually severe, persistent, or out of the range of your normal experience warrant immediate investigation.*

CASE EXAMPLE 1: A MEDICAL EMERGENCY

Frederick R., a sixty-five-year-old minister with a fairly healthy lifestyle and a strong commitment to natural medicine, came to me with the complaint of "worsening digestive pain of a year's duration." He said he wanted natural remedies for it, because he did not believe in allopathic medicine. The pain was episodic, beginning in the pit of the stomach, spreading upward to the chest and into the left arm, both sides of the jaw, and into his back. The episodes were becoming more frequent and recently had begun to wake him from sleep. Unable to control the pain himself, Frederick had gone to a gastroenterologist, who did various tests, including endoscopy—putting a tube into the stomach to visualize its lining. The tests revealed a hiatal hernia and a small gallstone that was probably causing no problems. The doctor prescribed a drug to suppress acid production in the stomach; Frederick took it for several months but got no relief. Then he consulted a naturopath who prescribed herbs and dietary changes, also to no avail. Now he was seeing a homeopathic doctor; but after trying several homeopathic remedies, he was no better. He told me the pain was made worse by exertion and by lying flat, made better by sitting up. It had no relation to what he ate or drank.

Burning pain in the chest that is worse lying down and better sitting up is typical of hiatal hernia (in which a portion of the stomach protrudes through the muscular ring at the esophageal junction and may become inflamed as a result of excess acidity), but hiatal hernia pain and digestive pain in general are not made worse by exertion. I questioned Frederick carefully about that association and got a very clear story from him of exertional chest pain, which suggested coronary heart disease, not a problem with his stomach. I asked him if the gastroenterologist or anyone else had taken a cardiogram; no one had. I was convinced from the history alone that this patient was experiencing unstable angina, a medical emergency, and I told him I would work with him only if he went immediately to a cardiologist for a treadmill stress test. I gave him the name of a nearby cardiologist, and he made an appointment for the next day. During the treadmill test, Frederick's heart went into a dangerously irregular rhythm, confirming the suspicion that it was seriously deprived of blood. The cardiologist stopped the test and told Frederick he would not be legally responsible for him if he left the office; he sent him directly to a hospital for emergency coronary artery bypass surgery. Frederick came through the operation well, is now in good health, and carefully follows a heart-healthy lifestyle.

Comment: Frederick's story illustrates the danger of paying insufficient attention to an unusual and persistent symptom that should have alarmed him and the health providers he saw. Any chest pain that wakes a person from sleep or occurs on exertion should be investigated allopathically. Both patients and doctors should know that exertional chest pain is more likely to be coming from the heart than from the digestive system. Without correct medical and surgical intervention Frederick would probably have had a heart attack, possibly a fatal one.

Common sense and intuition can help you analyze symptoms and decide whether they are serious or not. If you are suffering from headaches, for example, you should seek help if you have never before had headaches, if the headaches are more intense than any you have had before, if they last longer than any you have had before, if you have them regularly for a longer period of time than you have ever experienced, or if they are accompanied by other, novel symptoms (like vomiting or visual disturbance). The greater the sense you have of your body's normal range of changes, the more likely you are to pay attention to and seek professional help in diagnosing a symptom that is outside that range and may indicate a problem requiring conventional medical treatment.

Taking advantage of the diagnostic capability of standard medicine does not commit you to accepting its treatments. It is up to you to find out the success rates of conventional treatments as well as to determine their risks. If the treatments are suppressive and toxic, or if medicine has nothing to offer, then it is appropriate to look elsewhere for help. Remember also that whenever you visit conventional doctors—even if it is for diagnostic evaluation only—you must be on guard against their pessimism about healing.

CASE EXAMPLE 2: THE DOCTORS HAD NO IDEAS

Mary K., a forty-year-old intensive care nurse at a university hospital, thought she was in good health until she volunteered for a drug study and had to undergo a preliminary physical examination and blood tests. The blood tests showed elevated liver enzymes and high levels of iron and ferritin, the protein associated with iron storage in the body. She agreed to have a liver biopsy, which showed early cirrhosis and increased iron, but doctors were unable to determine a diagnosis. She told them she had had hepatitis twenty years before, following a period of intravenous drug use. Since then she had used no drugs, had had no recurrences of hepatitis, and had taken good care of herself.

Because she worked in a university medical center, Mary had access to outstanding allopathic specialists, several of whom became interested in her as a puzzling case. They ran further tests, pondered the results, and concluded that her cirrhosis was of unknown origin. They could find no reason for her elevated iron and had no treatments to suggest.

An intelligent person with medical training, Mary had some ideas of her own. She wondered, for example, whether phlebotomy—drawing off blood from a vein—might be a useful way to reduce the excessive iron in her system; but the doctors saw no merit in it. "Of the four specialists I saw initially, not one gave me any option for action or treatment," she wrote. "They did not even tell me there were dietary manipulations that could help reduce the iron load in my body. So where was any cause for hope?" Yet they certainly gave her cause for concern and fear. " 'I know you're thinking cancer,' one of them said to me during a consultation, and I remember saying to myself: 'The thought of cancer never entered my head until you just put it there.' At best, the doctors were tolerant of my ideas but not supportive. They displayed lack of common sense, no willingness to trust intuition, and no ability to be creative. In the end I felt disrespected."

Mary came to see me two years after the first abnormal blood tests. In that time she had avoided red meat and other iron-rich foods and kept up her good health habits. She still felt well but continued to worry about her liver and her iron metabolism. I began by reminding her that the liver has a remarkable capacity for regeneration, especially in a young, otherwise healthy person. I encouraged her to experiment and told her I thought phlebotomy would be worth a try. I also gave her additional suggestions about diet and vitamins and two herbal remedies for her liver: milk thistle (see page 177) and schizandra (the fruit of *Schisandra chinensis*), a Chinese medicine that helps the body heal chronic hepatitis. My impression was that Mary's primary problem was low-grade, chronic hepatitis that rendered her liver susceptible to damage from iron accumulation. Mary told me she knew a family-practice doctor at the university who was willing to supervise the bleeding. Over the next few weeks, she gave a number of units of blood and was delighted to see her iron levels drop and stay within the normal range. Over the next year her liver function gradually returned to normal and has stayed there, so that now she not only looks and feels as healthy as before but is also certified healthy by her medical test results. She no longer worries about cancer or other dire possibilities.

She wrote me recently:

You and the other doctors who were helpful listened to me, supported me in my desire to experiment, used common sense, and were open to other therapies. You understood that I wanted/needed to heal myself rather than be healed. I don't believe my healing began until I was able to follow my own instincts and act on them. You gave me permission to do that. That's when my faith that I could improve my health began to grow, and instead of just waiting passively I was able to act. I want to tell other patients to search until they find practitioners they can trust, who respect them, listen to them, care about them, *and are competent.*

Comment: Faced with pessimistic doctors who had absolutely nothing to offer her, this patient sought out other professionals who empowered her to experiment with measures that solved her problem. Although she knew intuitively that healing was possible, she needed permission from a doctor to act.

Let me summarize for you what allopathic medicine can and cannot do for you:

CAN:

- Manage trauma better than any other system of medicine.
- Diagnose and treat many medical and surgical emergencies.
- Treat acute bacterial infections with antibiotics.
- Treat some parasitic and fungal infections.

- Prevent many infectious diseases by immunization.
- Diagnose complex medical problems.
- Replace damaged hips and knees.
- Get good results with cosmetic and reconstructive surgery.
- Diagnose and correct hormonal deficiencies.

CANNOT:

- Treat viral infections.
- Cure most chronic degenerative diseases.
- Effectively manage most kinds of mental illness.
- Cure most forms of allergy or autoimmune disease.
- Effectively manage psychosomatic illnesses.
- Cure most forms of cancer.

Here is another good rule to follow: *Do not seek help from a conventional doctor for a condition that conventional medicine cannot treat, and do not rely on an alternative provider for a condition that conventional medicine can manage well.*

LET'S LOOK AT some more case examples of people who made the right decisions about how to resolve illness. I have chosen cases from my practice that are representative of broad classes of disease and that illustrate successful strategies for controlling them.

CASE EXAMPLE 3: NATURAL MEDICINE RELIEVES RHEUMATOID ARTHRITIS

Joyce N., a seventy-year-old retired teacher, has had rheumatoid arthritis for almost forty years. Despite pain and deformity in her hands and neck, she is a cheerful, positive woman, who, to my surprise, told me she had never taken any medication stronger than aspirin for her symptoms. "Many doctors over the years tried to talk me into taking gold, prednisone, and other strong drugs," she told me at our first meeting, "but I knew intuitively that they would not be good for me, and I always refused. I have a high tolerance for pain and have been able to manage using aspirin alone." Joyce came to see me at the beginning of one November, saying that her pain had increased recently, which worried her, because it was the beginning of the winter season, usually her worst time. "Is there anything you can suggest that might help me live with this condition more comfortably?" she asked.

I had never before met anyone with severe rheumatoid arthritis who had been able to avoid the strong suppressive drugs that allopathic doctors prescribe for it. Although Joyce was a quiet, retiring woman with significant deformity from her disease, she radiated a glow of emotional contentment. The glow increased when she described her marriage and family life, making me feel that this was the source of the inner strength that enabled her to live so well with chronic pain. I discovered also that she knew little about options for moderating rheumatoid arthritis without prescription drugs and told her I thought she could expect great improvement if she would make changes in her diet and activity, take a few supplements, and explore the mind/body connection. I asked her to eliminate all dairy products, eat less meat, add fish sources of omega-3 fatty acids, and eliminate all polyunsaturated and partially hydrogenated fats. I recommended an antioxidant formula (see pages 159–61) and an herbal remedy, feverfew (*Tanacetum parthenium*), which is nontoxic and known to alleviate rheumatoid arthritis. I recommended that she begin to swim regularly and to practice the relaxing breath (pages 206–7). Finally, I sent her to a hypnotherapist, who is skilled at working with chronically ill people. The patient reported back six weeks later that she had followed this program faithfully and was amazed at the degree of improvement she had experienced, all the more remarkable because it was now the coldest, wettest time of year, when she expected to suffer the most.

Comment: Rheumatoid arthritis is a prototypical autoimmune disease. (Others in this class are lupus, scleroderma, and multiple sclerosis.) Autoimmunity has an inherent tendency to wax and wane, with the ups and downs often mirroring emotional highs and lows. Conventional medicine has only immunosuppressive drugs to offer, which may be necessary for getting through periods of severe exacerbation of symptoms but are inappropriate for long-term treatment. The chronic inflammation of autoimmunity often causes pain and eventual damage to body structures, but inflammation can be moderated by a variety of nontoxic methods, especially dietary change and herbal remedies. Hypnotherapy and guided imagery therapy are often very effective at nudging the disease in the direction of remission. This patient's rapid and dramatic response to natural medicine, despite her age and the chronicity of her disease, may be due to two factors: her never having used suppressive medication and her psychospiritual good health, rooted in positive relationships and high self-esteem.

CASE EXAMPLE 4: TURNING AROUND
CHRONIC DERMATITIS

Nancy S., the forty-five-year-old wife of a successful surgeon, developed an itching, red rash on both hands that gradually spread to much of her body. The skin became thickened, cracked, and raw, causing her great discomfort. She saw several dermatologists, who told her the problem was dermatitis of unknown origin and prescribed steroid creams and oral prednisone. Prednisone made the rash disappear; but knowing its toxicity with long-term use, Nancy stopped it, whereupon the condition returned worse than before. This experience, repeated several times, made her wary of using steroids in any form. Eventually she went to a leading dermatologist in another city who biopsied the skin and told her that she might have a rare form of lymphoma, a cancer with a bad prognosis. This made her quite upset, although a subsequent biopsy by yet another dermatologist failed to support this possibility. The doctors had no treatments to offer other than steroids and antihistamines to control the itching. As the condition progressed, Nancy became fatigued, and her awareness of disfigurement led her to retreat from social contact into depression and isolation. She spent most of her time lying in bed or soaking her body in soothing baths.

When she came to see me, she had had the dermatitis for two years. One month before, she had consulted a homeopath, who gave her remedies that did not work, but she still felt there must be some way to solve the problem. In listening to her history, I thought it was significant that her children had left home about the time of the onset of her problem. Her husband's profession left him little time for home life, and she generally felt uprooted and isolated since they moved from another part of the country some years before. I assured her that her body could heal itself if given a chance, outlined a low-protein diet that excluded milk, and recommended supplementation with black currant oil, a source of an unusual fatty acid (GLA, gamma-linolenic acid), good for the health of the skin. I also taught her to make a tea of a desert shrub (chaparral, *Larrea divaricata*) for application to affected areas; recommended calendula lotion, another herbal product available in health food stores; and sent her to a hypnotherapist. This last suggestion frightened her, because she did not like the idea of "anyone taking over my mind," but she implemented the other recommendations, and her husband supported her in following them. He even bought her a little stove to brew the strong-smelling chaparral tea out of doors. She came to love this ritual and found the tea very soothing. After six weeks she began to experience some improvement but still had not made an appointment with the hypnotherapist. It took much urging to get her to overcome her reluctance; when she did, she was pleasantly surprised. The hypnotherapist taught her relaxation methods, which she now practices faithfully. Her improvement accelerated and has continued steadily; she has been able to dispense with the antihistamines and steroids and resume her social life.

Comment: Dermatitis is an allergic and psychosomatic condition, for which conventional medicine can offer only suppressive therapies. Diseases of the skin (and gastrointestinal tract) should be assumed to have an emotional basis until proved otherwise, because these systems are the most frequent sites of expression of stress-induced imbalances. Mind/body interventions combined with lifestyle change and nontoxic symptomatic management will often allow the body to heal itself completely from these conditions.

CASE EXAMPLE 5: CHILDREN WHO ARE ALWAYS SICK

Terry, age six, and Ryan, age four, were spending more of their time on antibiotics than off. Their frustrated parents brought them to me in the hope that I could suggest a way to change their pattern of continual ear infections, colds, and bronchitis. "We'll try anything," they told me, adding that they liked their pediatrician but felt he knew how to do only one thing: prescribe drugs. Both boys were active and well developed, apparently healthy except for the susceptibility to upper respiratory and ear infections. I explained to the parents that frequent use of antibiotics can worsen the very problem it is meant to alleviate, both by weakening immunity and by increasing the number and virulence of resistant germs. I suggested they try to reserve antibiotics for very severe infections after other remedies had failed. I taught them how to use echinacea, an herbal immune enhancer and antibiotic substitute made from the root of a native American plant (*Echinacea purpurea*, purple coneflower) that is nontoxic and readily available in health food stores. As general preventive measures I recommended excluding milk and milk products from the boys' diet, giving them daily doses of vitamin C, and taking them to an osteopath specializing in cranial therapy in order to relieve any restrictions in their breathing. The parents implemented all of these suggestions, and within three months the children's pattern of illness changed. Now episodes of infection are infrequent, and use of antibiotics in this household is unusual.

Comment: Antibiotics are powerful tools for containing susceptible infections but must be reserved for instances where they are really needed. The frequent use of antibiotics is not wise. In case of recurrent or chronic infections, it is important to increase natural resistance. Disease-causing germs are always present, but by enhancing immunity and natural healing capacity it is possible to reduce the chance that they can harm us. Doctors must bear much of the responsibility for getting us into our growing predicament with aggressive bacteria; by overprescribing and misprescribing antibiotics, they have brought on the coming catastrophe.

CASE EXAMPLE 6: REVERSING CHRONIC DISEASE BY CHANGING LIFESTYLE

When Henry D. was diagnosed with adult-onset diabetes at age sixty, his doctor started him on an oral hypoglycemic drug and advised him to exercise and lose weight. At about the same time Henry's blood pressure, which had long been in the high normal range, climbed to levels requiring treatment, so his doctor also prescribed an antihypertensive drug. Henry did not like its side effects and stopped taking it, but his doctor scared him into starting again by saying he would probably have a stroke without it. Henry took it but complained constantly. Shortly afterward, his wife, who was also overweight and hypertensive, read an article about a center that offered residential programs of lifestyle modification to treat cardiovascular diseases. The program emphasized a very low-fat diet (ten percent of total calories from fat), exercise, relaxation training, group discussion, and lectures aimed at helping people incorporate the program's changes into their lives upon returning home. Henry and his wife signed up for a ten-day program and loved it. On returning home they began cooking food according to the program's guidelines and exercising regularly. Henry's wife eventually lost twenty pounds, while Henry lost thirty-two. Both of them saw their blood pressure return to normal without medication, and Henry's diabetes disappeared as well. They say they feel much better now; both have more energy and greater confidence in their own healing abilities.

Comment: Lifestyle modification is a proven method for reversing a number of common, debilitating, chronic diseases, including hypertension, non-insulin-dependent diabetes, and coronary heart disease. The only requirement for patients is motivation.

CASE EXAMPLE 7: STOMACH PAIN

Ben K., a thirty-eight-year-old environmental consultant, suffered from chronic upper gastrointestinal pain and discomfort that he had lived with for several years. Eventually the episodes forced him to seek help from a family-practice doctor, who prescribed a course of antibiotics and a strong acid-suppressive drug. The doctor told Ben that he probably had an infection with *Helicobacter pylori,* the germ now believed to cause many cases of peptic ulcer and gastritis; hence the antibiotics. He did not give Ben any advice about changing his lifestyle or diet. On his own, Ben cut out coffee, which he had been drinking regularly, and started practicing relaxation techniques. When I saw him, three weeks into the treatment, the pain had lessened but was not entirely gone. I advised him to discontinue the acid-suppressive drug and to substitute a licorice extract called DGL,* which strengthens the mucus coating in the stomach, making it more resistant to acid. I encouraged him to eliminate caffeine entirely and to practice the relaxing breath. One month later, he was free of pain.

Comment: The doctor prescribed antibiotics without conducting a test to determine if *Helicobacter* was present. Antigen testing for this bacterium is very simple and should be done in all cases of persistent upper GI pain. If the test is positive, a course of antibiotic treatment (two different drugs) plus a course of bismuth subsalicylate (the active ingredient in Pepto Bismol) is definitely indicated. In this case, the doctor did not prescribe the correct antibiotic regimen and left out the bismuth. Of course, he did not know about DGL, since few conventional doctors are familiar with botanical remedies. This is a case where selective allopathic diagnostic work and treatment combined with alternative treatment was in the patient's best interest.

CASE EXAMPLE 8: IRREGULAR HEARTBEAT

Marjorie O., a sixty-two-year-old widow, was bothered by irregular heartbeats: frequent "skipped beats" and runs of rapid beats. Her internist examined her and took an electrocardiogram, which showed premature ventricular contractions, a common, usually benign arrhythmia that people perceive as skipped beats. He recommended an antiarrhythmic drug, but Marjorie declined to take it, because she was afraid of toxicity. When I saw her, I determined that her habits of diet and exercise were good. I advised her to avoid caffeine, to practice the relaxing breath twice a day, and to take supplemental magnesium, which helps stabilize irritable muscle tissue in the heart. With this regimen, her irregular heartbeats disappeared and have not returned.

Comment: Marjorie's use of conventional medicine to rule out a serious heart condition was appropriate, as was her refusal to take a strong chemical drug before exploring safer alternatives.

---

* Deglycyrrhizinated licorice is an extract of licorice root (*Glycyrrhiza glabra*) with a fraction removed that can cause sodium retention and elevated blood pressure. It is available in health food stores.

CASE EXAMPLE 9: ULCERATIVE
COLITIS AND CHINESE MEDICINE

Susan K. was diagnosed with ulcerative colitis in her mid-twenties. The disease had gone in and out of remission; but now, at age thirty-five, she required much suppressive medication, including prednisone, to keep the symptoms under control. She had frequent episodes of abdominal pain and diarrhea, and her doctor told her that if the condition worsened, the only remedy would be surgery to remove a length of affected colon. Although Susan hated being so dependent on doctors and drugs, she had been unable to find other ways to manage the colitis. She had been through psychotherapy, biofeedback, and several forms of relaxation training, and felt she had explored the mental/emotional roots of her illness without discovering practical solutions. I taught her the relaxing breath and urged her to keep exploring. Then on a trip away from home she suffered a severe exacerbation of symptoms and feared she might have to check in to a hospital. Instead she was able to find a Chinese doctor who practiced traditional Chinese medicine. He gave her instructions for making rice gruel, which he prescribed as her sole nourishment during the crisis, and treated her with acupuncture and herbal teas. After a few days the symptoms subsided without the need for allopathic intervention. With continued acupuncture and herbal treatment, the colitis went into remission, and Susan was able to eliminate most of the suppressive drugs.

Comment: Ulcerative colitis (and its relative, Crohn's disease) is a complex problem with genetic, autoimmune, and psychosomatic components. Suppressive medication is often required during periods of exacerbation but is never curative. Traditional Chinese medicine, with its unique therapies, may be able to manage illnesses of this sort with much less risk and expense.

CASE EXAMPLE 10: ASTHMA
AND AYURVEDIC MEDICINE

Michael B., a twenty-seven-year-old university student, had a long history of allergic asthma, controlled imperfectly with an array of allopathic drugs. He used a bronchodilator inhaler, a steroid inhaler, and oral theophylline, another bronchodilator; previously he had gone through several series of desensitization shots for some of the allergens that he reacted to most strongly. Nevertheless, his asthma attacks gradually became more frequent, forcing him to restrict his activities. When I saw him, he had just moved, because he felt the carpeting in his old apartment was a problem, and he now found it difficult to exercise because of breathing difficulties. Michael ate a healthy diet, took vitamins, and had experimented with a number of alternative treatments, including homeopathy, dietary change, and herbs. Nothing had given him substantial improvement. He worried that he was becoming more dependent on medication and might soon have to start taking oral prednisone, which he wanted to avoid at all costs.

I recommended further modifications in his diet, suggested he buy an air filter for his bedroom, and told him to take a natural product called quercetin, which reduces allergic responsiveness. I also sent him to an osteopath for manipulative treatment to free up restrictions in his chest. These measures helped some. Later, Michael called to tell me he had consulted a practitioner of Ayurvedic medicine in New Mexico, with wonderful results. Ayurveda is the traditional healing system of India, based on classifying people into constitutional types, then recommending appropriate dietary and herbal therapy. The practitioner had given Michael a list of foods to eat and a list of foods to avoid, along with herbal remedies and instructions for a detoxifying regimen. After two months on this program, Michael's asthma subsided to such an extent that he was able to dispense with most of his medication. He now uses his bronchodilator inhaler only occasionally, mainly before starting exercise, and finds that he can tolerate exposure to many allergens that he could not tolerate previously. This is the first time in his adult life that he has had long periods free of any breathing difficulties.

Comment: Bronchial asthma is not one disease but several. Some forms respond more easily to treatment than others. Allopathic measures are toxic and addictive, yet it is often impossible to do without them. The potential for spontaneous healing of asthma is significant, especially with major lifestyle change or application of alternative medical methods. The Ayurvedic approach, with its emphasis on the right diet for each person and its wealth of medicinal plants upon which to draw, might be worth exploring if you have a stubborn, chronic disease that conventional medicine cannot cure.

CASE EXAMPLE 11: LONG-TERM HIV INFECTION

Mark M. knows exactly when he got infected with the AIDS virus and from whom he got it. It was in 1983 from a male sexual partner; the man's previous partner died shortly afterward. One month after this contact Mark became very sick with a skin rash and a mysterious pneumonia that was never identified. He remained very sick for three months, then recovered and has been healthy ever since. In 1985 he tested positive for HIV. At that time his helper T cell count was over 1,000. (Helper T cells are the targets of HIV; as their numbers decline, people become more susceptible to opportunistic infections.) In 1989 his T cell count had dropped to 700.

Since his recovery from the initial infection, Mark has been very conscientious about his health, especially about his diet and mental state. He eats a lot of raw garlic—one head a day, chopped and mixed with food—because he read about garlic's beneficial effects on the immune system. He also eats a lot of hot chile peppers and buys only organically produced food, including some meat and chicken and a substantial quantity of fruits, fruit juice, and vegetables. He takes vitamins, drinks purified water, and walks, swims, and gardens regularly. He lives in a monogamous relationship, works as director of a program that provides counseling for persons with HIV, and creates art objects that he uses in healing rituals. In 1991, Mark's T cell count was up to 1,300; and when he was last tested, in 1994, it was still 1,300, which is in the normal range.

"The medical professionals gave me six to eighteen months to live when I was first diagnosed," Mark told me when I met him. "Since 1985 I can't tell you how many doctors have shown me the Curve— that is, the graph showing the percentage of people per year who develop AIDS after infection. They all try to tell me I'm somewhere along it, headed for destruction. This is really Western medicine's fascination with illness. Here I am with normal T cells, in great health, and they have the audacity to tell me I'm on this curve heading for death. When I see doctors now, I tell them right at the start:

'Look, I don't even want to hear about your curve. Just check me out, answer my questions, and keep your opinions to yourself!' They have also all tried to get me to take AZT [the antiviral drug that is conventional medicine's current treatment of choice for HIV], but all of the people I've known who have used it are dead, so I've refused. And none of them have been interested to hear what I'm doing to stay healthy. They pat me on the head and say, 'Whatever you're doing, just keep it up!'

"I have developed an ability not to buy into the medical system and a willingness to accept that I have control over what happens to me with HIV. I am also committed to not being afraid. I use visualization every day to neutralize fear; I've been doing it since I was a kid, because I came from a disastrous family and was subjected to incest and a lot of verbal and physical abuse. Things come up every day—like a funny spot on my arm recently. I visualized it going away, and it did. It was nothing. I'm also in ongoing psychotherapy. For the past seven years I've used it to keep centered. In my work I act as a healthy role model for persons newly diagnosed with HIV. I counsel them and don't reveal that I'm HIV-positive till later. It's an effective technique. Many of these people, especially as a result of their inter-actions with doctors, think they'll die within two years. I'm here to show them it doesn't have to be that way."

I did not have much to tell Mark except to make him aware of some of the Chinese herbal tonics that look promising for keeping HIV in remission.

Comment: With a life-threatening illness for which conventional medicine has no effective treatment, it takes conscious effort to get needed services from doctors (like monitoring of T cell counts) with-out taking on their pessimism. One of the most interesting and encouraging features of HIV infection is its tendency to go into a long latent period before it begins to compromise immunity. Conventional therapy centers on chemical weapons against the virus, but these drugs are all toxic and may select for strains of HIV that are less inclined to live in balance with their human hosts. For many years, medical doctors paid no attention to long-term survivors of HIV infection like Mark. Now enough cases have surfaced that re-searchers are beginning to study them. One possibility is that some of these people are infected with less virulent strains of HIV and may have developed immunity to them (which could help scientists develop an effective vaccine). Many long-term survivors have relied on healthy lifestyles and therapies to support the healing system, such as Chinese herbal remedies. If the latent period of HIV infection could be extended to twenty-five or thirty years, people with the virus might live out relatively normal lives. (They could, of course, still infect others.)

THESE CASE EXAMPLES show how correct decisions about treatment, particularly about whether and how to use conventional medicine, can allow the healing system to resolve a variety of serious health problems. Once you establish the right relationship with the conventional system, your next task is to make wise choices from among the great variety of alternative therapies now available.

16

CONSIDERING THE ALTERNATIVES

WHEN YOU VENTURE out of the world of standard medicine to look for alternative treatments, it is even more important to be an informed consumer. Alternative medical practices range from those that are grounded in long traditions of careful work to those that are nonsensical. In general, alternative treatments are less risky than allopathic drugs and surgery, but they can be expensive and wasteful of time and effort. I have written at length elsewhere about the history and philosophy of major systems of alternative medicine; what I will do here is give capsule summaries of a number of popular therapies, along with indications for their use. You will find a guide to locating practitioners in the Appendix to this book.

ACUPUNCTURE

Insertion of needles into particular points of the body is a unique therapeutic intervention of traditional Chinese medicine (TCM); Western doctors have taken the technique out of context, using it mostly to treat acute and chronic pain. As a symptomatic treatment for pain, acupuncture has the advantage of being free of the side effects of analgesic drugs, although relief is usually temporary, necessitating frequent visits to the therapist. I have known acupuncture to cure the pain, pressure, and congestion of acute sinus infections as well as to speed the healing of joint injuries. Some dentists use it as the sole form of anesthesia for dental work, including drilling and extraction of teeth. Another interesting use is in addiction treatment: placement of needles in points in the ear has helped some people quit smoking, withdraw from heroin and cocaine, and moderate addictive eating. In TCM acupuncture is used to manipulate energy flows around the body, not primarily to relieve pain or change behavior.

AYURVEDIC MEDICINE

One of the oldest medical systems in the world, Ayurveda has only recently become widely available in the West. Practitioners diagnose by observing patients, questioning them, touching them, and taking pulses. With this information the practitioner is able to assign patients to one of three major constitutional types and then to various subtypes. This classification dictates dietary modifications and selection of remedies. Ayurvedic remedies are primarily herbal, drawing on the vast botanical wealth of the Indian subcontinent, but may include animal and mineral ingredients, even powdered gemstones. Other treatments include steam baths and oil massages.

Although Ayurvedic herbs are little known outside India and few have been studied by modern methods, many may have great therapeutic value. For example, guggul (*Commiphora mukul*), a plant indicated traditionally for control of obesity, has been shown to lower cholesterol in a manner similar to pharmaceutical drugs used for that purpose, but with much less risk. An extract of it called gugulipid is now available in health food stores. Another Ayurvedic preparation, called triphala, is the best bowel regulator I have come across, much better than Western herbal remedies for constipation. It is a mixture of three fruits and can be found in capsule form in health food stores.

Finding a good Ayurvedic doctor takes some effort. Many practitioners in the West are members of the international religious organization of Maharishi Mahesh Yogi, the Holland-based billionaire, whose promotion of Ayurveda is definitely a for-profit endeavor. (In India Ayurveda is medicine of the people, an inexpensive alternative to allopathic treatment. Maharishi Ayurveda is anything but inexpensive.) This group offers training programs for physicians that certify them to be Ayurvedic practitioners after minimal exposure to the philosophy and methods of the system. I recommend seeking out practitioners who are independent of this organization. One way to find them is by inquiring in Indian communities, even in Indian restaurants and grocery stores.

BIOFEEDBACK

Training in biofeedback, a relaxation technique employing electronic equipment to amplify body responses until they become perceptible, is offered by certified therapists, many of them clinical psychologists. In the most common version, patients learn to raise the temperature of their hands and by so doing relax the whole sympathetic nervous system, which controls many involuntary functions. Biofeedback training is enjoyable, and almost everyone succeeds at it. It is especially useful for alleviating Raynaud's disease (see page 15), migraine, hypertension, bruxism (involuntary grinding of the teeth, especially during sleep), temporomandibular joint (TMJ) syndrome, and other ailments with a prominent stress component. Brainwave biofeedback, requiring more complex technology, may be helpful for people with seizure disorders, narcolepsy, and other central nervous system problems.

It is easy to find biofeedback therapists—they are usually listed in the yellow pages of the telephone book—but harder to find ones who are creative and do not use the technology in a mechanical fashion. A typical training program consists of ten one-hour sessions as well as daily practice on your own. Biofeedback teaches you what it feels like to be relaxed internally. It is then up to you to recreate the feeling and make it part of your way of being.

BODY WORK

In addition to prescribing massage therapy as a form of stress reduction, I often recommend specific kinds of body work. Here are the four I most prefer:

  • *Feldenkrais work* is a system of movements, floor exercises, and body work designed to retrain the central nervous system, particularly to help it find new pathways around any areas of blockage or damage. Feldenkrais work is innovative, gentle, and often strikingly effective at rehabilitating victims of trauma, cerebral palsy, stroke, and other serious disabilities. I find it to be much more useful than standard physical therapy.

• *Rolfing,* a more invasive form of body work, aims at restructuring the musculoskeletal system by working on patterns of tension held in deep tissue. The therapist applies firm pressure to different areas of the body, which can be painful while it is administered. "Getting Rolfed" means going through a basic series of ten sessions, each focusing on a different part of the body. Rolfing can release repressed emotions as well as dissipate habitual muscle tension.

• *Shiatsu,* a traditional healing art from Japan, makes use of firm finger pressure applied to specified points on the body and is intended to increase the circulation of vital energy. The client lies on the floor with the therapist seated alongside. Japanese practitioners use much firmer pressure than many Westerners find comfortable, but it is worth tolerating because shiatsu can be remarkably effective at dissipating muscle tension and recharging the body. Western practitioners generally use a lighter touch.

• *Trager work* is one of the least invasive forms of body work, using gentle rocking and bouncing motions to induce states of deep, pleasant relaxation. In addition to its relaxing effects, Trager work can also help facilitate the nervous system's communication with muscles, so that it can be helpful as a rehabilitation method, especially for people suffering from traumatic injuries, disabilities, post-polio syndrome, and other chronic neuromuscular problems.

TRADITIONAL CHINESE MEDICINE (TCM)

Traditional Chinese medicine is a comprehensive system of diagnosis and treatment that has now established itself throughout the world. Practitioners include Chinese immigrants and Westerners trained in China or in numerous schools in other countries. Diagnosis in TCM is based on history, on observation of the body (especially the

tongue), on palpation, and on pulse diagnosis, an elaborate procedure requiring considerable skill and experience. Treatment involves
dietary change, massage, medicinal teas and other preparations made
primarily from herbs but also including animal ingredients, and
acupuncture. The Chinese herbal pharmacopeia is vast, with many
plants now under serious scrutiny by Western pharmacologists.
Many Chinese remedies appear to have significant therapeutic value,
and some work on conditions for which Western doctors have no
pharmaceutical drugs.

In my experience, TCM is worth trying for a wide range of allergic,
autoimmune, infectious, and chronic degenerative conditions, including asthma, ulcerative colitis, Crohn's disease, chronic bronchitis,
chronic sinusitis, osteoarthritis, chronic fatigue syndrome, HIV infection and other states of immune deficiency, sexual deficiency, and general debility.

CHIROPRACTIC

Chiropractic has come a long way since the days of its invention a century ago. Today's chiropractors have had basic scientific education and
are not likely to claim that spinal adjustment alone can cure cancer,
diabetes, or any other serious disease. In my experience chiropractors
still take too many X-rays and are too likely to have patients commit
to long and costly treatment packages. (Some people see their chiropractors once or twice a week just to get adjusted, whether or not they
have anything wrong with them.) Chiropractic treatment can be helpful in cases of acute musculoskeletal pain, tension headaches, and
recovery from trauma; it is less effective with chronic pain syndromes.

GUIDED IMAGERY AND VISUALIZATION THERAPY

At several points in this book (see pages 93–7 and 199–201) I have
indicated my enthusiasm for these methods of employing the
mind/body connection to modify illness. Here I will simply repeat my
assertion that no disease process is beyond the reach of these therapies
and that it is best to work with a trained professional, at least initially,
to ensure you are using them correctly. Guided imagery and visualiza-

tion can enhance the effectiveness of other treatments, including allopathic drugs and surgery. Certainly try them for all autoimmune disorders and for any illness in which healing seems blocked or stalled.

HERBAL MEDICINE

As a physician with botanical training, I recommend herbal treatments for a wide range of diseases. Unfortunately, few allopathic physicians have the knowledge or experience to do this. You are more likely to find knowledgeable practitioners in the fields of Ayurvedic medicine, traditional Chinese medicine, and naturopathy. There are also professional herbalists, persons who do not have degrees in any of the major systems of medicine but who have studied on their own or with experienced preceptors.

To be a wise consumer of the great variety of herbal remedies available in health food stores, you must buy reliable preparations and brands. Tinctures (alcoholic extracts), freeze-dried extracts, and standardized extracts are recommended. Herbal medicines tend to be milder than chemical drugs and produce their effects more slowly; they are also much less likely to cause toxicity, because they are dilute forms of drugs rather than concentrated ones.

HOLISTIC MEDICINE

Holistic doctors subscribe to the principles that human beings are more than their physical bodies and that good medicine should embrace the whole spectrum of available treatments, not just the drugs and surgery of conventional medicine. Although holistic doctors share a common general philosophy, there is little uniformity of practice from one to the next, nor is there any assurance that a doctor is good just because he or she is a member of a holistic medical association.

HOMEOPATHY

Homeopathic medicine, a system of diagnosis and treatment based on the use of highly diluted remedies made from natural substances, has a distinguished two-hundred-year history and is now enjoying new popularity. Its main virtue is that it cannot possibly cause harm, because the medicines it employs are so diluted. Homeopaths say that the diluted substances work on the body's energy field, catalyzing natural healing responses; critics charge that homeopathic remedies are nothing but placebos.

It is confusing to seek homeopathic treatment today, because it is practiced in many different forms by people with very different training. Classical homeopathy—the kind taught by the founder of the system—specifies the administration of one dose of one remedy selected on the basis of information gained during a lengthy interview with the patient. Nonclassical homeopathy prescribes multiple or regular doses of formulas combining several remedies. Homeopathic practitioners may be M.D.'s, osteopaths, naturopaths, chiropractors, or lay persons without formal training as health professionals. My own preference would be to seek out classical homeopathy from an M.D., but I have met a few highly accomplished lay homeopaths. Homeopathic remedies are now widely sold in both drugstores and health food stores, another deviation from the classical system, which requires the expertise of a doctor to pick the proper remedy for each individual.

Although I cannot explain how homeopathy works in scientific terms, I have known it to be effective for a diversity of health problems, including allergies, skin and digestive ailments, rheumatoid arthritis, ear and upper respiratory infections in children, gynecological problems, and headaches. Homeopaths often object to combining their treatment with other types of treatment, especially allopathic drugs, herbal medicines, and vitamins and supplements. They also believe that coffee, camphor, mint, and a few other substances act as antidotes to the remedies and must be avoided once you begin treatment with this system.

HYPNOTHERAPY

Hypnotherapy takes advantage of the mind/body connection by encouraging patients to enter a trance, a state of heightened suggestibility. In this state, verbal suggestions are often able to pass from the mind to the nervous system, influencing the body in ways that seem impossible in ordinary states of awareness. I frequently refer patients to hypnotherapists because I have seen it produce excellent results in many illnesses that are managed poorly by conventional medicine, among them a wide range of skin and gastrointestinal ailments, allergy and autoimmune disease, and chronic pain. Some people fear hypnotherapy, seeing it as mind control; but, in fact, hypnotherapists simply arrange circumstances to allow patients to move on their own into natural states of focused concentration, similar to daydreaming or watching a movie. Patients then learn to recreate the experience on their own. It is important to shop around for a therapist you trust and feel comfortable with. One problem I encounter as a referring physician is that many hypnotherapists lack imagination and limit their work to relaxation, pain control, and overcoming bad habits. If I send them patients with challenging physical diseases like multiple sclerosis or ulcerative colitis, they are likely to regard these problems as beyond their expertise and are reluctant to take them on. So as well as being someone you can trust, a good hypnotherapist should be inventive and willing to try new strategies to access spontaneous healing.

NATUROPATHY

Many people think of naturopathic physicians as being "New Age." In fact, naturopathy comes from the old tradition of European health spas with their emphasis on hydrotherapy, massage, and nutritional and herbal treatment. Older naturopaths may actually be chiropractors with mail-order degrees in naturopathy. Younger naturopaths are well trained in basic sciences and have had exposure to subjects omitted from the conventional medical curriculum, such as nutritional and herbal medicine. Except for their adherence to a general philosophy of taking advantage of the body's natural healing capacity and avoiding the drugs and surgery of conventional medicine, naturopaths show a great deal of individuality in their styles of practice. Some use acupuncture, some use body work, some practice herbalism, others practice homeopathy.

As a profession, naturopathy is smaller than the other major systems of alternative medicine, licensed in only a few states in the United States, mostly in the West. Good naturopaths are worth consulting for childhood illnesses, recurrent upper respiratory infections and sinusitis, gynecological problems, and all ailments for which conventional doctors have only suppressive treatments. Naturopaths can be valuable as advisors to help people design healthy lifestyles.

OSTEOPATHIC MANIPULATIVE THERAPY (OMT)

Most osteopaths (D.O.'s) today are indistinguishable from M.D.'s in their reliance on drugs and surgery; only a small percentage of them still use manipulation as a primary therapeutic modality. Unlike chiropractic, osteopathic manipulation does not focus solely on the spine but works on all parts of the body, often with gentler techniques than the high-velocity adjustments favored by chiropractors. Since osteopaths have the same educational background as M.D.'s, they are much more competent than chiropractors in assessing general health problems. Skilled practitioners of OMT can relieve a variety of acute and chronic musculoskeletal problems, undo effects of past traumas (like automobile accidents), and help treat headaches and TMJ syndrome. Cranial therapy, a specialized form of OMT, may benefit asthma, recurrent ear infections in children, sleep disorders, and other conditions rooted in nervous system imbalances. I frequently refer patients to D.O.'s for OMT and often encourage medical students to learn the technique, because I have found it to be safe and highly effective.

RELIGIOUS HEALING

A considerable body of research data supports the beneficial effects of prayer on health. Good documentation also exists for the efficacy of Christian Science healing. It is reasonable to think that belief on the part of patients is the crucial factor here; however, some research shows prayer to be effective even when sick people are unaware that they are the objects of prayer, suggesting that unknown mechanisms might also be at work. Since religious practices can clearly activate healing responses and cannot cause direct harm, there is no reason not to use them as adjunctive or primary treatments in cases of medically hopeless disease.

THERAPEUTIC TOUCH

Therapeutic touch, a form of energy healing taught and practiced mostly by nurses, is a learnable skill of great utility. It can relieve pain without the side effects of drugs, can speed healing from injury, and can identify and dissipate energy blockages that may be impeding the healing system. As with prayer, therapeutic touch cannot harm, so there is no reason not to try it. Many healers outside the therapeutic touch movement also work by the laying on of hands and achieve good results. In addition, you can learn to use this therapy on yourself. Put yourself in a relaxed state and begin by trying to sense and transmit energy with the palms of the hands; then direct it to a part of the body that is hurting.

17

SEVEN STRATEGIES
OF SUCCESSFUL PATIENTS

IN ADDITION TO the case reports already recounted, I have known and interviewed many other patients who have experienced spontaneous healing. Reflecting on their stories, I have identified a few common strategies they used, strategies that would benefit anyone who is sick and struggling with difficult decisions. If more patients adopted them, I believe, the incidence of spontaneous healing would rise dramatically.

I observe that successful patients:

1. DO NOT TAKE "NO" FOR AN ANSWER

Most of the people whose experiences I have related heard discouraging words from health professionals, especially from medical doctors who told them there was no hope, nothing more to be done, and no possibility of getting better. They did not buy it. Instead they never gave up hope that there was help to be found somewhere.

The young man with chronic autoimmune disease, described on page 99, had been told for years by hematologists that nothing could be done for him but to maintain him on the high doses of steroids that were destroying his health. For years he accepted that view, but as the toxicity of suppressive treatment became more and more obvious, he acted on his intuitive belief that other methods had to exist and began a search that led him to me. I told him I thought he could alter the behavior of his immune system by making significant changes in his lifestyle, exploring alternative therapies, and working with mind/body approaches. He was interested but skeptical. I gave him reading assignments about psychoneuroimmunology, and he followed up on these by going to the University of Arizona medical library to look up more articles on the subject. After reading this material, he was excited and motivated to begin the work. He told me he wanted his hematologist on his team as well, in order to monitor his blood counts and be there in case of a crisis. I agreed and said I would be happy to review a treatment plan with his doctor.

A few days later he came back to see me. The hematologist had told him his ideas were crazy; that if he tried to discontinue his medication, he would land in the hospital in a matter of days. He had tried to give the hematologist copies of the articles he had found on mind/body approaches to autoimmunity, but the doctor had laughed at him and said he would not waste his time "reading garbage." This remark so infuriated the patient that he worked up his courage to fire his doctor, the first time in his life that he had defied a medical authority and taken into his own hands responsibility for treatment. With some effort he found another hematologist, who, despite some discomfort, was willing to watch over him and let him experiment. The patient made the recommended changes in his life and weaned himself from prednisone. His blood counts fluctuated for a period, then stabilized at better levels than when he was on the drug. This convinced him he was on the right track and bolstered his motivation to proceed.

2. ACTIVELY SEARCH FOR HELP

Successful patients search out possibilities for treatments and cures and follow up every lead they come across. They ask questions, read books and articles, go to libraries, write to authors, ask friends and neighbors for ideas, and travel to meet with practitioners who seem promising. Such behavior leads some doctors to label these patients difficult, noncompliant, or simply obnoxious, but there is reason to think that difficult patients are more likely to get better while nice ones finish last.

Remember the words of Kristin, the young woman who was healed from aplastic anemia (page 20): "There may be different ways to healing for different people but there is always a way. Keep searching!"

3. SEEK OUT OTHERS WHO HAVE BEEN HEALED

One of the most effective ways to neutralize medical pessimism is to find someone who had the same problem you do and is now healed. Whenever I come across people who have solved serious health problems, I ask them if they will allow me from time to time to send similarly affected patients for advice and guidance. For example, I know a man in his late thirties who developed rheumatoid arthritis fifteen years ago. For years he took larger and larger doses of suppressive medication, and he required several surgeries to correct worsening deformity of one hand. Then he began to notice that the fluctuating course of the disease followed his emotional ups and downs. He made a conscientious effort to develop a healthy lifestyle and cultivate evenness of mood; as a result, he has been able to stop the progression of the arthritis and eliminate the medication. I have sent him several patients with rheumatoid arthritis—young people who knew only the perspective of conventional rheumatologists and had no reason to believe they could take charge of their health. He helped convince them that they could modify their disease without depending on drugs and then got them started on the road to healing.

4. FORM CONSTRUCTIVE PARTNERSHIPS WITH HEALTH PROFESSIONALS

Successful patients often ally themselves with health professionals who support them in their search for answers. An ally can simply be a doctor who says, "I don't know what you're doing, but whatever it is, keep it up!" Or it can be a practitioner who takes an active hand in suggesting experiments. What you want is a professional who believes in you and in your ability to heal yourself, someone who empowers you in your search and makes you feel that you are not alone. Good doctors are willing to say "I don't know," and they will take the greatest pleasure in seeing you heal, whatever methods you decide to use.

5. DO NOT HESITATE TO MAKE RADICAL LIFE CHANGES

Many of the successful patients I have known are not the same people they were at the onset of illness. Their search for healing made them aware that they had to make significant changes in their lives: changes in relationships, jobs, places of residence, diet, habits, and so forth. In retrospect they see these changes as steps that were necessary to personal growth, but at the time the process was wrenching. Change is always difficult; major change can be very painful. Illness often forces us to look at issues and conflicts in our lives that we have ignored in the hope that they would disappear. Continuing to ignore them may block any possibility of spontaneous healing, while willingness to change may be a strong predictor of success.

6. REGARD ILLNESS AS A GIFT

Because illness can be such a powerful stimulus to change, perhaps the only thing that can force some people to resolve their deepest conflicts, successful patients often come to regard it as the greatest opportunity they have ever had for personal growth and development—truly a gift. Seeing illness as a misfortune, especially one that is undeserved, may obstruct the healing system. Coming to see illness as a gift that allows you to grow may unlock it.

7. CULTIVATE SELF-ACCEPTANCE

To accept oneself, with all of the imperfections, limitations, and defects that characterize every human being, represents a surrender to a higher will. Change seems more likely to occur in this climate of surrender than in a climate of confrontation with the universe. When you are sick, surrender does not mean giving up hope of renewed health. Rather it means accepting all the circumstances of your life, including present sickness, in order to move beyond them. Recall the stages of the process of grieving (see page 83): only with acceptance of loss does it become possible to move on to completion and healing. Recall also the words of one man who experienced spontaneous healing: "The trick is to get your ego out of the way, get your concepts out of the way, and just let the body heal itself. It knows how to do it."

18

MANAGING GENERAL CATEGORIES OF ILLNESS: SECRETS OF A HYGEIAN PRACTITIONER

IF YOU GET SICK, it is useful to know about therapeutic approaches that can give the healing system a boost, especially dietary modifications, specific supplements, herbal medicines, and alternative methods unknown to most conventional doctors. It is not my purpose to go through an exhaustive list of diseases with complete treatment plans, particularly since I believe that treatment must be customized for each individual, but I can offer you advice about the management of general categories of illness. Bear in mind that the suggestions in this chapter are not meant to be total replacements for standard medicine. Remember also that people react in different ways to substances they ingest. Although the treatments outlined below are safe and effective in my experience, idiosyncratic adverse reactions can occur in response to taking any herb or supplement. Stop using any remedy that causes problems. Also be patient with natural treatments; they usually take longer to work than strong, suppressive drugs. If you change your diet and begin a regimen of natural therapies, it may be six to eight weeks before you notice improvement. The improvement will be gradual, steady, and solid, because it represents lasting activity of the healing system rather than suppression of symptoms.

ALLERGY

Allergy is a learned response of the immune system to environmental agents that are not intrinsically harmful. The goal of good treatment should be to calm an overreactive immune system so that you can live with allergens and not sneeze, cough, or itch. Conventional treatments are more or less toxic and, because they are purely suppressive, may increase immune reactivity over time. The fact that allergies can suddenly come and suddenly go is encouraging; it indicates that the learned patterns of response are not fixed, that what the immune system has learned, it can unlearn. Spontaneous healing of allergy is not an infrequent occurrence. To increase its likelihood, it is a good idea to work on several fronts:

Dietary modification can reduce allergic responsiveness. The most important suggestions I can give are to follow a low-protein diet, to cut down on animal protein in general and, specifically, to eliminate cow's milk and products made from it, since milk protein acts as an irritant of the immune system in many people. Additionally, I recommend eating organically grown foods as much as possible, because I think residues of agricultural chemicals frequently contribute to immune system reactivity.

Supplement the diet with quercetin, a natural product obtained from buckwheat and citrus fruits. Quercetin stabilizes the membranes of cells that release histamine, the mediator of many allergic reactions. You can buy quercetin tablets in health food stores (some brands contain vitamin C and other related compounds). The recommended dose is 400 milligrams twice a day between meals. Quercetin is a preventive, not a symptomatic, treatment, so it is best to use it regularly. If allergies are seasonal, start taking it several weeks before you expect the onset of symptoms. Otherwise try it for two to three months, then gradually reduce the dose to determine if the improvements are maintained.

A good *herbal treatment* for hay fever, especially for allergic sneezing and itching eyes, ears, and throats, is stinging nettles (*Urtica dioica*), especially a freeze-dried extract of the leaves of this plant. (See Appendix for a source.) One to two capsules every two to four hours as needed will control symptoms with none of the toxicity of antihistamines and steroids. The safest standard drug for this problem is cromolyn sodium in the form of a nasal spray (Nasalcrom nasal solution), which works by a mechanism similar to that of quercetin.

Environmental modifications, such as installing air filters in the home, can reduce the allergenic load on the immune system and give it a better chance to calm down.

Mind/body interventions are important. Some people strongly allergic to roses will have allergic reactions on being shown plastic roses, indicating that learning at the level of the higher brain is involved in these misdirected responses of the immune system. Interactive guided imagery therapy may be especially helpful for allergic skin conditions like chronic hives and eczema.

AUTOIMMUNE DISEASE

In autoimmune disease, immune responses are directed against the body's own tissues, causing inflammatory changes and eventual damage to body structures. Predisposition to autoimmune disease may be inherited, and the disease may be triggered by infection or other physical stress or by emotional trauma. Any number of tissues and organs can become targets for the abnormal immune responses: nerves (multiple sclerosis), joints (rheumatoid arthritis), endocrine glands (myasthenia gravis and forms of thyroiditis), muscles (polymyositis), connective tissues throughout the body (systemic lupus erythematosus), kidneys (glomerulonephritis), and so on. The natural history of all of these diseases is marked by alternating periods of exacerbation and remission—a welcome pattern because it demonstrates the potential of the healing system to curb autoimmune disease. The conventional medical approach to this type of illness is unsatisfactory, relying as it does on suppressive drugs that are highly toxic.

Because autoimmune disease has multiple roots (among them heredity, stress, and environmental interactions), good treatment should address the total lifestyle of each patient. In addition to helping the healing system modulate immunity, it is useful to make adjustments in the diet that aim to reduce inflammation, since inflammatory changes mediate the tissue damage in these diseases.

Dietary modification would be the same as it is for allergy: a low-protein diet with minimal intake of foods of animal origin, especially milk and milk products; plenty of organically grown fruits, vegetables, and grains; elimination of polyunsaturated vegetable oils and artificially hydrogenated fats; inclusion of fish or other sources of omega-3 fatty acids, such as flax seeds.

Supplement the diet with antioxidant vitamins and minerals.

Herbal treatments include ginger for its anti-inflammatory effect (capsules of powdered, dried ginger are best; start with one twice a day) and feverfew, which shows efficacy in the treatment of autoimmune arthritis. (I recommend one to two capsules of freeze-dried feverfew leaves twice a day; see the Appendix for a source.) Another possibility is turmeric (*Curcuma longa*), the spice that makes curry and much prepared mustard yellow. Obtained from the rhizome of a ginger relative, turmeric has significant anti-inflammatory properties and can simply be added to food; however, it is more efficient to take curcumin, the yellow pigment that is the active component, in doses of 400 to 600 milligrams three times a day. Health food stores sell products that combine curcumin with bromelain, an enzyme from pineapple that enhances curcumin's absorption and has anti-inflammatory effects of its own.

Alternative medical treatments may be of great benefit, especially traditional Chinese medicine and Ayurvedic medicine. I have also seen cases of autoimmune disease respond to homeopathic treatment. (See Appendix for information on finding practitioners.)

Mind/body interventions are key in autoimmune disease, because the ups and downs of these diseases often correlate with emotional ups and downs, and because we know that mental factors influence immune responses. Psychotherapy, hypnotherapy, and guided imagery therapy are all useful and worth exploring.

CARDIOVASCULAR DISEASE

Most diseases of the heart and blood vessels are diseases of lifestyle that can be prevented by following a heart-healthy diet, by not smoking, by getting proper exercise, and by working at building nurturing emotional relationships and neutralizing anger and stress. Even when these diseases appear, their progress can be slowed, halted, or even reversed by changing lifestyle in the proper manner. Here are some additional suggestions:

Dietary modification should stress reduction of fat, especially saturated fat, and substitution of olive oil for other kinds of fat in the diet. A high-fiber, low-fat, vegetarian or semivegetarian diet with fish or other sources of omega-3 fatty acids is probably most protective of the heart. Garlic, onions, chili peppers, green tea, and turmeric all have protective effects on the cardiovascular system.

Supplement the diet with antioxidant vitamins and minerals, especially vitamin E. Two other natural products that I recommend are coenzyme Q (also known as Co-Q-10) and L carnitine. The former improves the use of oxygen at the cellular level, especially in heart muscle cells. I recommend taking 60 milligrams once a day, more if you can afford it, up to 200 milligrams a day. (It is not worth buying Co-Q-10 in dosage forms less than 60 milligrams per capsule.) L carnitine is an amino acid that also improves the metabolism of heart muscle cells (it, too, is not cheap). The recommended dose is 250–500 milligrams twice a day. Both products are available in health food stores and from vitamin suppliers. For cardiac arrhythmias, supplementation with magnesium may be very helpful. Try 1,000 milligrams of magnesium (citrate, gluconate, or chelate) at bedtime plus another 500 milligrams in the morning, along with equal amounts of calcium (citrate). I recommend the same doses of calcium and magnesium for help in managing high blood pressure.

Herbal treatments for the cardiovascular system include hawthorn (*Crataegus oxycantha*), a natural diuretic and heart tonic, useful in persons with coronary heart disease and heart failure, and tree ear mushrooms (*Auricularia polytricha*), an ingredient in Chinese cuisine that has an anticoagulant effect similar to that of aspirin. Encapsulated, freeze-dried extract of hawthorn is available (see Appendix); the dose is one to two capsules two to four times a day. You can buy dried tree ears in Oriental grocery stores. Reconstitute them by soaking in hot water until they expand and become soft; then discard any hard bits and add the mushrooms to soups or stir-fries. A reasonable dose is one tablespoon of the soaked mushrooms a day. Horse chestnut (*Aesculus hippocastanum*) provides a topical treatment for varicose veins. Creams containing horse chestnut extract, sometimes called "escin," are available in health food stores.

Regular aerobic exercise is one of the best influences on the heart and blood vessels, as are all techniques of relaxation and stress reduction.

DIGESTIVE DISORDERS

Here is another large category of diseases that are mostly related to lifestyle, especially to poor habits of eating and managing stress. Conventional medicine controls them poorly. Alternative medicine offers many safe and effective treatments, probably because the healing system, if given a chance, is often able to resolve these conditions completely. A common root cause of many digestive disorders, from esophageal reflux to constipation, is an imbalance between the intrinsic motility of the gastrointestinal musculature and the regulating influence of involuntary nerves that coordinate the whole system. There is so much nervous input to the GI tract that it is very susceptible to stress-induced distortions. In fact, along with the skin, the digestive system is the most common site of expression of stress-related illness.

Dietary modification should always be employed to improve digestive health and function. As a start, eliminate caffeine (especially coffee), tobacco, and other stimulant drugs. Alcohol can be a major irritant of the esophagus and stomach. Pay attention to which foods and combinations of foods cause distress, and change eating habits accordingly. Sometimes eating smaller amounts more frequently will make your digestive system function more smoothly.

Herbal treatment for digestive disorders is often quite effective. Chamomile and peppermint teas both work for simple heartburn and nausea; but peppermint, because it relaxes the sphincter muscle where the esophagus joins the stomach, may make esophageal reflux worse. Ginger in any form works for nausea. For severe gastritis, reflux, or peptic ulcer, try the licorice preparation DGL (see footnote on page 232), which increases the natural, protective mucus that coats the stomach lining. Peppermint oil in enteric-coated capsules, available at health food stores, is an excellent treatment for irritable bowel syndrome, diverticulitis, and other intestinal ailments. A good natural remedy for diarrhea and intestinal inflammation is carob powder, available at health food stores. Start with one tablespoon, mixed with some applesauce and honey to make it palatable. Take it with acidophilus (liquid or capsules from the health food store) on an empty stomach (at least an hour and a half before or three hours after eating). For constipation, the Ayurvedic preparation triphala is excellent; follow dosage recommendations on the product.

Relaxation is all-important. The breathing exercise described on pages 206–7 has especially beneficial effects on the GI system, but it must be practiced regularly. Biofeedback and yoga can be helpful, and I cannot recommend hypnotherapy and guided imagery therapy too highly.

Alternative medical approaches to digestive disorders that give the best results are naturopathy, homeopathy, traditional Chinese medicine, and Ayurvedic medicine. I would try these systems before resorting to allopathic drugs and surgery.

INFECTION

I have noted more than once in this book that the effectiveness of antibiotics for bacterial infections is rapidly declining as organisms develop resistance to them. Infections that are severe, fast moving, or involve vital organs are emergencies requiring allopathic supervision, but even in those cases it is worth using complementary methods to stimulate healing responses. For less severe infections and for chronic or recurrent infections that resist allopathic treatments, the primary focus should be to rouse the healing system to action. For accessible, localized infections, one of the best ways to accomplish this is to increase blood flow to affected areas by applying heat—for example, by using hot, wet compresses or soaks. You can also help the healing system fight infection by giving the body more rest, eating less, increasing fluid intake, and sweating in a steam room or sauna.

Dietary modification can reduce susceptibility to some kinds of infection. For example, cutting down on sugar of all sorts may decrease the frequency of urinary tract infections in women, and increasing intake of fresh fruits and vegetables will help build immunity.

Supplement the diet with antioxidant vitamins and minerals, especially with vitamin C, 2,000 milligrams two to three times a day for chronic or recurrent infections.

Herbal treatments abound for infections, from the familiar (garlic) to the exotic (Oriental mushrooms). Add raw garlic to the diet as a general measure and experiment with echinacea (*Echinacea purpurea* and related species), a native American herb with antibiotic and immune-enhancing properties. Echinacea preparations are readily available in health food stores and some drugstores. Taste them to make sure they cause a distinct numbing sensation on the tongue after a minute; otherwise they are not effective. Follow dosage recommendations on the product or use one dropperful of the tincture in a little warm water four times a day. For topical infections, try tea tree oil, obtained from an Australian tree (*Melaleuca alternifolia*).

Buy only one hundred percent pure tea tree oil from a health food store; it is an excellent disinfectant, useful in first-aid kits for the home and when traveling. For chronic or recurrent viral infections, try astragalus (see pages 177–79).

Alternative medicine can sometimes succeed with infectious illnesses when conventional medicine cannot. My first choice would be traditional Chinese medicine, which has a vast array of medicinal plants with antiviral, antibacterial, and immunomodulating properties.

Mind/body approaches should always be tried. At the least, they can enhance the efficacy of conventional drugs. At best, they can change the balance between the immune system and pathogenic germs in a way that favors resolution of the infection.

MEN'S HEALTH PROBLEMS

The prostate gland is a vulnerable point of male anatomy, often harboring stubborn infections in youth and enlarging in age to the point of interfering with urination. The main irritants of the prostate are coffee and other forms of caffeine, decaffeinated coffee, alcohol, tobacco, red pepper, dehydration, and either too frequent or too infrequent ejaculation. Prolonged sitting and repetitive jarring motion (as from riding a horse, bicycle, or motorcycle) also stress the gland.

Supplement the diet with zinc, 30 milligrams a day of the picolinate form. Also increase intake of soy foods; their phytoestrogens might protect the prostate from the unbalanced influence of male sex hormones.

Herbal treatment for prostatic enlargement relies on two plants: saw palmetto (*Serenoa repens*) and pygeum (*Pygeum africanum*). Use one or both, following dosage recommendations on the products. You can continue taking them indefinitely.

For sexual deficiency, traditional Chinese medicine offers many treatments, including ginseng (see pages 179–80), the preeminent male sexual tonic. Ayurvedic medicine contributes ashwaganda (*Withania somnifera*), newly available in health food stores. Follow dosages recommended on the product.

Mind/body methods are worth exploring in all sexual and genital problems, hypnotherapy and guided imagery therapy being especially useful.

MENTAL, EMOTIONAL, AND NERVOUS DISORDERS

For anxiety, even the most severe forms of anxiety, the best treatment I know is the breathing exercise on pages 206–7. By gradually changing the tone of the involuntary system, it allows deep, internal relaxation that promotes emotional healing. If you start practicing it now, you will have it ready to use in case of need. Regular exercise is also important, and, obviously, relaxation training can be very helpful. Two herbal treatments that I recommend frequently are passion flower (*Passiflora incarnata*) and valerian (*Valeriana officinalis*). The former, which is quite mild, can be taken as a tincture: one dropperful in a little warm water as needed, up to four times a day. The latter is a strong enough sedative to be used for insomnia, but small doses—say, ten drops of the tincture in a little warm water—can be used for daytime calming.

For depression, the best single treatment is vigorous, regular aerobic exercise, at least thirty minutes a day, five days a week. Avoidance of alcohol, sedatives, antihistamines, and other depressant drugs is advisable. Dietary modification—less protein and fat, more starches, fruits, and vegetables—may also make a difference. Try this regimen of supplements as well: In the morning, on arising, take 1,500 milligrams of DL-phenylalanine (DLPA, an amino acid), 100 milligrams of vitamin B-6, 500 milligrams of vitamin C, and a piece of fruit or a small glass of juice. Do not eat breakfast for at least an hour. (Use this formula cautiously if you have high blood pressure, as DLPA may worsen that condition temporarily. Start with a lower dose of the amino acid and monitor blood pressure frequently.)

MUSCULOSKELETAL DISORDERS

Acute and chronic musculoskeletal pain brings more patients to doctors' offices than many other categories of illness combined. Conventional drugs and surgery should be regarded as last resorts to be used only after aggressive experimentation with natural and alternative methods has failed to provide relief.

Dietary modification is less important here, except that it is useful to manipulate dietary fats to reduce any inflammatory processes.

That means eliminating polyunsaturated and artificially saturated fats and increasing intake of omega-3 fatty acids in any form.

Supplementation with the B-vitamin niacinamide can be very helpful for osteoarthritis. Start with 500 milligrams twice a day, increasing by 500 milligrams at three-week intervals if necessary to a maximum daily dose of 2,000 milligrams.

Herbal treatments for musculoskeletal pain include ginger, especially in dried form, and the Ayurvedic herb *Boswellia,* or the extract made from it, boswellin. Health food stores sell it; follow dosage recommendations on the products. Ginger and boswellin may provide relief in fibromyalgia and other conditions in which people complain that "it hurts all over." Also consider using curcumin, the anti-inflammatory agent from turmeric, as described under "Autoimmune Disease." For extensive bruises and hematomas resulting from trauma, an excellent treatment is bromelain, the pineapple enzyme you can find in capsules at health food stores. Take 200 to 400 milligrams three times a day on an empty stomach. Bromelain promotes healing of tissue injuries, but occasional individuals may develop an allergic rash from it; discontinue it if you develop any itching.

Mind/body interventions, again, are critical. Hypnotherapy can teach people how to distance themselves from chronic pain, which can help the pain to resolve more quickly. Other forms of stress reduction, including guided meditation, have worked for chronic pain syndromes after all conventional approaches have failed.

Alternative treatment is always worth trying for these maladies, especially osteopathic manipulation, chiropractic, therapeutic massages, and other forms of body work. Acupuncture can provide dramatic temporary relief of musculoskeletal pain and may promote healing of some conditions. In combination with Chinese herbal treatment, it may do wonders for individuals with arthritis and other chronically painful musculoskeletal ailments.

PAIN

Pain has two aspects: the physical sensation arising from some disturbance of body structure or function and the psychic perception of it. The latter aspect can be modified in several ways. My preference is for hypnotherapy, guided imagery, meditation, and acupuncture. Review the story of Ethan's back pain on pages 118–22, which describes the healing of chronic pain through purely psychic intervention.

To the extent that pain is the result of inflammation at the tissue level, it can be approached through all of the dietary changes, herbal treatments, and alternative medical approaches listed under "Autoimmune Disease" and "Musculoskeletal Disorders."

Therapeutic touch and other forms of energy healing can be dramatically effective in relieving pain.

SKIN DISORDERS

Because the skin has so many nerve endings, it is another very frequent site for stress-related problems. Again, conventional treatments for many skin diseases, especially topical steroid preparations, are suppressive in nature and potentially toxic.

Lifestyle changes can make a huge difference to the health of the skin, particularly protection from the damaging effects of sun exposure; decrease in frequency of washing with soap, which removes natural protective oils; assiduous use of moisturizers immediately after a bath or shower; and elimination of cosmetic products containing dyes and other harsh chemicals.

Dietary modification is also important in order to eliminate foods that may promote allergic and inflammatory changes and to provide nutrients needed for healthy development of skin, hair, and nails. In general, make the changes recommended under "Autoimmune Disease," being sure to provide adequate sources of omega-3 fatty acids. ·

Supplement the diet with antioxidant vitamins and minerals and with GLA (gamma-linolenic acid, an essential fatty acid of particular benefit to the skin); best sources are black currant oil and evening primrose oil, available in capsules at health food stores. The recommended dose of black currant oil is 500 milligrams twice a day. You will see changes in the skin, hair, and nails after six to eight weeks of continuous use.

Mind/body interventions should be tried in all cases of skin disease to take advantage of the high level of innervation of the skin. I usually send patients to skilled hypnotherapists and guided imagery therapists.

Alternative medicine can be more effective and less toxic than conventional medicine in managing skin disorders. In my experience the greatest chance for success is with homeopathy, Ayurvedic medicine, and traditional Chinese medicine, even for cases of psoriasis and other severe, chronic problems.

STRESS-RELATED DISORDERS

All illnesses should be assumed to be stress-related until proved otherwise. Even if stress is not the primary cause of illness, it is frequently an aggravating factor. To say that a bodily complaint is stress-related does not in any way mean that it is unreal or unimportant; it simply means that time spent at stress reduction and relaxation training may be very worthwhile in terms of obtaining relief. Some of the most common stress-related ailments are headache, insomnia, musculoskeletal pain (especially in the back and neck), gastrointestinal disorders of all sorts, skin disorders of all sorts, sexual deficiency, menstrual problems, and increased susceptibility to infection; that accounts for quite a few symptoms, visits to doctors, and prescriptions for suppressive drugs. In all of these conditions, regardless of what other interventions you try, I recommend working with the relaxing breath, using mind/body approaches, and all relaxation methods that appeal to you in order to give the healing system the best possible chance to solve any problems on the physical level.

URINARY SYSTEM DISORDERS

Lifestyle change is critical here, because the most common stressors of the kidneys are tobacco; high blood pressure; dehydration; alcohol, caffeine, and other stimulant drugs; and high-protein diets. The metabolism of protein puts a huge workload on the kidneys. If you know that you have abnormal kidneys or have had any kidney disease in the past, the most important preventive strategies you can employ are to adopt a very low-protein diet and never to allow yourself to become dehydrated.

Because the urinary system filters toxins from the blood and concentrates them in urine, it is susceptible to toxic injury that may initiate malignant transformation, especially in the bladder. Following the advice in Chapter 10 of this book on protecting yourself from toxins will help you, as will the regular use of antioxidant supplements.

Women are much more vulnerable than men to urinary tract infections. They can reduce susceptibility by eliminating or minimizing the use of tobacco, alcohol, and caffeine, by avoiding traumatic or excessive sexual activity, and by always maintaining good urinary output by drinking plenty of water. Also, cranberries contain a substance that makes it harder for bacteria to stick to the bladder wall. If you are experiencing frequent urinary tract infections, try drinking cranberry juice often or use unsweetened cranberry concentrate from the health food store that you can dilute to your own taste with water or sparkling water. Taking acidophilus in liquid or capsule form after meals can also help increase resistance to bladder infections.

An *herbal treatment* that can help the urinary tract is bearberry, or uva ursi (*Arctostaphylos uva-ursi*). Tinctures and encapsulated extracts of the leaves can be found at health food stores and are useful for a variety of urinary problems. The dose is one dropperful of the tincture in a little water or one or two capsules of extract three to four times a day. This should be used as a short-term remedy only, since prolonged use may cause irritation.

Mind/body methods can be extremely valuable in managing urinary problems. Guided imagery with a trained therapist would be my first choice.

Alternative medicine can also be helpful, especially naturopathy, homeopathy, and traditional Chinese medicine.

WOMEN'S HEALTH PROBLEMS

Menstrual problems, including painful periods and premenstrual syndrome (PMS), can be moderated by eliminating caffeine and inflammation-promoting fats (see "Autoimmune Disease," pages 255–56) and by supplementing the diet with GLA (see "Skin Disorders," pages 263–64), vitamin E, and vitamin B-6 (100 milligrams twice a day). Dong quai (*Angelica sinensis*) is a useful tonic for a wide range of female problems (see page 181). Another useful herbal treatment is chaste tree (*Vitex agnus-castus*), which may be taken in tincture or capsule form (one dropperful of the tincture in water or one or two capsules twice a day); it helps regulate the female reproductive cycle. Regular, moderate aerobic exercise is also important.

To avoid imbalances of estrogen metabolism, it is essential to avoid consuming foods with added estrogen (commercially raised meats and poultry), to avoid exposure to pollutants that may have estrogenic activity, to minimize consumption of alcohol, to eat a low-fat diet, and to increase intake of soy foods for their protective phytoestrogens.

Menopausal symptoms can be managed without resorting to hormone replacement therapy, although women who are already losing bone density or are at high risk for coronary heart disease may choose hormone replacement for those reasons. An herbal formula that will reduce or eliminate hot flashes in most women consists of dong quai, chaste tree, and damiana (*Turnera diffusa*). Take one dropperful of the tinctures of each, or two capsules of each, once a day at noon.

Mind/body approaches are invaluable in all disorders of the female reproductive system. Results of hypnotherapy and guided imagery therapy can be rapid, dramatic, and surprisingly effective.

19

CANCER AS A SPECIAL CASE

CANCER HAS ALWAYS been with us. All living organisms are susceptible to it, and the more complex the organism, the higher the risk. A great many pressures on cells push them toward malignant transformation; malignant cells are dangerous because they do not die when they are supposed to, do not stay in place, and do not limit their growth to conform to the general laws that regulate the economies of whole organisms.

Nevertheless, there is a radical difference between a transformed cell and a cancerous growth with power to kill its host. When cells become malignant, they announce their new identity by displaying abnormal antigens on their surface membranes. An ongoing job of the immune system is to scan cells in order to recognize and eliminate those that are not-self, that do not belong in the body. Given the number of cell divisions constantly occurring, and given all the possibilities for malignant transformation, the seeds of cancers are surely being created unceasingly, and just as surely the immune system eliminates them. Immune surveillance to weed out malignant cells is a key function of the healing system, a defense against cancer that our bodies developed in the course of evolution. Yet the incidence of cancer is rising sharply in the world today, because our defenses are overwhelmed. In addition to the natural carcinogenic agents that have always been with us, we have added to the environment a great number of manmade ones. By following the advice in Part Two of this book on optimizing the healing system, you can strengthen your defenses and reduce your risks of getting cancer.

Given the inadequacy of current treatments for this disease, prevention is all-important.

Once cancer becomes established in the body, and particularly when it has spread from its initial site (metastasis), it is very difficult to cure. We fear cancer because it develops insidiously from within, because it resists our best technological weaponry, and because it has great destructive potential. To understand why cancer presents such a difficult challenge, you need grasp only one basic fact: *The presence of cancer in the body, even in its earliest stages, already represents significant failure of the healing system.* In order for a transformed cell to give rise to a detectable tumor, it must have escaped immune destruction, undergone many divisions, and produced countless generations of daughter cells, all without interference. With most other diseases, even severe ones like coronary heart disease and multiple sclerosis, it is reasonable to expect much of the healing system. With cancer, by the time a lump is noticed, failure of healing mechanisms is already a fixed pattern.

Current therapies for cancer, both conventional and alternative, are far from satisfactory. Conventional medicine has three main treatments: surgery, radiation, and chemotherapy, of which only the first makes sense. If cancer is in one location only and accessible to a surgeon's knife, it can be excised and eliminated permanently. Unfortunately, only a small percentage of cancers meet those criteria, principally cancers of the skin and uterine cervix. In far too many cases cancer has already spread to more than one site by the time of its discovery or is somewhere in the body that is beyond the reach of a surgical cure.

Radiation and chemotherapy are crude treatments that will be obsolete before long. Both work by killing dividing cells; the assumption made by doctors who use them is that cancerous cells divide faster than normal ones. Unfortunately, that is true only for a small percentage of cancers, principally childhood cancers, leukemias, lymphomas, testicular cancer, and a few others. In most cases, cells of cancers have lower division rates than the most active normal tissues of the body: the skin, the lining of the gastrointestinal tract, the bone marrow, and other immune structures. The well-known side effects of radiation and chemotherapy—loss of hair, loss of appetite, nausea, and vomiting—represent damage to the skin and the GI tract. Damage to the immune system is less obvious and much more of a concern. If you have cancer and are faced with a decision about whether to use conventional therapies, the question you must try to answer is this: Will the damage done to the cancer justify the damage done to the immune system?

Ultimately, hopes for cures of cancer are equivalent to hopes for immune responses, because the immune system has the potential to recognize and eliminate malignant tissue. The future of cancer treatment is not in bigger and better cytotoxic weapons (which will never be capable of killing malignant cells without also killing fast-growing normal cells). Instead, the future will bring immunotherapy capable of rousing a slumbering immune system to action. Some forms of immunotherapy are now available, but most are still experimental.

Spontaneous remission of cancer—an all-too-rare event—appears to result from sudden immune activation, which demonstrates the potential of the immune system to react against malignant growth, sometimes with such vigor that large masses of tumor tissue dissolve in a matter of hours or days. Here is an account of that kind of cancer remission, sent to me by Robert Anderson, M.D., of Edmonds, Washington, a past president of the American Holistic Medical Association.

The patient, Helen B., was a sixty-seven-year-old hairdresser who came to him in 1985 for a routine checkup. Dr. Anderson felt a suggestion of a mass during the vaginal examination; he thought it might be scar tissue from a previous hysterectomy but worried when blood tests revealed the patient to be anemic with abnormal liver function. Dr. Anderson referred her to a gynecologist, but she procrastinated, believing that her previous physician had described these same findings several years before. Both of her former doctors had died, and her records could not be located. When Dr. Anderson re-examined her six weeks later, the mass was "significantly larger," and blood test results were significantly worse. He insisted that she see a gynecologist and undergo further tests, one of which, an ultrasound examination, revealed "a left pelvic mass consistent with ovarian origin."

One month later, Helen B. underwent exploratory surgery. The surgeon found a large tumor mass in the left and central pelvis, extensively involving the small and large bowel, and noted that "widespread 3–9 mm peritoneal lesions were studded throughout the pelvic and abdominal cavities, exceeding one hundred in number;

five of them were biopsied." The pathology report of the biopsies described "malignant tumor with moderate variation in cell size and shape. . . . The tumor appears as a poorly differentiated carcinoma, possibly of ovarian origin." Several days later, Helen underwent more surgery, for removal of the mass and attached portions of small and large bowel. She was left with a colostomy and obvious tumor still in her abdomen. The pathologist's final diagnosis was "poorly differentiated carcinoma of probable ovarian origin."

Poorly differentiated carcinoma of any origin is not a good kind of tumor to have. The primitive cells tend to be highly malignant and invasive; in Helen B.'s case, widespread metastasis had already occurred throughout the abdominal cavity, making for a poor prognosis. The surgeon wrote to Dr. Anderson: "I recommend oncological consultation and commencement of chemotherapy. The colostomy does not need to be considered permanent. After the first course of chemotherapy, probably within six months, we should re-explore her, and at that time we could close the colostomy." But Helen did not want to go to an oncologist or to take chemotherapy. She went to Dr. Anderson again and said, "I want you to tell me what I have to do to recover." He outlined for her a comprehensive program that included a low-fat, low-sugar, high-fiber vegetarian diet, supplementation with antioxidant vitamins and minerals, regular exercise when possible, regular meditation incorporating visualization of tumor shrinkage, and "modifying her attitude toward her husband, including forgiveness," since marital discord was a major source of stress in her life. He also insisted on a visit to an oncologist, and Helen went, albeit reluctantly. The oncologist, who was very concerned about the residual cancer, urged chemotherapy "now rather than later when the tumor is bulkier and our chances for a good outcome are much less," but Helen refused, saying that she and God would win the battle.

A month after the surgery her anemia resolved and her liver function returned to normal. She felt strong and confident. Dr. Anderson encouraged her, noting that "her belief in the divine was evangelistic; I reinforced her hope with every encouragement." Helen hated the colostomy and began to demand that the surgeon undo it. He was unwilling to operate until she had undergone chemotherapy, but her refusal was so adamant and so persistent that he finally relented and reoperated two and a half months after the removal of the tumor. He reported of this operation that "the surgery was long and tedious. The adhesions encountered merely entering the peritoneal cavity were among the worst I had ever seen. . . . The hundreds of 3–9 mm peritoneal tumors appeared as before. Seven of them from various locations were biopsied." But this time the pathology report on the biopsies was quite different; it showed "inflammatory tissue with moderate cell variation and no malignant characteristics." The surgeon's comment on receiving this news was, "She is a very interesting lady."

Helen B. quickly returned to normal life and health, continuing the program that Dr. Anderson had recommended to her. Two years later she was divorced from her husband, which seemed to provide emotional relief. Dr. Anderson wrote: "In 1987, approximately two years following her first visit with me, she developed an incisional hernia at the site of the previous surgical operation. It became problematic, and she underwent surgery for yet a fourth time to repair it. At the time of operation, the surgeon, with my assistance, took advantage of the opportunity to reexplore her abdomen briefly. The adhesions were totally gone; *there were no residual peritoneal tumors and no evidence of cancer anywhere.*" Helen B. died at seventy-five of unrelated causes, nearly eight years after her original diagnosis.

What happened in this woman's abdomen that eliminated widely disseminated cancer and restored her internal organs to good health? Her healing system, probably making use of immune mechanisms, was surely responsible; but why did it not act before? Did removal of the main mass of tumor tissue somehow activate a healing response? If so, why doesn't this happen more often? In most patients with metastatic cancer of this sort, tumors will regrow, often in spite of aggressive cytotoxic therapy and often with fatal results. If an immune response is the best hope for a total cure of cancer, then one must be cautious indeed about using cytotoxic treatments that can damage the immune system.

Cancer treatments abound in the world of alternative medicine, most of them much less toxic than radiation and chemotherapy, but none of them works reliably for large numbers of patients. Many of the therapies I have looked into appear to have induced remissions in some people; in many more they improve quality of life for a time, yet the cancers remain and continue to grow. If there were a reliably effective alternative treatment for cancer, we would all know about it soon enough.

Let me summarize the information in this chapter so far: Cells turn malignant constantly, and normally the healing system eliminates them. Given the increasing environmental pressures toward malignant transformation and the inadequacy of cancer treatments, it is imperative to maintain our healing systems in good working order and to know how to reduce cancer risks. Spontaneous healing of cancer occurs but is much less common than spontaneous healing of most other diseases because the healing system has already failed if a malignant cell is able to give rise to a detectable tumor. When remission does occur, the mechanism is immune activation; therefore, great care must be exercised in deciding whether or not to use cytotoxic treatments (radiation and chemotherapy), because damage to the immune system may reduce the long-term possibility of a curative healing response.

So how should you proceed if you or a loved one develops cancer? The first step must be to determine whether, and how, to use conventional treatments. Here are some guidelines:

• If surgical excision of a tumor is possible, have it done. Even partial removal of a large tumor mass ("debulking") may help the healing system contain cancerous growth.

• Find out whether any forms of immunotherapy are available for your particular type of cancer. If your oncologist does not know of any, call the National Cancer Institute or cancer research centers at universities.

• If radiation and chemotherapy are urged on you, obtain statistics on their success rates for the particular type and stage of cancer you have. You cannot always rely on oncologists here, since they have a vested interest in promoting these therapies and are usually unfamiliar with alternatives. I have known oncologists to represent a regimen of chemotherapy as producing an "eighty percent cure rate" when all the scientific literature showed was an eighty-percent five-year cancer-free survival. What happened to the patients after five years? If you are trying to place your bet wisely, you want to know the accurate odds. In a few cases, books exist to guide patients in making these difficult decisions. More often than not, the only way you will acquire the information you need is to visit a medical library and look up articles on the proposed treatment.

• Remember that radiation and chemotherapy are themselves mutagenic and carcinogenic. It is possible to calculate the percentage of patients exposed to these therapies who, if they survive long enough, will develop independent cancers that are direct results of treatment.

• Natural chemotherapeutic agents like vincristine from the Madagascar periwinkle and taxol from the Pacific yew tree are no safer than synthetic ones. All forms of chemotherapy—natural or chemical, old or new, singly or in combination—are cell-killing agents that damage DNA and injure actively dividing cells, including those of the immune system.

• In general, radiation is safer than chemotherapy because it can be directed to one part of the body. Still, it may cause severe scarring that can interfere with future organ function.

• If immunotherapy is not an option and if the success rates of conventional therapies are good for your type and stage of cancer, then avail yourself of them without worrying about the risks. Those therapies may give you time to explore other options; and by working to optimize your healing system, you can moderate their side effects.

• If you decide to proceed with radiation or chemotherapy, discontinue use of antioxidant supplements during treatment, since they may protect cancer cells along with normal cells. Resume the supplements as soon as treatment ends.

• If, after reviewing the statistical evidence for the usefulness of radiation and chemotherapy for your particular type and stage of cancer, you decide not to undergo those treatments, you should then investigate alternative therapies.

Here are a few suggestions regarding alternative cancer therapies:

• It is just as important to seek good statistical information on outcomes from the use of alternative treatments. Ask to see any published data supporting treatments that interest you. Published data may be scant or lacking here, so you may have to rely on the statements of providers.

• Try to determine whether there is any risk of toxicity or harm from the therapies in question.

• Ask for names of patients you might contact who have undergone the therapies. If providers will not give you this information, be wary.

Regardless of whether you choose conventional or alternative treatment, there are general recommendations that everyone with cancer should follow:

• Because it represents failure of the healing system, cancer, even in its early and localized stages, is a systemic disease. Patients must work to improve general health and resistance by making changes on all levels: physical, mental/emotional, and spiritual.

• As a minimum, I recommend changing diet according to the principles reviewed in Part Two, Chapter 2; maintaining a program of regular exercise; taking antioxidant supplements; using tonic herbs, especially those with immune-enhancing effects; learning visualization or guided imagery techniques to help the healing system contain the cancer; working to heal relationships (with parents, children, and spouses, for example); and making whatever changes in lifestyle are necessary to give yourself the best chance for healing to occur.

• In addition, try to find people who have experienced healing of cancer, preferably those who have had your particular kind of cancer. Read accounts of healing and books that increase your confidence in your own healing capacity.

• Seek out healers. Get all the help you can find.

If the healing system is not able to eliminate cancer completely, it may be able to do something else: slow or contain malignant growth to allow a period of relatively good health. Here is the story of one patient who did remarkably well even though cancer eventually caused her death.

Barbara S. came to me at the beginning of 1989, five and a half years after she was diagnosed with breast cancer and had undergone standard treatment: mastectomy and chemotherapy. She believed that if she made it through five years without a recurrence, she would be out of danger; but just at the fifth anniversary of her diagnosis, she fell and injured her right hip, which would not heal. Tests revealed the bone to be weakened by the presence of tumor. The cancer was not gone; it was now present as bone metastases throughout her skeleton—shocking news for Barbara and her family. Her doctor started her on tamoxifen, an estrogen antagonist, and told her he would order another course of chemotherapy if that did not shrink the tumors in her bones.

In the next few months Barbara made drastic changes in her life. She took a sabbatical from her job as a college dean, visited a number of counselors and psychotherapists, started yoga, began practicing visualization therapy, inaugurated a vitamin regimen, improved her diet, began swimming regularly, made arrangements to receive regular shiatsu treatments, took a Chinese herbal formula for cancer, and worked with healers. For the next three years, contrary to all the statistics for disseminated breast cancer, Barbara was in good health and looked so well that most people who met her could not believe she had cancer. During this period, I sent to Barbara several patients of mine newly diagnosed with breast cancer, who were frightened and confused about which steps to take. She was a great help to them. I also invited her to my classes to tell her story to groups of medical students. They found her to be an inspiring speaker who made a great case for taking charge of one's life and learning how to combine conventional and alternative therapies. Above all she demonstrated that recurrence of cancer does not automatically condemn a patient to sickness and rapid decline.

In the fall of 1992, Barbara's cancer advanced, with new metastases in her liver. She underwent chemotherapy and a trial of an experimental drug, investigated other alternative therapies, and continued most of the program she had developed to maintain her general health. She lived for another year and a half, during which she was very close to her family. Her doctors constantly expressed amazement at her longevity and vigor in the face of an overwhelming disease, and she continued to inspire many people with whom she came in contact. Barbara's healing system was unable to eradicate her cancer, but it held it in check for a long time, during which she accomplished a great deal.

CANCER WILL ALWAYS be with us. Prevention remains the best strategy for managing it, and that depends on the integrity of the healing system. As environmental pressures toward malignant transformation of cells increase, it will be ever more important to know how to optimize your healing potential. New and better cancer treatment is on the horizon in the form of immunotherapy, methods that will take advantage of natural healing mechanisms to recognize and destroy malignant cells without harming normal ones. In the meantime, a concerted effort to discover and study cases of spontaneous remission may help us understand that phenomenon and increase its incidence. To make wise decisions regarding the use of existing therapies for cancer you must have reliable information about their benefits and risks. Whatever specific treatments people decide to use, they must also work with all due diligence to improve general health in order to give the healing system the best chance to check cancer's spread.

AFTERWORD:
PRESCRIPTIONS FOR SOCIETY

IMAGINE A FUTURE world in which medicine was oriented toward healing rather than disease, where doctors believed in the natural healing capacity of human beings and emphasized prevention above treatment. Except for urgent care facilities, hospitals in such a world might more resemble spas, where patients could learn and practice the principles of healthy living, where they would learn to eat and prepare healthy food, learn to take care of the physical needs of their bodies, learn to use their minds in the service of healing, and become less rather than more dependent on health professionals. Even in urgent care facilities, technology would be used to help the healing system, as by stimulating regeneration of damaged organs. In these facilities the best ideas and methods of both conventional and alternative medicine would be available to all patients. In such a world doctors and patients would be partners working toward the same ends, with malpractice litigation a rare event rather than a commonplace. Insurance companies would happily reimburse for preventive education and natural treatments, knowing that these efforts were in their own best interests.

What stands in the way of moving health care in these directions? Here are the main obstacles that I see:

• Medical education is frozen in a disease-oriented mode. The clinical training of doctors remains a brutal initiation that makes it very difficult for students to maintain healthy lifestyles and develop the mental and spiritual qualities of healers.

• Insurance companies dictate how medicine is practiced by their policies of reimbursement. They will not pay for most of the interventions described in this book because they say they do not have research data to support their effectiveness or their cost-effectiveness compared to conventional treatments.

• Research on healing and on alternative medicine is primitive or nonexistent because the people who set research priorities and disburse research funds are not interested in these fields.

• The biomedical model from which medical scientists work stifles movement toward Hygeian medicine. From that model's materialistic perspective, doctors can easily dismiss most of the ideas in this book as unscientific and unworthy of investigation.

And what are the remedies for this situation?

I believe that the root problem is medical eduction. If future doctors were taught alternative models of science and health, were encouraged to study the healing power of nature, and were allowed to develop themselves into healthy role models for patients, all the obstacles listed above would begin to melt away. These new doctors would want to do the research that will eventually change standards of practice and lead insurance companies to spend their money in better ways. They would know how to take belief projected onto them by patients and reflect it back in ways that increase the occurrence of spontaneous healing. They would be able to design and staff new kinds of health care institutions that would be more like spas than hospitals, and they would recreate the trust between doctors and patients that makes lawsuits unthinkable.

Having said that, I must also say that I am cynical about the prospects for radical reform of medical education, even though I am committed to trying to bring it about. My cynicism goes back to my days as a first-year medical student in 1964 and has been reinforced by my experience on a medical school faculty. Many of my classmates at Harvard had majored in humanities rather than science as undergraduates, and many were not sure they wanted to be doctors. We were a restive group, and we were dismayed by the quality of instruction we received in our basic science course. Instead of being taught how to think about science and health, instead of learning general principles of human biology, we were inundated with masses of detail that we were expected to regurgitate on frequent exams. Many of us had experienced much better teaching in college, and we complained bitterly. The faculty put us off by saying that a brand-new curriculum, the product of much work by committees and subcommittees, was to be unveiled in the second semester: an integrated curriculum that was to be a model for medical schools of the future. What you are getting now is the old stuff, they told us, so please stop complaining and be patient.

Came the first day of the new curriculum. Instead of studying traditional subjects like embryology, anatomy, physiology, and biochemistry, we were now going to study systems of the body, and the first unit was to focus on the heart. An embryologist delivered an incredibly detailed sixty-minute lecture on the embryology of the heart. Then an anatomist gave an equally detailed lecture on cardiac anatomy. And so on for physiology and biochemistry. At the end of four hours, we were dazed, confused, and angry. This was supposed to be integrated teaching? It was integration by juxtaposition, nothing more. And I am sorry to say that in all the years since, I have listened to committees and subcommittees proposing ideas for curriculum reform and there has been no progress whatsoever. It all amounts to reshuffling the deck and dealing out the same cards in a different order.

What I mean by radical reform of medical education is this:

• Basic instruction in the philosophy of science, with reference to new models based on quantum physics that replace old concepts of Newtonian mechanism and Cartesian dualism. Such instruction would include information on probability and gambling theory, would discuss possible interactions of the observer and the observed, and would present models that could account for the nonphysical causation of physical events.

• Instruction in the history of medicine with reference to the development of major systems like traditional Chinese medicine, homeopathy, and osteopathy.

• Emphasis on the healing power of nature and the body's healing system.

- Emphasis on mind/body interactions, including placebo responses, medical hexing, and psychoneuroimmunology.

- Instruction in psychology and spirituality in addition to information about the physical body.

- Reduction in the amount of factual knowledge students are now required to memorize to pass certifying examinations. If students learn how to learn and know the general structure of knowledge in the various medical sciences, they will be able to look up the details as they need them, especially as this information becomes available in computerized formats.

- Provision of practical experience in the areas of nutrition, exercise, relaxation, meditation, and visualization. Students should be evaluated not only on factual knowledge but on personal progress in developing healthy lifestyles.

- Practical experience with the basic techniques of alternative medicine, such as herbalism, nutritional medicine, manipulation, body work, breath work, acupuncture, and guided imagery, in addition to the basic techniques of allopathic medicine.

- Instruction on how to design and conduct research in medicine and how to evaluate published research.

- Instruction in the art of communication, including interviewing patients, taking medical histories, and presenting treatments in ways that are likely to activate the body's healing system.

In addition to these changes in the training of doctors, I would insist on the creation of a National Institute of Health and Healing within the National Institutes of Health. The mission of this institute would be to investigate all healing phenomena, including spontaneous remissions of cancer and other diseases, placebo responses, and faith healing. The present Office of Alternative Medicine should operate within this organization with a greatly expanded budget to conduct research on the efficacy of alternative treatments and their cost-effectiveness compared to conventional treatments. Another goal of the Institute of Health and Healing should be to develop a National Registry of Healing, classified by diseases and extensively cross-referenced. This information should be available to all health professionals and patients, so that if you develop scleroderma, for example, you can obtain a list of persons in your area of the country who have experienced healing of scleroderma, and you or your doctor can contact them to discover what steps they took. Not only will this information permit researchers to compile data on the most promising treatments for particular diseases, it will also, I predict, increase the incidence of spontaneous healing.

The specifics of health care differ from country to country, but in all countries conventional medicine is caught in an economic crunch because of its reliance on technology that is inherently expensive. In addition a powerful consumer movement is responsible for a renaissance of alternative medicine worldwide and the growing openness to it within the medical profession. Doctors, hospitals, and universities are starting to consider ideas about health care that would have been unthinkable a decade ago. As a consumer of health care, you have great power to help accelerate this change and direct attention to spontaneous healing in your society. The time is right for change. The direction in which medicine needs to move is clear.

ACKNOWLEDGMENTS

This book was written mostly during a summer of record heat and dryness in the Sonoran Desert of southern Arizona and in the midst of a major move my family made from one end of the Tucson valley to the other. Early in the move I lost my office and a comfortable place to write. Mel Zuckerman of Canyon Ranch came to the rescue by offering me a guest house to use as a writing studio. Without his help, this book would not have seen the light of day so soon. I am much indebted to him and to Enid Zuckerman, and to Gary Frost, Jerry Cohen, Jonah Liebrecht, and other personnel at Canyon Ranch for their generous hospitality.

My agent, Richard Pine of Arthur Pine Associates, was instrumental in finding the right publisher for the book and motivating me to get to work on it. He also contributed useful insights and facts. And I thank Marly Rusoff and Sara Davidson for introducing me to Richard. Jonathan Segal, my editor at Alfred A. Knopf, gave the manuscript great attention while it was in preparation, for which I am most grateful.

Persons who contributed information to the book include Dr. James Dalen and Dr. Jean Wilson of the University of Arizona Health Sciences Center; Dr. Robert Anderson, Dr. William Manahan, Dr. Amy Stine, Dr. Michael T. Murray, Mark Blumenthal, Stephen Foster, Deborah Coryell, Kay Swetnam, Paul Stamets, and all the patients who graciously consented to let me use their stories of healing in these pages. Pete Craig of the University of Arizona College of Medicine gave me excellent research assistance, and a number of readers of the manuscript made valuable suggestions: Melanie Anderson, Brian Becker, Sue Fleishman, Woody Wickham, and Sabine Kremp especially.

Kevin Barry, senior hydrotherapist at Canyon Ranch, kept me relaxed and in good spirits while I was writing, and Dr. Dean Ornish gave me pep talks when I was feeling overwhelmed.

Finally, I must express special thanks to my old friend and sometime coauthor, Winifred Rosen, who spent a great deal of time and energy helping me polish the writing to a point that satisfied both of us.

Andrew Weil
Tucson, Arizona
Spring 1995

Appendix:

Finding Practitioners, Supplies, and Information

UNITED STATES OF AMERICA

Here is a listing of organizations that can help you find practitioners of therapies mentioned in this book:

Acupuncture

American Academy of Medical Acupuncture
5820 Wilshire Boulevard, Suite 500
Los Angeles, California 90036
213 937-5514

Biofeedback

Biofeedback Certification Institute of America
10200 West 44th Avenue, Suite 304
Wheat Ridge, Colorado 80033
303 420-2902

Cranial Therapy

Cranial Academy
3500 De Pauw Boulevard, Suite 1080
Indianapolis, Indiana 46268
317 879-0713

Feldenkrais Work

The Feldenkrais Guild
P.O. Box 489
Albany, Oregon 97321
800 775-2118

Guided Imagery Therapy

Academy for Guided Imagery
P.O. Box 2070
Mill Valley, California 94942
415 389-9324

Herbal Medicine

American Herbalists Guild
P.O. Box 1683
Soquel, California 95073
408 464-2441

Herb Research Foundation
1007 Pearl Street, Suite 200
Boulder, Colorado 80302
303 449-2265

Holistic Medicine

American Holistic Medical Association
4101 Lake Boone Trail, Suite 201
Raleigh, North Carolina 27607
919 787-5146

Homeopathy

National Center for Homeopathy
801 North Fairfax Street, Suite 306
Alexandria, Virginia 22314
703 548-7790

Hypnotherapy

American Society of Clinical Hypnosis
2250 East Devon Avenue, Suite 336
Des Plaines, Illinois 60018
708 297-3317

Naturopathy

American Association of Naturopathic Physicians
2366 Eastlake Avenue East, Suite 322
Seattle, Washington 98102
206 323-7610

Osteopathic Manipulative Therapy

American Academy of Osteopathy
3500 De Pauw Boulevard, Suite 1080
Indianapolis, Indiana 46268
317 879-1881

Rolfing

Rolf Institute
205 Canyon Boulevard
Boulder, Colorado 80306
303 449-5903

Traditional Chinese Medicine

The American Foundation of Traditional Chinese Medicine
505 Beach Street
San Francisco, California 94133
415 776-0502

Institute for Traditional Medicine
2017 Southeast Hawthorne
Portland, Oregon 97214
503 233-4907

Trager Work

The Trager Institute
33 Millwood
Mill Valley, California 94941
415 388-2688

Resources and Supplies

The following companies sell products mentioned in this book:

Chinese Tonics and Medicinal Herbs

The Tea Garden Herbal Emporium
903 Colorado Boulevard, Suite 200
Santa Monica, California 90405
310 450-0188

Freeze-Dried Herbal Extracts and Tinctures

Eclectic Institute
14385 Southeast Lusted Road
Sandy, Oregon 97055
800 332-4372

Ginger Preparations

New Moon Extracts, Inc.
99 Main Street
Brattleboro, Vermont 05301
802 257-0018

Maitake Mushrooms

Maitake Products, Inc.
P.O. Box 1354
Paramus, New Jersey 07653
800 747-7418

Fungi Perfecti
P.O. Box 7634
Olympia, Washington 98507
800 780-9126

Organic Produce

Eden Acres, Inc.
12100 Lina Center Road
Clinton, Michigan 49236
517 456-4288
Distributes directories of organic growers.

Mothers & Others for a Livable Planet
40 West 20th Street
New York, New York 10011
212 242-0010

Radiation Shields for Computer Displays

NoRad Corporation
1549 11th Street
Santa Monica, California 90401
800 262-3260

Vitamins and Supplements

L & H Vitamins
37–10 Crescent Street
Long Island City, New York 11101
800 221-1152

The Vitamin Shoppe
4700 Westside Avenue
North Bergen, New Jersey 07047
800 223-1216

Detailed instructions for management of common medical conditions with natural remedies that take advantage of the body's healing system will be found in my book *Natural Health, Natural Medicine: A Comprehensive Manual for Wellness and Self-Care* (Boston: Houghton Mifflin, revised edition, 1995).

If you would like information on my seminars, lectures, and informational products, including a monthly newsletter I write on health and healing, please write to:

Andrew Weil, M.D.
P.O. Box 697
Vail, Arizona 85641

UNITED KINGDOM

Some practitioners for therapies mentioned in the text might be difficulty to locate, for example, practitioners of biofeedback, visualisation therapy or feldenkrais, so contact the Institute of Complementary Medicine:

Institute of Complementary Medicine
P.O. Box 194
London SE16 1QZ
0171 237 5165
Holds the British Register of Complementary Practitioners.

Other general and useful contacts include:

British Complementary Medicine Association
39 Prestbury Road
Pittville
Cheltenham
Gloucestershire GL52 2PT
01242 226770

Council for Complementary and Alternative Medicine
Park House
206 Latimer Road
London W10 6RE
0181 968 3862

Centre for Complementary Health Studies
University of Exeter
Streatham Court
Rennes Drive
Exeter EX4 4PU
01392 433828

Acupuncture

British Acupuncture Council
Park House
206 Latimer Road
London W10 6RE
0181 964 0222
Publishes a Directory of British Acupuncturists.

Aromatherapy

Aromatherapy Organisations Council
3 Latymer Close
Braybrooke
Market Harborough
Leicestershire LE16 8LN
01858 434242
This is the umbrella organisation with 4,500 practitioners. It also represents the leading aromatherapy organisations in the United Kingdom.

Aromatherapy Trade Council
P.O. Box 52
Market Harborough
Leicestershire LE16 8ZX
01858 465731

International Federation of Aromatherapists
Stamford House
2–4 Chiswick High Road
London W4 1TH
0181 742 2605

Autogenic Training

Centre for Autogenic Training
100 Harley Street
London W1N 1AF
0171 935 1811

Chiropractic

British Chiropractic Association
29 Whitley Street
Reading RG2 0EG
01734 757557

Cranial Osteopathy

Cranial Osteopathic Association
478 Baker Street
Enfield
Middlesex EN1 3QS
0181 367 5561

Guided Imagery Therapy

Visualisation, autogenic training, biofeedback, psychotherapy, stress management – many practitioners of these also use guided image therapy. Contact the Institute for Complementary Medicine (see above) for information and recommendations.

Healing

British Alliance of Healing Organisations
01502 742224

National Federation of Spiritual Healers
Old Manor Farm Studio
Church Street
Sunbury-on-Thames
Middlesex TW16 6RG
01932 783164

Herbal Medicine

National Institute of Medical Herbalism
56 Longbrook Street
Exeter EX4 6AH
01392 426022

Holistic Medicine

British Holistic Medicine Association
Trust House
Royal Shrewsbury Hospital South
Shrewsbury SY3 8XF
01743 261155

Homeopathy

Faculty of Homeopathy
Royal London Homeopathic Hospital
60 Great Ormond Street
London WC1N 3HR
0171 837 8833

Hahnemann Society
Hahnemann House
2 Powis Place
London WC1N 3HT
0171 837 9469

Hypnotherapy

British Hypnotherapy Association
67 Upper Berkeley Street
London W1H 7DH
0171 723 4443

Naturopathy

General Council and Register of Naturopaths
Goswell House
2 Goswell Road
Street
Somerset BA16 0JG
01458 840072

Osteopathy

General Council and Register of Osteopaths
56 London Street
Reading
Berkshire RG1 4SQ
01734 576585

Osteopathic Information Service
P.O. Box 2074
Reading
Berkshire RG1 4TR
01734 512051

Shiatsu

The Shiatsu Society
31 Pullman Lane
Godalming
Surrey GU7 1XY
01483 860771

Traditional Chinese Medicine

Register of Chinese Herbal Medicine
P.O. Box 400
Wembley
Middlesex HA9 9NZ
0181 904 1357

Trager

Jill Dunley, UK Trager Representative
The Wilbury Clinic of Natural Therapy
Wilbury Road
Hove
Sussex BN3 3PY
01273 324420

Resources and Supplies

While most of the products mentioned have been located by the author in the United States, the following resource list should help locate the products mentioned in the United Kingdom. Many also provide a mail order service.

Acumedic Centre
101–5 Camden High Street
London NW1 7JN
0171 388 5783

Ainsworths Homeopathic Pharmacy
36 New Cavendish Street
London W1M 7LH
0171 935 5330

Essential Oil Company
(Dept SH)
Freepost (BZ 704)
Basingstoke
Hampshire RG22 4BR
01256 332737

Health Plus Ltd
Dolphin House
30 Lushington Road
Eastbourne
East Sussex BN21 4LL
01323 737374

Helios Homeopath Pharmacy
97 Camden Road
Tunbridge Wells
Kent TN1 2QR
01892 537254

Natural Remedies
35 Brecknock Road
London N7 0BT
0171 267 3884

For information about organic produce, and a directory of suppliers, contact:

Soil Association
86 Colston Street
Bristol BS1 5BB
0117 929 0661

AUSTRALIA

Herbal Medicine

National Herbalist Association of Australia
Suite 14/249 Kingsgrove Road
Kingsgrove
New South Wales 2208

Victorian Herbalists Association
24 Russell Stret
Northcote
Victoria 3070

Homeopathy

Australian College of Alternative Medicine
P.O. Box 625
Box Hill Arcade
Victoria 3128

Australian Centre for Homeopathy
P.O. Box 234
Tanunda
South Australia 5352

Hypnotherapy

Australian College of Hypnotherapy
1082 Maroondah Highway
Box Hill
Victoria 3128

Australian Society of Hypnosis
Austin Hospital
Studley Road
Heidelberg
Victoria 3084

Naturopathy

Australian Natural Therapist Association Ltd
P.O. Box 522
Sutherland
New South Wales 2232

Australian College of Natural Medicine
609 Camberwell Road
Camberwell
Victoria 3124

Traditional Chinese Medicine

Association of Traditional Health Practitioners Inc.
P.O. Box 346
Elizabeth
South Australia 5112

Chinese Tonics and Medicinal Herbs

Australia-wide supplier:

Brauer Biotherapies
Reply Paid 10 (no postage stamp required within Australia)
P.O. Box 234
Tanunda
South Australia 5352

For other herbal suppliers and organisations within Australia:

Kim Fletcher
Focus on Herbs
P.O. Box 203
Launceston
Tasmania 7250

SOUTH AFRICA

Acupuncture Association
5 Protea Road
Kempton Park Ext. 3
1619

Chiropractors, Homeopaths and Allied Health Professions Council
P.O. Box 36207
Menlo Park
0102

Holistic Massage Practitioners Association
P.O. Box 505
Constantia
7848
021 782 5909

Natural Health Association
P.O. Box 39556
Bramley
2018

Natural Health Clinic
Complementary Therapies
P.O. Box 5299
Halfway House
1685
011 805-0374

Organic Growing Association
P.O. Box 67726
Bryanston
2021

Polarity Therapy Association
P.O. Box 441
Constantia
7848
(021) 794-7838

Postural Integration
2 Jessie Avenue
Norwood
2192

SA Association of Hypnology
(021) 761-4829

SA Homeopathy Association
29 Alamein Road
Southdale
2135

Vitamin Information Centre
P.O. Box 182
Isando
1600

NOTES

Introduction

4 Quotation from René Dubos: *Mirage of Health: Utopias, Progress, and Biological Change* (New York: Harper & Brothers, 1959), 110–11.

5 Resistance to antimicrobial agents: Michael D. Katz in *Clinical Research News for Arizona Physicians* 5 (September 1994):9 (published by the University of Arizona Health Sciences Center, Office of Public Affairs). For further information on this subject, see A. Tomascz, "Multiple-Antibiotic-Resistant Pathogenic Bacteria: A Report on the Rockefeller University Workshop," *New England Journal of Medicine* 330 (1994):1247–51; and J. A. Fisher, *The Plague Makers: How We Are Creating Catastrophic New Epidemics—and What We Must Do to Avert Them* (New York: Simon & Schuster, 1994).

PART ONE: THE HEALING SYSTEM

1. Prologue in the Rain Forest

15 Hahnemann on disease suppression: Samuel Hahnemann, *The Chronic Diseases: Theoretical Part* (New Delhi: B. Jain, 1993). This was originally published in German in 1835.

19 The fate of the Kofán: See Joe Kane, "Letter from the Amazon," *New Yorker*, September 27, 1993.

2. Right in My Own Backyard

31 Confirmation of cranial motion: V. M. Frymann, "A Study of the Rhythmic Motions of the Living Cranium," *Journal of the American Osteo-

pathic Association 70 (1971):928–45; D. K. Michael and E. W. Retzlaff, "A Preliminary Study of Cranial Bone Movement in the Squirrel Monkey," *Journal of the American Osteopathic Association* 74 (1975):866–9; E. W. Retzlaff et al., "Cranial Bone Mobility," *Journal of the American Osteopathic Association* 74 (1975):869–73.

36 Documentary film of Dr. Fulford: *Robert Fulford: An Osteopathic Alternative,* available from Biomedical Communications, University of Arizona Health Sciences Center, Tucson, Arizona 85724.

3. Testimonials

51 Effects of *Ginkgo biloba:* J. Kleijnen and P. Knipschild, "*Ginkgo biloba* for Cerebral Insufficiency," *British Journal of Clinical Pharmacology* 34 (1992):352–8.

4. Medical Pessimism

60 People who go to alternative practitioners: D. M. Eisenberg et al., "Unconventional Medicine in the United States: Prevalence, Costs, and Patterns of Use," *New England Journal of Medicine* 328 (1993):246–52.

61 Voodoo death: See W. B. Cannon, "Voodoo Death," *Psychosomatic Medicine* 19 (1957):182–90.
   Hexing in exotic cultures: See, for example, R. A. Kirkpatrick, "Witchcraft and Lupus Erythematosus," *Journal of the American Medical Association* 245 (1981):1937.

66 Bibliography of spontaneous remission: Brendan O'Regan and Carlyle Hirshberg, *Spontaneous Remission: An Annotated Bibliography* (Sausalito, California: Institute of Noetic Sciences, 1993).
   Quotation on remission and cancer: O'Regan and Hirshberg, *Spontaneous Remission,* 13.
   Wart cures: See "Why Warts Fall Off," Chapter 18 of my book *Health and Healing* (Boston: Houghton Mifflin, 1988).

5. The Healing System

73 Enzymes: See Donald Voet and Judith G. Voet, *Biochemistry* (New York: John Wiley & Sons, 1990), Chapter 12, "Introduction to Enzymes," 316–28, and Chapter 14, "Enzymatic Catalysis," 355–90.

74 DNA repair enzymes: See E. C. Friedberg, *DNA Repair* (New York: Freeman, 1985). Also, A. Sancar and G. B. Sancar, "DNA Repair Enzymes," *Annual Review of Biochemistry* 57 (1988):29–67.

75 Many different enzymes available for the healing of DNA: See Voet and Voet, *Biochemistry,* Chapter 31, "DNA Replication, Repair, and Recombination," 948–86.

77 Recycling of LDL receptors: J. L. Goldstein et al., "Receptor-mediated Endocytosis," *Annual Review of Cell Biology* 1 (1985):1–39.

79 Growth factors in wound healing: Ramzi S. Cotran, Vinay Kumar, and Stanley L. Robbins, *Robbins Pathologic Basis of Disease,* 4th ed. (Philadelphia: W. B. Saunders, 1989), 74–77.

80 Bone healing: Cotran, Kumar, and Robbins, *Robbins Pathologic Basis,* 1322–33.
Becker on bone healing and regeneration: Robert O. Becker and Gary Selden, *The Body Electric: Electromagnetism and the Foundation of Life* (New York: William Morrow, 1985).
Regeneration of the liver: Cotran, Kumar, and Robbins, *Robbins Pathologic Basis,* 72, 913.

81 Absence of regeneration in heart and nerve cells: Cotran, Kumar, and Robbins, *Robbins Pathologic Basis,* 72–73.

82 Reversibility of atherosclerosis: Dean Ornish, *Dr. Dean Ornish's Program for Reversing Heart Disease Without Drugs or Surgery* (New York: Ballantine, 1992).

84 Case report from Lourdes: J. Garner, "Spontaneous Regressions: Scientific Documentation as a Basis for the Declaration of Miracles," *Canadian Medical Association Journal* 111 (1974):1254–64.

85 Case of Vittorio Micheli: J. Garner, "Spontaneous Regressions," quoted in Brendan O'Regan and Carlyle Hirshberg, *Spontaneous Remission: An Annotated Bibliography* (Sausalito, California: Institute of Noetic Sciences, 1993), 548.

6. The Role of the Mind in Healing

90 Article on ulcerative colitis and smoking: E. J. Boyko et al., "Risk of Ulcerative Colitis Among Former and Current Cigarette Smokers," *New England Journal of Medicine* 316 (1987):707–10.

91 Ulcer as an infectious disease: See Terence Monmaney, "Annals of Medicine," *New Yorker,* September 20, 1993.

92 Candace Pert on neuropeptides: C. B. Pert et al., "Neuropeptides and Their Receptors: A Psychosomatic Network," *Journal of Immunology* 135 (1985):820s–826s.

93 Quotation from Pert: C. B. Pert et al., "Neuropeptides," 824s.

103 Quotation from Lao-tzu: *The Way of Life According to Lao Tzu,* translated by Witter Bynner (New York: Perigee Books, 1972), verses 43 and 55.

7. The Tao of Healing

110 The art of dying: See, for example, Mary Catharine O'Connor, *Art of Dying Well: Development of the* Ars Moriendi (New York: Columbia University Press, 1967).

113 Cancer seems almost to be an occupational hazard of sainthood: Larry Dossey, *Meaning in Medicine* (New York: Bantam, 1991), 208–9.

119 Book by John Sarno: John E. Sarno, *Healing Back Pain: The Mind-Body Connection* (New York: Warner Books, 1991).

120 Lack of correlation between subjective experience of back pain and objective measures: M. C. Jensen et al., "Magnetic Resonance Imaging of the Lumbar Spine in People Without Back Pain," *New England Journal of Medicine* 331 (1994):69–73.

PART TWO: OPTIMIZING THE HEALING SYSTEM

8. Optimizing Your Healing System: An Overview

133 Lupus in Nogales, Arizona: K. Bagwell, "Lupus Is Found at Highest Rate in Nogales, Ariz.," *Arizona Daily Star,* November 7, 1993.

9. A Healing Diet

136 Low-fat diet and longevity: S. A. Grover et al., "Life Expectancy Following Dietary Modification or Smoking Cessation," *Archives of Internal Medicine* 154 (1994):1697–704.

137 Animals live longer with less disease on fewer calories: E. J. Masoro, "Assessment of Nutritional Components in Prolongation of Life and Health by Diet," *Proceedings of the Society for Experimental Biology and Medicine* 193 (1990):31–34.

142 Olive oil and better health: M. Aviram and K. Eias, "Dietary Olive Oil Reduces Low-Density Lipoprotein Uptake by Macrophages and Decreases the Susceptibility of the Lipoprotein to Undergo Lipid Peroxidation," *Annals of Nutrition and Metabolism* 37 (1995):75–84.

143 Omega-3 fatty acids and health: For example, see A. Leaf, "Cardiovascular Effects of Omega-3 Fatty Acids," *New England Journal of Medicine* 318 (1988):549–57; W. Hermann, "The Influence of Dietary Supplementation with Omega-3 Fatty Acids on Serum Lipids, Apolipoproteins, Coagulation, and Fibrinolytic Parameters," *Zeitschrift für Klinische Medizin* 46 (1991):1363–69; R. A. Karmali, "Omega-3 Fatty Acids and Cancer," *Journal of Internal Medicine* 225 (suppl. 1, 1989):197–200; J. M. Kremer, "Clinical Studies of Omega-3 Fatty Acid Supplementation in Patients Who Have Rheumatoid Arthritis," *Rheumatic Disease Clinics of North America* 17 (1991):391–402; and H. R. Knapp, "Omega-3 Fatty Acids, Endogenous Prostaglandins, and Blood Pressure Regulation in Humans," *Nutrition Reviews* 47 (1989):301–13.

149 Soy phytoestrogens: A. Cassidy et al., "Biological Effects of a Diet of Soy Protein Rich in Isoflavones on the Menstrual Cycle of Premenopausal Women," *American Journal of Clinical Nutrition* 60 (1994):333–40.

10. Protecting Yourself from Toxins

154 Quotation on pesticides on food crops: T. H. Jukes, "Organic Food," *CRC Critical Reviews in Food Science & Nutrition* 9 (1977):395–418.

155 Quotation on aldicarb in watermelon: A. M. Fan and R. J. Jackson, "Pesticides and Food Safety," *Regulatory Toxicology and Pharmacology* 9 (1989): 158–74, 168.

163 Quotation on DDT in fish: Fan and Jackson, "Pesticides," 169.

165 Most heavily contaminated vegetable crops: R. Wiles et al., *Washed, Peeled, Contaminated* (Washington, D.C.: Environmental Working Group, 1994).

169 Biological hazards of energy: Robert O. Becker, *Cross Currents: The Perils of Electropollution, The Promise of Electromedicine* (Los Angeles: Tarcher, 1991).

11. Using Tonics

173 Garlic lowers blood pressure: J. E. Brody, "Personal Health: Modern Doctors Confirm the Ancient Wisdom That Garlic Has Many Benefits," *New York Times,* July 27, 1994.
Effects of garlic on cholesterol and blood clotting: "Garlic," *Lawrence Review of Natural Products* (St. Louis, Missouri: Facts and Comparisons), April 1994. See also S. Warshafsky et al., "Effect of Garlic on Total Serum Cholesterol: A Meta-analysis," *Annals of Internal Medicine* 119 (1993): 599–605.
Garlic as an anticancer agent: Brody, "Modern Doctors Confirm."

174 Effects of ginger on the digestive system: Paul Schulick, *Ginger: Common Spice & Wonder Drug* (Brattleboro, Vermont: Herbal Free Press, rev. ed., 1994), passim. This book contains an excellent list of references to the scientific literature.

175 Anti-inflammatory effect of ginger: Schulick, *Ginger.*

176 Health benefits of green tea: Jean Carper, *Food—Your Miracle Medicine* (New York: HarperCollins, 1993), 212–3. See also H. N. Graham, "Green Tea Composition, Consumption, and Polyphenol Chemistry," *Preventive Medicine* 21 (1992) 334–50; Y. Sagesaka-Mitane et al., "Platelet Aggregation Inhibitors in Hot Water Extract of Green Tea," *Chemical and Pharmacological Bulletin* (Tokyo) 38 (1990):790–93.

177 Protective effect of milk thistle on liver: V. Fintelmann and A. Albert, *Therapiewoche* 30 (1980):5589–94; H. Hikino and Y. Kiso, "Natural Products for Liver Disease," in H. Wagner, H. Hikino, and N. R. Farnsworth, *Eco-*

nomic and Medicinal Plant Research, Vol. 2 (New York: Academic Press, 1988), 39–72.

178 Fu zheng therapy: Subhuti Dharmananda, *Chinese Herbal Therapies* (Portland, Oregon: Institute for Traditional Medicine, 1988), Chapter 2.

Astragalus enhances immune function: See "Astragalus" in A. Y. Leung and S. Foster, *Encyclopedia of Common Natural Ingredients* (New York: John Wiley & Sons, 1995).

179 Protective effects of Siberian ginseng: N. R. Farnsworth et al., "Siberian Ginseng (*Eleutherococcus senticosus*): Current Status as an Adaptogen," in H. Wagner, H. Hikino, and N. R. Farnsworth (eds.), *Economic and Medicinal Plant Research,* Vol. 1 (Orlando, Florida: Academic Press, 1985), 155–215; and B. W. Halstead and L. L. Hood, *Eleutherococcus senticosus, Siberian Ginseng: An Introduction to the Concept of Adaptogenic Medicine* (Long Beach, California: Oriental Healing Arts Institutre, 1984).

182 Quotation on maitake: From H. Namba, "Maitake Mushroom: Promising Immune Therapy for Cancer Treatment," *New Editions Health World,* October 1994, 20–24.

183 Anticancer and immune-enhancing effects of maitake: N. Ohno et al., "Structural Characterization and Antitumor Activity of the Extracts from Matted Mycelium of Cultured *Grifola frondosa,*" *Chemical and Pharmacological Bulletin* (Tokyo) 33 (1985):3395–401; also, I. Suzuki, "Antitumor and Immunomodulating Activities of a β-Glucan Obtained from Liquid-cultured *Grifola frondosa,*" *Chemical and Pharmacological Bulletin* (Tokyo) 37 (1989):410–13.

184 Quotation on Chinese distance runners: Cameron Smith, "Gold Medal Herbs," *Natural Health,* May/June 1994, 85–7.

13. Mind and Spirit

202 Quotation from Rabbi Nachman of Bratislav: Edward Hoffman, *The Way of Splendor: Jewish Mysticism and Modern Psychology* (Northvale, New Jersey: Jason Aronson, 1992), 124.

203 Quotation on breath: Andrew Weil, *Natural Health, Natural Medicine* (Boston: Houghton Mifflin, 2nd rev. ed., 1995), 89.

207 Few books about breathing are available: An excellent one of recent publication is *Conscious Breathing* by Gay Hendricks, Ph.D. (New York: Bantam, 1995). It has detailed instructions for working with breath to improve physical, mental, and spiritual health.

208 Italian-Americans of Roseto, Pennsylvania: C. Stout et al., "Unusually Low Incidence of Death from Myocardial Infarction: Study of an Italian American Community in Pennsylvania," *Journal of the American Medical Association* 188 (1964):845–49; A. Keys, "Arteriosclerotic Heart Disease in Roseto, Pennsylvania," *Journal of the American Medical Association*

195 (1966):137–39. The conclusions of these papers are questioned in a more recent article by S. Wolf et al., "Roseto Revisited: Further Data on the Incidence of Myocardial Infarction in Roseto and Neighboring Pennsylvania Communities," *Transactions of the American Clinical and Climatological Association* 85 (1973):100–08.

PART THREE: IF YOU GET SICK

15. Making the Right Decisions

224 Schizandra and chronic hepatitis: L. Geng-tao, "Pharmacological Actions and Clinical Use of Fructus Schizandrae," *Chinese Medical Journal* 102 (1989):740–49.

227 Feverfew and rheumatoid arthritis: H. O. Collier et al., "Extract of Feverfew Inhibits Prostaglandin Biosynthesis," *Lancet* 11 (1981):1054; M. I. Berry, "Feverfew Faces the Future," *Pharmacy Journal* 232 (1984):611–14.

229 GLA for eczema: V. A. Ziboh, "Implications of Dietary Oils and Polyunsaturated Fatty Acids in the Management of Cutaneous Disorders," *Archives of Dermatology* 125 (1989):241–5.

230 Echinacea as an immune enhancer: B. Bräunig et al., "Echinacea purpureae Radix for Strengthening the Immune Response in Flu-like Infections," *Zeitschrift für Phytotherapie* 13 (1992):7–13.

232 DGL (licorice extract): See Bardhan et al., "Clinical Trial of Deglycyrrhizinated Liquorice in Gastric Ulcer," *Gut* 19 (1978):779–82; A. G. Morgan et al., "Comparison Between Cimetidine and Caved-S in the Treatment of Gastric Ulceration, and Subsequent Maintenance Therapy," *Gut* 23 (1982):545–51.

234 Quercetin reduces allergic responsiveness: E. Middleton and G. Drzewieki, "Naturally Occurring Flavonoids and Human Basophil Histamine Release," *International Archives of Allergy and Applied Immunology* 77 (1985): 155–77; M. Amelia et al., "Inhibition of Mast Cell Histamine Release by Flavonoids and Bioflavonoids," *Planta Medica* 51 (1985):16–20; E. Middleton and C. Kundaswami, "Effects of Flavonoids on Immune and Inflammatory Cell Functions," *Biochemical Pharmacology* 43 (1992):1167–79.

16. Considering the Alternatives

238 I have written elsewhere about alternative medicine: See Andrew Weil, *Health and Healing* (Boston: Houghton Mifflin, rev. ed., 1988).

239 Guggul lowers cholesterol: G. V. Satyavati, "Gum *Guggul (Commiphora mukul)*—the Success Story of an Ancient Insight Leading to a Modern Discovery," *Indian Journal of Medical Research* 87 (1988):327–35; S. Nityanand et al., "Clinical Trials with Gugulipid, a New Hypolipi-

daemic Agent," *Journal of the Association of Physicians of India* 37 (1989):323–28.

246 Beneficial effects of prayer on health: Larry Dossey, *Healing Words: The Power of Prayer and the Practice of Medicine* (San Francisco: Harper San Francisco, 1993).

18. Managing General Categories of Illness: Secrets of a Hygeian Practitioner

254 Stinging nettles for hay fever: P. Mittman, "Randomized, Double-Blind Study of Freeze-Dried *Urtica dioica* in the Treatment of Allergic Rhinitis," *Planta Medica* 56 (1990):44–46.

256 Anti-Inflammatory effect of feverfew: See "Feverfew," *Lawrence Review of Natural Products* (St. Louis, Missouri: Facts and Comparisons), September 1994.

Turmeric and curcumin: M. Murray, "Curcumin: A Potent Anti-inflammatory Agent," *American Journal of Natural Medicine* 1 (1994):10–13.

257 Coenzyme Q: T. Kawasaki, "Antioxidant Function of Coenzyme Q," *Journal of Nutritional Science and Vitaminology* 38 (1992), special number, 552–55.

L carnitine improves the metabolism of heart muscle cells: C. J. Pepine, "The Therapeutic Potential of Carnitine in Cardiovascular Disorders," *Clinical Therapeutics* 13 (1991):2–21.

Tree ear mushrooms have an anticoagulant effect: D. E. Hammerschmidt, "Szechuan Purpura," *New England Journal of Medicine* 302 (1980): 1191–93.

259 Antibiotic and immune-enhancing properties of echinacea: B. Bräunig et al., "Echinacea purpureae Radix for Strengthening the Immune Response in Flu-like Infections," *Zeitschrift für Phytotherapie* 13 (1992):7–13.

260 Saw palmetto and *Pygeum* for prostatic enlargement: G. Champault et al., "A Double-blind Trial of an Extract of the Plant *Serenoa repens* in Benign Prostatic Hyperplasia," *British Journal of Clinical Pharmacology* 18 (1984):461–62; A. Barlet et al., "Efficacy of *Pygeum africanum* Extract in the Medical Therapy of Urination Disorders Due to Benign Prostatic Hyperplasia: Evaluation of Objective and Subjective Parameters: A Placebo-controlled Double-blind Multicenter Study," *Wiener Klinische Wochenschrifte* 102 (1990):667–73.

262 Niacinamide can be very helpful for osteoarthritis: W. Kaufman, "The Use of Vitamin Therapy to Reverse Certain Concomitants of Aging," *Journal of the American Geriatric Society* 3 (1955):927–36.

Boswellia for musculoskeletal pain: C. K. Reddy et al., "Studies on the Metabolism of Glycosaminoglycans Under the Influence of New Herbal Anti-inflammatory Agents," *Biochemical Pharmacology* 20 (1989): 3527–34.

19. Cancer as a Special Case

269 Account of Helen B.: Dr. R. A. Anderson, "Carcinoma of the Ovary: A Case Report," December 1992.

271 Alternative treatment for cancer: For a review of this subject with detailed information on the nature and availability of therapies, see Michael Lerner, *Choices in Healing* (Boston: MIT Press, 1994).

272 It is imperative to maintain our healing systems in good working order: In addition to the information in Part Two of this book, see my previous book, *Natural Health, Natural Medicine* (Boston: Houghton Mifflin, 2nd rev. ed., 1995), especially Chapter 11, "How Not to Get Cancer," and Chapter 12, "How to Protect Your Immune System."

Books exist to guide patients in making these difficult decisions: For example, S. Austin and C. Hitchcock, *Breast Cancer: What You Should Know (But May Not Be Told) About Prevention, Diagnosis, and Treatment* (Rocklin, California: Prima Publishing, 1994), which includes an excellent analysis of the choices facing women with breast cancer.

INDEX

HEALTH AND HEALING

Andrew Weil, M:D.

'A warm and clear-cut spectrum of health and healing. I recommend this book to all who are involved in or interested in wellness' *Dr Bernie Siegel*

In this groundbreaking handbook, Dr Andrew Weil – international bestselling author of *Spontaneous Healing* – explains the principles and practice of conventional and alternative medicine and presents an intelligent and persuasive philosophy of health, treatment and healing.

Dr Weil presents the full spectrum of alternative healing practices, including holistic medicine, homeopathy, osteopathy, chiropractic, acupuncture and Chinese medicine, outlining their differences from conventional approaches and assessing their strengths and limitations. Some problems call for drugs or surgery, whereas others cannot be treated by allopathic medicine and benefit from alternative treatments.

Drawing on his vast clinical and personal experience, as well as on case studies from around the world, Dr Weil explores the ways in which the body stays healthy and argues that we each need to choose wisely among the available forms of medicine – to take control of our health and our health care.

'Andrew Weil knows how to make us think . . . Read this book and learn' *Dean Ornish, M.D.*

'Offers the clear non-judgmental investigation we have come to expect from Weil'
San Francisco Chronicle

WARNER
0 7515 1766 6

Warner Books now offers an exciting range of quality titles by both established and new authors which can be ordered from the following address:
   Little, Brown and Company (UK),
   P.O. Box 11,
   Falmouth,
   Cornwall TR10 9EN.

Alternatively you may fax your order to the above address. Fax No. 01326 317444.

Payments can be made as follows: cheque, postal order (payable to Little, Brown and Company) or by credit cards, Visa/Access. Do not send cash or currency. UK customers and B.F.P.O. please allow £1.00 for postage and packing for the first book, plus 50p for the second book, plus 30p for each additional book up to a maximum charge of £3.00 (7 books plus).

Overseas customers including Ireland, please allow £2.00 for the first book plus £1.00 for the second book, plus 50p for each additional book.

NAME (Block Letters) ....

....

ADDRESS ....

....

....

☐ I enclose my remittance for ....

☐ I wish to pay by Access/Visa Card

Number ☐☐☐☐☐☐☐☐☐☐☐☐☐☐☐☐

Card Expiry Date ☐☐☐☐